CASTLE
LOVES
FANDOM

CASTLE LOVES FANDOM

CELEBRATING THE DETECTIVE SHOW'S QUIPS, HOMAGES, AND META-SALUTES

VALERIE ESTELLE FRANKEL

Other Works by Valerie Estelle Frankel

Henry Potty and the Pet Rock: A Harry Potter Parody
Henry Potty and the Deathly Paper Shortage: A Harry Potter Parody
Buffy and the Heroine's Journey
From Girl to Goddess: The Heroine's Journey in Myth and Legend
Katniss the Cattail: The Unauthorized Guide to Name and Symbols
The Many Faces of Katniss Everdeen: The Heroine of The Hunger Games
Harry Potter, Still Recruiting: A Look at Harry Potter Fandom
Teaching with Harry Potter
An Unexpected Parody: The Spoof of The Hobbit Movie
Teaching with Harry Potter
Myths and Motifs in The Mortal Instruments
Winning the Game of Thrones: The Host of Characters & their Agendas
Winter is Coming: Symbols, Portents, and Hidden Meanings in A Game of Thrones
Bloodsuckers on the Bayou: The Myths, Symbols, and Tales Behind HBO's True Blood
The Girl's Guide to the Heroine's Journey
Choosing to be Insurgent or Allegiant: Symbols, Themes & Analysis of the Divergent Trilogy
Doctor Who and the Hero's Journey: The Doctor and Companions as Chosen Ones
Doctor Who: The What Where and How
Sherlock: Every Canon Reference You May Have Missed in BBC's Series
Symbols in Game of Thrones
How Game of Thrones Will End
Joss Whedon's Names
Pop Culture in the Whedonverse
Women in Game of Thrones: Power, Conformity, and Resistance
History, Homages and the Highlands: An Outlander Guide
The Catch-Up Guide to Doctor Who
Remember All Their Faces: A Deeper Look at Character, Gender and the Prison World of Orange Is The New Black
Everything I Learned in Life I Know from Joss Whedon
Empowered: The Symbolism, Feminism, and Superheroism of Wonder Woman
The Avengers Face their Dark Sides
The Comics of Joss Whedon: Critical Essays
Mythology in Game of Thrones

This book is an unauthorized guide and commentary on the *Castle* show and its associated comics and books. None of the individuals or companies associated with the comics, television show or any merchandise based on this series has in any way sponsored, approved, endorsed, or authorized this book.

ISBN-13: 978-0692544266 (LitCrit Press)
ISBN-10: 0692544267

Contents

Introduction

New York is stuffed with tiny communities of subculture, whether one goes for fashion week or bird watching. For viewers across the world, these episodes provide deeper looks into these strange cultures, even the ones right next door. Other episodes are homages to beloved shows like *Grey's Anatomy* or *Dancing with the Stars*. There's a Steampunk, a Western, a space adventure and several hardboiled mysteries. Each time, Castle or one of the detectives displays a crazy fannishness, meant as a wink to the other fans watching from their couches.

This show also allows Fillion to flaunt his geek cred. "It's easy to keep the geek fan base stoked by simply remaining true to the inner geek," he says. "I just continue to be excited by the things I am excited by. I love sci-fi. I love computer games. I love technology. I like flashlights that are really small but really bright. If it has buttons, batteries, performs some kind of unusual function – yeah, I got it. I want it" (Bierly et al.)

Fillion's own enthusiasm for these small communities and his own fannishness are central. Fillion notes: "I have been very fortunate in my career to have a long streak of projects where I'm thrilled to be part of them," he says. "I don't think I've ever done a job where I said, 'Well, I really need the money.' Everything I've done I've done with an excitement of 'I can't wait to do this!'" (Bierly et al.). Indeed, in many ways he *is* Castle, the man who hurls himself into fandom with all the passion of an actor or writer. Show creator Andrew Marlowe adds on the concept of theme episodes:

We are in a very challenged television environment, where it's hard to break through the noise. We try to do everything we can to have the idea behind the show be its own promotional entity so that you can grasp what the show is easily. We approach it from the point of view of, "What is the poster of this episode?" It's something that, in my feature background, people talk about all the time. If they're going to spend $100 million or, these days, closer to $150 million or $200 million, people are going to know what this movie's about. Bringing that to the television landscape helped us evolve to where we do have these themed episodes, where we go into a world or subculture that we find fascinating as storytellers and think about what Castle and Beckett will respond to. (Ng)

The storytellers' passion indeed shines through the episodes, as many are described as "love letters" to fans of soap operas or zombie walks. Stana Katic, Beckett's actress, says of the show, "It appeals to an audience that wants dessert after dinner. It's charming in a classic kind of way. I think people love a bit of heart, humor, drama and stakes, so I suppose it has a nice mix of a lot of different emotions." (Ng).

Just as beloved as these are all the self-references. The show explodes with *Firefly* references, celebrating Nathan Fillion's most cherished show with more fannishness than the fans. Crafting a truly meta world, the *Castle* producers finally came out with Nikki Heat novels and Derrick Storm comic books, all of which nod to the show and to Nathan Fillion as well. Richard Castle has a book website and author appearances as the art comes full circle, feeding itself until the show celebrates each comic or novel release.

This book lays out all the references – all the winks at Fillion's time on *Firefly*, *Buffy*, and *One Life to Live*, all the times Castle riffs on *Star Wars* and *Godfather*, all the times he breaks the fourth wall to wink at his audience and why those moments are so great. For in the end, *Castle* is a show made for fans…and made by the biggest fans of all.

Enter the Worlds of...

Mystery Writers ("Flowers for Your Grave," 101)

Murder, mystery, the macabre. What is it about a hard-boiled detective, the femme fatale, and the cold steel of a gun that keeps our bedside lamp burning into the wee hours of the morning? However the spell is cast, tonight we honor a master of the form and celebrate the launch of *Storm Fall*.

With this introduction (by Castle's publisher and ex-wife Meredith) this is clearly set up as a show for the fans. Castle begins the show at his latest book party, signing autograph after autograph. While the party itself is glamorous and he's the toast of the town, he's bored. That's why he killed off his bestselling character, Derrick Storm. Now he's suffering from writer's block, sitting around in his underwear while his book is weeks past deadline. At his own party, he's moping by the bar with Alexis. He complains, "Life should be an adventure. You want to know why I killed Derrick? There were no more surprises. I knew exactly what was going to happen every moment of every scene. It's just like these parties they've become so predictable. 'I'm your biggest fan!' 'Where do you get your ideas?'" Certainly, writers attending book parties and conventions hear these words over and over. It's rare to get a different question from the public.

CASTLE: Just once I'd like someone to come up to me and say something new.
BECKETT: Mr. Castle?
CASTLE: (Takes out his pen) Where would you like it?

11

> BECKETT: Detective Kate Beckett, NYPD, we need to ask you a few questions about a murder that took place earlier tonight.
> ALEXIS: That's new.

Castle, asked to consult when a copycat killer imitates the scenes of his books, is delighted. He tells Beckett, "I have this poker game, it's mostly other writers, Patterson, Cannell, you know, bestsellers. You have no idea how jealous those would make them...That I have a copycat. Oh my gosh, in my world that's the red badge of honor. That's the criminal Cooperstown." Social worker Allison Tisdale was murdered in an homage to *Flowers For Your Grave*, while lawyer Marvin Fisk was staged from *Hell Hath No Fury*. To Beckett's dismay, Castle realizes she's a big fan. "*Hell Hath No Fury?* Angry wiccans out for blood? C'mon! Only hardcore Castle groupies read that one," he tells her. A discussion of fandom comes up, with Beckett's fellow detectives more skeptical:

> ESPOSITO: I work dead bodies all day, the last thing I want to do when I go home is read murder books.
> BECKETT: Aren't you curious?
> ESPOSITO: Curious?
> BECKETT: About how people can do these kinds of things to one another?

She appears to find mystery novels a source of deep truth, even as she solves crimes in real life.

Meanwhile, Castle's fans seem to make him miserable rather than proud as he tells Alexis, "No, we had a deal. Surf all the Internet you want, but stay off the fan sites." He adds to Beckett that "all my fan mail is disturbing. It's an occupational hazard." Nonetheless, he's poignantly obsessed with the story – the motives that drive people to commit horrific acts. As such, on some level he's devoted to his craft, just not to the superficial life that comes with it.

His poker game provides another inside look at the writing life as James Patterson and Stephen J. Cannell solve cases as stories. They appear as themselves and discuss their own books, in a wave to mystery fans that helps establish Richard Castle as a real author like them. They also crack the case by dissecting the episode they're in in a truly meta examination:

> JAMES PATTERSON: So what's the problem, Ricky? Maybe we can help.
> CASTLE: I'm working on this thing. It starts with a famous author. Some psycho starts staging murders like he does in his books.
> STEPHEN J. CANNELL: Ha! That's pretty self-aggrandizing, isn't it?
> JAMES PATTERSON: This is Castle we're talking about.
> CASTLE: So, crime scenes are clean. Doesn't leave any fingerprints, doesn't leave any DNA, but the psycho writes the author a fan letter with his prints all over it. Well that leads the police to his apartment where they find enough evidence to convict him.
> STEPHEN J. CANNELL: And then?
> CASTLE: That's it.
> STEPHEN J. CANNELL: That's it?
> CASTLE: Yeah, they arrest him.
> JAMES PATTERSON: That's terrible. No wonder you're blocked.
> STEPHEN J. CANNELL: And here's another thing, the guy doesn't leave his prints at the scene of the crime, but he sends a letter with his prints on it. You lost me there. And what about a twist?
> ...
> CASTLE: Yeah, right, like maybe someone set this kid up.
> STEPHEN J. CANNELL: That's what your story needs, the character who thinks the kid's innocent, keeps digging 'til he finds the truth.
> CASTLE: Oh, I have just the guy.

He casts himself as the character they've invented and helps Beckett solve the mystery, using their combined experience. After, he's hooked on crime-solving and living the mysteries rather than just imagining them. While his character Derrick Storm is a wish-fulfillment James Bond type, his Nikki Heat and Jameson Rook are based on himself and Beckett, writing the true story of his life in a new series he finds truly thrilling.

Private Academies ("Hedge Fund Homeboys," 103)

CASTLE: Oh, I've been kicked out of all of New York's finer educational institutions at least once. The irony is, now that I'm rich and famous, they all claim me as alum and want money.
BECKETT: *[sarcastically]* It is just so rough being you.
CASTLE: My cross to bear. ("Hedge Fund Homeboys," 103)

In fact, growing up in the private school environment showed Castle how the rich, spoiled teens think. Through the investigation, he points out how much money they have and how this colors their thinking. As he explains, they would be likely to buy their way out of trouble, yet would be cruel and exclude someone no longer their social equal. The murder victim, one of their friends, loses his family fortune but continues attending the school and dating a rich girl. Of course, one of his peers hates him for continuing to push in where he's not wanted and takes a brutal revenge. It's Castle who gets the murderer to crack:

CASTLE: *[In order to get Brandon to admit to his crime]* If only Max had been strong enough just to man up... If only Donny realized he didn't belong with you guys anymore, he and Amanda were through, well, then none of this would have been necessary. (Lowered voice) Weak people just don't get it, do they, Brandon? Sometimes they just have to be led to the truth.
BRANDON: (Whispers) Exactly.
CASTLE: *[Smiling at Beckett]* Did he just say "exactly"?

African Immigrants ("Always Buy Retail," 106)

Jamal, the victim this time, is laid out on a large square of red flannel. A burned-down white candle is clutched in his left hand, while a glass bowl of blood waits by his head. Castle's knowledge of obscure rituals points to someone conducting a Voodoo findsman's ritual. This allows a person

VALERIE ESTELLE FRANKEL

to beseech the spirits for their favor. He tells the team to open the victim's mouth, where they find a small pouch.

> CASTLE: The, uh, blood in the bowl? Most likely animal. Part of the ceremony. The pouch is an offering to the spirits, but I don't recognize the symbol.
> ESPOSITO: If you did, you'd be a suspect. So, how do you know about all this?
> CASTLE: Research for my sixth Derrick Storm novel.
> RYAN: *Unholy Storm.*
> CASTLE: Yes, thank you. And uh, Vodun's not just limited to West Africa. It's also practiced by Haitian and Dominican communities right here in New York.

Unholy Storm (allegedly a Richard Castle novel, actually available as a graphic "adaptation") takes Storm and Clara Strike to New Orleans. Chased by zombies and plagued by a voodoo doll, Storm thinks, "I'm no expert, but I know enough to realize that voodoo gets a *bad rap.* The media paints the religion as something sinister and evil. It's an easy target." He adds to himself that it's neither good nor evil, but can be used for both. The murderer is invoking the *loa* Lenglensou, who punishes those who can't keep secrets. Thus the killer, like the practitioner in the episode, is simply using this religion as a tool to accomplish goals.

Of course, it's finally revealed that Castle gets his lore from an African-American restaurant owner who studied in Africa. As she insists, "Your killer may be voudoun, but that's not why this man's dead. He was killed because he has something the killer desperately wants. And he's not going to stop until he finds it."

Onscreen, their search directs them to slum housing, up six flights of stairs where many immigrants huddle in fear of INS. Though Beckett threatens them with deportation, they are more frightened of the man who controls their lives:

> AZI: His name is Charles, Charles Oni.
> BECKETT: Charles Oni.
> AZI: Immigrants know this man. He owns the places where we live, he owns the places where we work.

15

CASTLE: And what about Jamal, did he work for him too?
AZI: At his store on Canal Street. But it was only temporary.
He was going to save his money to apply for a visa,
become legal.
CASTLE: And Oni had a problem with that?
AZI: No. Yesterday when Oni came looking for Jamal he
said Jamal had taken something. Jamal was not a thief but
Oni insisted. He say he knew my father was the priest of
our village, so he made to show him how to invoke the
spirits.

Oni, as it turns out, makes illegal passports and sells some
to a very dangerous man. Muhkta Baylor, a former child
soldier, is called the Butcher of Benin. "He traffics. Drugs,
women, whatever will make him money. It is him that killed
Jamal and the woman." Today, parts of Africa still use
children as soldiers and even send them on suicide missions,
leaving the survivors with their instincts brutalized.

The first use of child soldiers in Rwanda occurred during
the 1994 genocide between the ethnic groups of Tutsis and
Hutus. Over 800,000 of the seven million people in Rwanda
were slaughtered. The terribly young soldiers from this war
often grew up savage, with their morality corrupted from a
young age. Children are uniquely vulnerable to kidnapping,
manipulation, and control by outside forces as they're
recruited often before they can understand the consequences
of their actions. Newly conscripted youngsters are told that
it's their duty to revenge themselves on the killers of their
families, that fighting will make them wealthy, or even that
dying in battle will send them to heaven. This pattern has
repeated in the Central African Republic, Darfur, the
Democratic Republic of the Congo, Uganda, Nepal, Syria and
Sri Lanka. Hundreds of thousands of children under eighteen
still serve in government forces or armed rebel groups. Some
are as young as eight years old. Most countries have no
rehabilitation programs, leaving the children with nowhere to
go but back to a world of violence.

In the episode, no solution is offered for this tragedy
gripping the world. Further, the immigrants are presented

sympathetically but trapped, all under the thumb of someone more powerful, with no source of protection that isn't exploitative. Unfortunately, their problems are never truly solved either – none are offered asylum or police protection. Thus the story backs away from doing a hard-hitting exposé and merely presents a slice of life among the unfortunate.

Rich and Elite ("Home is Where the Heart Stops," 107)

> CASTLE: In a building like this, this part of town? You'd think she'd be safe. No pun intended. How often are people killed in neighborhoods like this?
> BECKETT: Same as anywhere else, Castle. Just the once.

It's soon discovered that there's a pattern of similar robberies, each in a different high-end part of the city. The thieves are well-informed, specifically targeting wall safes and high-end jewelry. Beckett and her team search for a pattern and discover escalating violence among only the wealthy homes. Seeking information from his ex-thief friend Powell, Castle hears that the opportunity is key here: "Seeing comes before wanting, Rick. These chaps may actually live among their victims and move through their world."

As Beckett searches for someone who touches the world of the rich, she suggests, "A waiter. Dog-walker. Doorman. Personal trainer." Castle takes the puzzle on head on, getting tickets for himself and Beckett to the next charity event:

> BECKETT: What are those?
> CASTLE: The gateway to another world.
> BECKETT: Castle.
> CASTLE: They hold four fundraisers a year. The last one took place a week before the robberies began.
> BECKETT: No.
> CASTLE: It is perfect. You don't have to ask who the donors are, because they'll be there wearing their jewelry.

He escorts her in, him in black tie, her in an amazing

gown sent by a "fairy godmother" and Martha's necklace. They step out of a town car into a salvo of flashbulbs, in a perfect fairy-tale moment. This too is a visit to another world, specifically Castle's world of privilege and charity drives. There a young woman tells Beckett about being "on the circuit…breast cancer, land mines. Oh, you know what the best one is? Um, uh, that project what do you call it - the one with the lips? There are a lot of, uh, plastic surgeons there. Fish in a barrel." Of course, she regards these drives as opportunities to find a husband. She also describes young women's attempts on Castle – "Oh, most of the girls on the register have tried to land him. Rich and handsome. We call him The White Whale." However, one woman's boyfriend is taking photos of the guests. Castle explains, "It's perfect. He IDs the jewels and then uses his girlfriend's research to build profiles on the victims." Thus they capture the criminal and end the violence. Beckett finishes the story of entering Castle's world by sharing a family breakfast with Martha, Castle, and Alexis.

Cosmetic Surgery ("A Death in the Family," 110)

A cosmetic surgeon is killed after being tortured. When the team investigates, they interview his disgruntled client, Jacey Goldberg. With her giant lips, she's become deformed, and worse, addicted to surgery, suing in anger after the doctor refuses to do a fourth face lift. In the end, Jacey's husband Jack had her committed to Bellevue for psychiatric treatment for her obsession. The team find her creepy looking.

> ESPOSITO: Wow, look at her. How can anyone do that to themselves?
> CASTLE: Right? It's like she escaped from the Island of Dr. Moreau.
> BECKETT: Come on guys, she's not an animal. She's a human being.
> CASTLE: Yeah, I know but…wait, are you being sincere, or quoting the Elephant Man?

Nathan Fillion, Castle himself, adds, "There are episodes

where we do go pretty dramatic, but by and large, we don't take ourselves terribly seriously. We keep it fairly light. I think it makes it easy to like" (Ng). Thus he and his friends use humor, though they do explore this weighty real-life problem.

In the same episode, Martha takes Alexis prom dress shopping and explains, "What men don't understand is, the right clothes, the right shoes, the right make-up... just, it hides the flaws we think we have. They make us look beautiful, to ourselves. That's what makes us look beautiful to others." While Castle worries Alexis will develop body issues, he tries Martha's way of encouraging Alexis to look beautiful and find a vision of herself she adores.

The doctor is a good person, performing surgery on a crucial witness in federal protection and getting killed for the information. However, his assistant is a spy and killer. As she sneaks into the hospital to perform another hit, and gives her victim a lethal injection in an IV, there's a creepy moment of body horror. Thus, the surgeon's assistant is the story's real monster. She's even switched faces with another woman in order to get away with it. The horrors of plastic surgery thus get a few nods, as the story explores the creepy and dysfunctional side of striving for beauty.

Fashion Models ("Inventing the Girl," 202)

> CASTLE: Well, she's tall, she's gorgeous, 10 pounds underweight. Her hair is fried, she's wearing too much eye makeup. She's a model. Which means she was probably at a club last night. It's is, after all, Fashion Week, when all the hottest women in the world descend upon the hippest nightspots like locusts. Only, locusts eat.

Teddy Farrow, a major designer, hired the murder victim, Jenna, to be his new star model. As he fusses that the scandal will destroy his entire spring line of his clothing, Beckett is disgusted. He also callously requests the dress she was murdered in back. As he gives a speech about the value of his own insular world, Farrow insists clothing is as important as homicide – "clothes are what separate us from animals" and that they define civilization. He also describes a lifestyle of constant stress:

> Jenna was a small town girl straight of the bus from Ohio. She was a rising star but she wasn't ready for what was coming her way. I mean... I was thinking of making her the face of my campaign. That would have meant photo shoots magazines, billboards in Times Square and a very generous pay check. In the recent week she had become so bad tempered, paranoid. I started to wonder if she wasn't too inexperienced for a major campaign.

Her husband adds, "These parties you know, everyone's so phony" and describes a stalker writing her disturbing messages and taking photos. The photographer sabotaged her photo shoot when she refused to sleep with him. She was taking Addmair for weight loss, adding to her stress. It's finally revealed that she was killed with a photography trophy, emphasizing the cruel and deranged nature of the business.

The story hits closer to home as Castle offers Alexis's old babysitter, now a model, a safe haven in hopes the business won't take her down as well. During the episode, it's revealed that Beckett was a teen model, to her embarrassment, though she gave it up to pursue more serious work. Thus the industry is framed as a world where the models get out quickly or suffer.

Vampires ("Vampire Weekend," 206)

When a boy dressed as a vampire, with custom fangs is staked through the heart in a graveyard, Castle leaps to investigate. Creepy music and gloomy lighting add to the atmosphere of the scenes. But as Ryan tells them, vampires are nothing that startling:

> RYAN: Yeah, a vampire coven is like joining a church or a club. You like to play golf. I like to play golf. You like to drink blood. I like to drink blood. What? I...I used to go out with a girl who was into the lifestyle.
> ESPOSITO: What happened? Did the relationship suck?

CASTLE: Oh!
RYAN: The deal breaker? She wanted to have sex in a coffin.

They visit one of these clubs, complete with candelabras, red velvet and Gothic arches, only to find a place of high-end Halloween fun and romance amid the Victorian costumes and fake fangs. There they learn the boy's real life story. He was haunted by a strange dream, and turned to this alternative world for comfort and to explore the deep sadness in his life. They also track down his friend, who liked to dress as a werewolf. However, both boys dressed this way for entertainment and release rather than descending into some form of wickedness.

This world is presented sympathetically, as a place where the misfits and dark, gothic brooders can find a place to belong. The creepy psychopath Morlock who truly believes he's a vampire was trying to save his friend's life, and the murderer came from outside, framing the community to unfairly suggest the boy's lifestyle killed him.

Appropriately for the vampire episode, there's also a celebration of Joss Whedon's works – Nathan Fillion's Halloween costume is his own Captain Mal outfit from *Firefly*. Fillion adds, "That whole Halloween episode where I dressed as Mal Reynolds—the audience loves that. They know it's a TV show. So to see those little nudges and winks, it's great" (Nussbaum).

Alexis snarks that a space cowboy is an illogical concept with no cows in space, and that he wore the outfit "five years ago" when the film *Serenity* was made. Of course, Fillion also played a villain in season seven of *Buffy the Vampire Slayer*, so he takes the time to nod to the show. In the episode, he patrols a graveyard and quips, "Looks like Buffy visited the Big Apple."

Punk Bands ("Famous Last Words," 207)
Hayley Blue, lead singer of The Blue Pill, is found in an

alley, body staged, song "Here Kitty Kitty" playing. Since the song and the staging resemble a music video where Hayley described a stalker, he becomes the lead suspect. It's soon revealed that everyone in Hayley's world was troubled including Hayley herself. The investigation leads them to "Alison King Rehab Center. It's where all the stars go to clean up," as Beckett puts it. Hayley's sister Sky is still using, while her abusive guitarist tried to get them both high to suck them back into the life. Everyone in her life feels Hayley betrayed them by getting clean and being successful.

The only good, nonexploitative people in her life appear to be producers Ian and Bree Busch.

> BECKETT: Mrs. Busch, the rehab center said that you and your husband paid for her treatment and that she moved in with you after she left the facility.
> BREE BUSCH: Yeah. She'd become like family.
> CASTLE: Do all record producers pay for their artists to go to rehab?
> IAN BUSCH: No. Most just score them drugs and then look the other way. Manager gets them some pot so they can relax. The producer gets them some blow so they can... so they can work. Then someone gets them heroin. By the time we got to Hayley, she was already hooked. We told her our door was always open if she wanted to get clean.

Her old producer is a vile human being, exploiting Hayley's memory with "A Hayley Blue Tribute Tour." He was the one who addicted her to drugs after discovering her. He didn't kill her but is eager to be arrested for the publicity. "I never fully appreciated the nuances of the word 'skeevy' until just now," Castle notes as they walk away. Despite all these horrible people in her life, Hayley was actually killed by Ian Busch. First Bree tried to end her hard-won sobriety:

> BREE BUSCH: You have to understand, I had put so much money into this record. If she didn't finish it, I was gonna lose this studio. So I had to get her to stay, right? She was using anyway.
> CASTLE: You offered her drugs.

BREE BUSCH: A bag. I offered her a bag. I said, "There's plenty more where that came from." I – I would have gotten her help after she finished. I couldn't let her walk away.

After this, Ian, her rapist, killed her to cover his crime. The story thus unfolds all the hideous exploitation of the business, with everyone desperate to take whatever they came from Hayley, even those who promise to protect her.

Fandom is central to this episode as Alexis begins it in tears, informing Castle of the murder which she's learned of via the fan site. Alexis is the one to reveal the significance of the staging and the importance of the song lyrics. She knows everything about the pop star's time in rehab and struggle to get clean. She even reveals Hayley's obsession with Tarot – death means change, not murder. Castle sympathetically tells her, "Sometimes when we lose an artist we like, it's kind of like losing a friend. You know, I remember when John Lennon died, I didn't leave my room for a week." Alexis, Castle, and Beckett attend the singer's tribute concert as fans, finding a way to say goodbye. Thus fandom gets a gentler wave even during this episode's condemnation of the industry.

Call Girls ("Love Me Dead," 209)

SCARLETT PRICE: I came to New York in this ancient blue Beetle. The floor was so rusted, it literally sagged in the middle. But I can still remember coming over the bridge, and seeing the city right there in front of me. I thought everything was going to be perfect.
CASTLE: Something tells me this story takes a turn for the worse.
SCARLETT PRICE: The first night, somebody broke into my car and stole all my stuff. Then, the college friend I was going to stay with told me her boyfriend was moving in. I had to find another place.
CASTLE: Oh.
SCARLETT PRICE: But somehow I survived. Spent a year barely eating, living in a closet. When a friend mentioned doing this, I thought, "It couldn't be worse."
CASTLE: And is it?

SCARLETT PRICE: Mostly, no. Thanks for listening.

Her story is a cliché, and a further cliché follows as she arrives bruised at Castle's place then tries to kiss him and he gently rejects her, promising her safety and protection without strings. As she explains, her business has moved with the times, so much so that she only interacts with her pimp online. She adds:

> I know he runs the business, but I've never met him. It's not like I'm a street walker and he's in a fedora and a long fur coat. He's organized the entire operation to protect his identity. The girls are independent contractors. The clients are all given numbers so we don't know their last names. They pay the business by credit card, and our fees get deposited directly into our bank accounts.

Scarlett claims she's a call girl putting herself through law school (another cliché) until a prosecutor took pity on her and hired her as an intern so she could give up the life (another cliché again). As is finally reveled, she's the pimp herself, not surprising as her last name suggests she's anything but altruistic. Castle tells her (in terribly clichéd fashion once again) "You never stop manipulating, do you, Scarlett? I should be impressed, really. How easily you played me. But all I can think about is how sad it is. All that brains and beauty wasted on a heart gone rotten. You're so busy building up walls to keep people out...you don't even realize that you're the one trapped inside. All alone."

This story barely touches the real plight of real call girls, only a single terribly manipulative young woman whose entire story appears a lie. Only a few moments consider the real truth of her plight:

> CASTLE: Do you think she'll be okay?
> BECKETT: I don't know. Girls in sex industry usually come from a history of childhood dysfunction. It's hard to escape that.
> CASTLE: But it's possible, right?
> BECKETT: Yeah.

Clearly those in need of real saving must wait for another story.

Professional Baseball ("Suicide Squeeze," 215)

> CASTLE: What is it with professional sports? Even the agencies are on steroids.
> BECKETT: Fox's client list is a veritable who's-who of star athletes. Five percent of their endorsements and salaries? You could pay for half of lower Manhattan.

As Beckett and Castle gush, Joe Torre guest stars as himself. The episode had no licensing from Major League Baseball or any affiliate organization, so they vaguely mention Torre's "big move" but call the players winners of the "World Championship" instead of "World Series."

Their victim is famous – with many fans in the NYPD. Between the team's fannishness and Torre's appearance, this episode seems another big wave to the fans, reminding them that the NYPD is as starstruck as they are.

> BECKETT: Cano Vega, the baseball player.
> ESPOSITO: Yep.
> CASTLE: Cano Vega? Are you sure?
> ESPOSITO: He was my first-round draft pick in my fantasy league three years running. .314 batting average, 4 gold gloves, and one... championship ring.
> BECKETT: I almost caught one of his homers once. He had just came to the States from Cuba, and my dad took us out to the bleachers over at Shea.
> CASTLE: I didn't know you were a baseball fan.
> BECKETT: It's genetic, on my dad's side. He's been taking me to games since I was 3.

The victim is killed with a baseball bat on a practice field, and then pummeled with balls from the automatic machine. He seemed a good man, supporting the unfortunate by having that field built in the first place. Though beloved by many fans, he also had enemies. Alfredo

Quintana, editor of a Cuban magazine in the US, considers him a traitor willing to support Castro's regime. Vega's wife explains:

> A-a few months ago, the Cuban tourism department approached him. They wanted Cano to be the poster boy for the new Cuba...While Cano was down there, the locals treated him like a hero – their hero. At a state dinner, Castro came over and shook his hand. When he got home, his friends called him a traitor for going, said he was a lapdog for Fidel. The same people who cheered when he built that ballpark came up and told him to go to hell.

As a gifted player, everyone values him – the Cuban government and his manager, but all want to use him for their own aims – the government as a poster boy and Bobby Fox, Cano's agent, for money. It's the latter who smuggled him out of Cuba but made him leave his fiancée behind, a brutal betrayal that defined Cano Vega's life. Despite the contrasting pictures that other people offer of him, Vega appears to be a good person trying to give back to the community. It's the exploitation of others in this multimillion dollar industry that finally kills him.

Bondage and Dominatrices ("The Mistress Always Spanks Twice," 216)

The episode starts smutty, with a dead woman cuffed and covered in caramel sauce, hanging in the park. However, on closer examination, nothing is what it appears.

The custom cuffs were actually a gift from Tyler Benton for his girlfriend Jessica, the murder victim. He had been just about to propose. Jessica was a doctoral student in sociology, masquerading as Mistress Venom to aid her academic research. While they interrogate her masochistic, semi-aggressive, client (who had caramel fantasies), he's found innocent. As with the vampire case, someone not involved in this insular and misunderstood world committed the murder and tried to frame the victim's lifestyle as the motive for it.

As usual, Castle has fun plunging into the life, but Beckett does as well, booking a session for herself and her "boyfriend Ricky" who's been a "bad bad boy" and interrogating a client dominatrix-style. Ryan and Esposito have opposite reactions to the women as their "work outfits" don't seem to bother Ryan at all, while Esposito interviews a dominatrix who orders him to untie the laces of her knee-high boots and slaps him with her riding crop as he gets down on his knees. The episode provides a fun exploration, allowing characters to enact their fantasies, but can't stop itself from playing up the salacious angle.

Mummies ("Wrapped Up in Death," 219)

Mr. Medina, associate curator at the New York History Museum, is the victim. He had recently led an expedition to the tomb of Kan-Xul, the legendary Mayan king. They discovered "the single most important archaeological find in Mayan history – his burial chamber – where he was entombed with a dozen of his mummified slaves." Like the Egyptians, the Mayans mummified important figures, particularly kings, and filled their tombs with grave goods so they could live on. This was a form of worship, allowing the people to commemorate and revere the powerful among them. Sometimes they would kill the servants and mummify them beside their ruler.

Inevitably, questions arise of a mummy's curse for disturbing the sacred resting place.

> RUPERT BENTLEY: Tell them, Stanford. Tell them what was written at the entrance to the burial chamber. "All who gaze on the face of the Mayan king shall be struck down by his wrath."
> CASTLE: Mayan king? This Mayan king?
> RUPERT BENTLEY: That very one. They all looked inside, and they're all dead.
> BECKETT: There were other incidents?
> DR. RAYNES: All easily explainable. One of our grad students, Nicole Graham, was mauled to death by a jaguar outside the dig site.

RACHEL: And Professor Fisher died of dengue fever.
DR. RAYNES: Which is common in that region, as are curses written above grave sites. It's how they kept people from robbing them for thousands of years.

Unfortunately for Castle, he has already opened the mummy's tomb (while playing Indiana Jones) and laid himself open...to his friends' humor and possibly a curse. The precinct follow his encounter with practical jokes, as they remove bolts from his chair so it collapses, then have the bomb squad rig the coffee maker to spew steam at him. Beckett quips, "Castle, you sure you don't want to stay in the car? We don't want the curse to get you." However, when the elevator traps him within, they tell him even they're not that cruel. A dog attack likewise might be coincidence...or not.

RYAN: (holding a book) You know, Castle, this Kan-Xul was no joke. Legend has, he personally conducted hundreds of human sacrifices. (Points to a picture in the book)
ESPOSITO: You know why his burial chamber was so hard to find, right? Because his own People buried it so that he couldn't come back from the grave and get them.
CASTLE: Yes, yes, yes. Scary mummy, I get it. Thank you.

Meanwhile, activist Cacaw Te raises a legitimate concern, saying, "The Mayans are not a dead race. There are seven million of us in Mexico and Central America – the direct descendants of Kan-Xul. His remains and all that was buried with him belong to us." Indeed, archeologists through history have disrespected local peoples to raid tombs and steal treasure. This is one factor leading to the stories of ancestral curses.

There are several actor jokes. Gil Birmingham, Cacaw Te, played a mummy's bodyguard in *Buffy's* "Inca Mummy Girl." Erick Avari from *The Mummy* (1999) also cameos.

The curse gains more power, as the murder weapon, a pushed gargoyle, is revealed to have traces on it of sodium nitrate, iron oxide, decomposed hemp fibers and ancient human tissue. Either the killer touched the mummy, or as Castle fears, "The mummy himself has risen from the grave and is roaming New York seeking vengeance."

Meanwhile the mummy trip, when investigated, offers many dirty secrets, as its leader was sleeping with his grad student before she got killed out in the woods. Dr. Raynes adds, "What happened to Will wasn't the curse. It was karma." Will also sold his gathered treasures to private collectors. The museum is quick to capitalize on the deaths, as they advertise "Do you dare see... The mummy of the Mayan king," and refuse to let tragedy stop them from profiting.

One reportedly ancient mummy is finally revealed to be a recent murder victim, killed because of a lover's obsession, not because of the job. The museum generously returns the mummies to the Mayans, in return for Chacaw Te telling Castle how to break the curse. Thus everyone gets a happy ending. Nonetheless, Castle ends the episode by cutting himself with a bread knife and asking, "What's the difference between 'curse' and 'clumsy'?" The mystique lives on.

Talk Shows ("The Late Shaft," 220)

"And that's our show for tonight. Stay tuned for "Late Talk with Mickey Reed." I'm Bobby Mann. Remember, folks... The boys'll be back on duty tomorrow night," Bobby announces broadly. As the cameras click off, Bobby whispers "They want me dead," to Castle, who's guest-starring on the show. Indeed, Bobby turns up murdered shortly after. He is reminiscent of Conan O'Brien, complete with Dwight Eisenhower mug, offering a particular homage for viewers.

The talk show hosts are terribly immoral – as Beckett points out, they're professional liars. One woman sleeps with Castle to secure the casting of Nikki Heat. The murder victim has a collection of lovely blonde ex-wives (every five years he gets another) and is sleeping with the show's young intern, the producer's daughter.

> JANINE: He was banging my daughter right under my nose?! I will kill him!
> CASTLE: He's already dead.
> JANINE: Well I will kill him again! I don't care! Where's the corpse?!
> BECKETT: Ms. Marks, we just...
> JANINE: Kayla! My office, now! Move it! Move it!

She isn't the only one hot under the collar about the industry:

> WEISBERG: Hell, I'll sick God on you! (To Castle) And you? I don't ever want to see you on my network again. You're banned! (To Beckett) And you?! I don't know you. You're all a bunch of nobodies! I could buy this precinct!
> MONTGOMERY: Howard Weisberg, President of the network. He just found out about the search warrant for Mickey Reed. And he also found out that we think Bobby Mann was murdered.
> BECKETT: How?
> MONTGOMERY: Breaking news on a different network. The guy got scooped on his own star's murder.

As the solution is found, the victim was planning to replace his old war buddy and co-anchor to save his own career. Thus his old friend, horribly betrayed, plotted a swift revenge. This murder was driven by the cutthroat industry, with millions at stake, as the story makes clear. The episode's plot has many similarities to the Jay Leno/Conan O'Brien controversy on *The Tonight Show*, as well as elements of David Letterman's affair and its scandal.

Celebrity Chefs ("Food to Die For," 222)

Food and the restaurant experience are central in New York, as Castle protests: "The murder is at Q3? This place has only been open three months. I can't even get a reservation here. I've been dying to eat here." The restaurant served fois gras sandwiches and popcorn soup, while the chef specialized in molecular gastronomy. Later Castle and restaurant PR specialist Madison go out for a tasting menu of caviar parfait and black truffle risotto with crispy shrimp. Castle adds, "The waiter was about to come out with the duck confit en croute, Rocco Dispirito's pumpkin gnocchi, not to mention the langoustine, the lavender crème brûlee that was coming up. And don't even get me started on the wine pairings."

The victim, Balthazar Wolf, was the head chef. Castle calls him "Big Bad Wolf, winner of Kitchen Wars, season six." Allegedly, he was "the bad boy America loved to hate." Meanwhile, "Kitchen Wars" isn't a real show, but it appears based on cooking competition series *Top Chef.* The episode emphasizes how much of the *Kitchen Wars* animosity is fake – Wolf and rival Jennifer Wong fought onscreen and she even threatened to kill him, but she reveals that offscreen they were friends and loaned each other cooking equipment. She adds, "And win or lose, you want people to remember your name when it's over. That's how you build your brand." Mitchell Olson, a contestant on *Survivor: Australia*, revealed that all the laughter and sing-alongs by the campfire always got edited out: "I guess because it's not as dramatic – it doesn't show us being stressed out and starving" (Robinson 182). Only the fights and cattiness stayed onscreen.

Nonetheless, winning the TV competition brought Balthasar incredible fame, leading to a starring role at the new restaurant as well as the $100,000 prize. Women drape themselves all over him, even married ones. It's a world of fun and glamour as New Yorkers try the newest, hottest dishes on the cutting edge of cuisine. While Wolf's personal life caught up with him, his restaurant goes forward with a grand reopening, emphasizing that restaurants in New York will always be king.

Simulated Spy Game ("A Deadly Game," 224)

A man runs through the park at night like he's being chased. He runs to a pay phone.

31

MAN (on phone): This is Blackbird. Identification?
ROGER FARRADAY: Designate 223. I am blown. I am blown!
MAN (on phone): This call is unauthorized, 223. This line is not secure.
ROGER FARRADAY: Where is the safe house?
MAN (on phone): Negative, 223. You know the rules. (click)

The story opens on a spy adventure, with the pay phone at the beginning as an homage to the spy movie *Three Days of the Condor*, according to Andrew Marlowe's commentary.

Castle, meanwhile, is at home watching *His Girl Friday* when he gets his call that there's been a murder ("A Deadly Game," 224). They find the victim professionally shot with false ID and a bag of euros in the car.

BECKETT: I tried information, our database...They even did an internet search, and it's like these guys don't even exist.
CASTLE: Who?
BECKETT: Fastwater Global Services.
CASTLE: Ah! See? I told you. CIA cover. No, I mean, they probably just don't like to advertise.
BECKETT: Yeah, well, I thought so as well. So I checked their address, 1747 West 43rd Street. It's in the middle of the Hudson River. So, I went back and checked through his wallet, and looked at his IDs, his gym membership, health insurance, even his ATM card. They're all fakes.

On finding a pen that plays a message, Castle realizes to his delight that their victim is a spy. As shown from the beginning, they're using all the clichés from the movies – code words, public identifiers, a pen that plays a message and self-destructs. Beckett has to ask, "This all feel a little odd to you? The old cloak-and-dagger, secret meetings, code words. It all feels a little old-fashioned. I mean, why meet face-to-face when you can just send an encrypted e-mail?"

In fact, she is right. When Castle finds documents on the target, a diplomat from the Republic of Luvania, he realizes it's all fake. With his innate fannishness, he immediately understands who would set up fake spies with code words to assassinate a fake diplomat.

> ESPOSITO: The company is called Spy Ventures. They specialize in high-end spy-cations for thrill seekers.
> CASTLE: Spy-cations?
> ESPOSITO: Yeah. You want to be kidnapped and interrogated? They got a package. You want to be a super spy? They got a package. Their motto is "authenticity."
> CASTLE: Right down to the offshore accounts, false identifications, and realistic weaponry.
> BECKETT: All right, find out who the hell's in charge. Let's see if "authenticity" includes murder.

SpyVentures is actually based on a French company called Ultime Realite, which specializes in giving its players the illicit thrill of kidnapping and interrogation. Beckett is sarcastic about the game's value, noting, "You know, it used to be if you were gonna have a midlife crisis, you'd just buy a Ferrari, get a new girlfriend, even jump out of a plane." Even Castle seems in no rush to sign up for this one.

The problem is that people aren't playing and creating the game for its fun – they're exploiting it. One of the handlers is selling fake IDs, which his players deliver. Two players are using the game to indulge in their affair. And one is using it to cover a murder. Thus the game allows its player to revel in the worst of human behavior, not its best.

Psychics ("He's Dead, She's Dead," 303)

> RYAN: Mediums are the ones that can see ghosts, right, Castle?
> CASTLE: Yes, psychics can tell the future. Mediums can tell the future and talk to the dead.
> BECKETT: That's like saying psychics are con artists and mediums are con artists and charlatans.
> CASTLE: You sound pretty certain of yourself. ("He's Dead, She's Dead," 302)

In "He's Dead, She's Dead," Castle is the believer, as usual, and Beckett is the skeptic. Martha reveals that Castle comes from a long line of "mind readers" who were actually carnival folk swindling the public. Despite this, Castle pounces on every one of the psychic's revelations. "Castle always wants everything to be fantastic. He wants the stories to be amazing," Fillion notes in the commentary for "The Final Frontier" (507).

Several of her predictions come true: the psychic told a criminal that if he wanted to find happiness, he should invest in a real estate offer. He does so and the deal goes bust, but he meets his high school sweetheart and they fall in love once more. More intriguingly, the psychic writes a note with details of the crime. "The psychic predicted her own murder!" Castle shouts with glee.

It's revealed that the psychic did some detective work and spied on her clients, but also that she knew more than can be explained away. As such, it treats her business with a mixture of faith and realism. The show takes a mystery angle, leaving it ultimately unclear whether the murderer wrote the note as a diversion or whether the psychic really did see the future. Her daughter's final message is also intriguing: that Alexander will be very important to Beckett and save her life. The writers get in a wave to the audience with this one:

> CASTLE: Oh, before I forget... what did Penny say about Alexander?
> BECKETT: Oh, nothing. Just some silly stuff that didn't really make any sense. Why?
> CASTLE: Because my middle name is Alexander.
> BECKETT: I thought your middle name was Edgar.
> CASTLE: Been perusing the personal section of the Richard Castle website again, have we? No, I changed my middle name to Edgar for Edgar Allen Poe back when I changed my last name to Castle. My given name is Richard Alexander Rodgers. What a coincidence, huh?

Steampunk ("Punked," 304)

The team find a murder victim shot with an antique bullet, as well as century-old clothing. Tracking the victim's favorite address, they discover a hidden steampunk club. There, the members dress in corsets and bustles, celebrating the Victorian era, though with science fiction gadgets added.

The club president rides up on a penny-farthing with exhaust pipes and proceeds to help with the investigation.

After *NCIS: LA*'s "steampunk episode," in which Abbey goes on a date at a rather generic LA Goth bar named SteamPunk, where a few of the Goths wear Steampunk accessories – that's it – a blogger at Tor issued a challenge for someone to produce a real "steampunk episode." He adds:

> I have been told by *Castle* creator and executive producer Andrew Marlowe that "Punked" was their answer to that challenge, and let me say that they have more than exceeded my wildest expectations. *Castle*'s "Punked" was everything that the *NCIS: LA* episode was not, and it should go down in television history as the first real "steampunk episode" of a mainstream TV show. (Falksen)

He adds glowingly, "The club has just the vintage Victorian feel one would expect to attract steampunk clientele (indeed, speaking personally I wish the club really did exist in New York City; I'd join in a heartbeat)" (Falksen). The Steampunk community in L.A. were extras, strutting in their top hats and goggles as they reveled in the fun. The doorman offers Jules Verne trivia, which Castle guesses (while the less romantic Beckett flashes her badge). They find themselves entering Victorian London, 1892, but with rock music, colorful drinks, and a time machine. Their club president calls their club "an oasis where human potential and ingenuity is limitless. Where there's poetry and wonder and meaning even in death." Castle looks spellbound and requests to try the penny-farthing.

Castle explains steampunk to Beckett, describing it as "a subculture that embraces the simplicity and romance of the past and at the same time couples it with the hope and promise and sheer supercoolness of futuristic design." This definition pleased the steampunk community, establishing an excellent summary for non-fans. This, like the vampire episode, was a respectful and loving look at the culture. "The characters display a lovely blend of eccentricity, jovial humor and artistic romanticism. It is subtly but accurately pointed out that the members of the steampunk community are intelligent, respectable, educated people who, though a bit geeky and certainly eccentric, are well-spoken and good-hearted" (Falksen). As often occurs on the show, while the members of the world were having a romantic and impetuous but ultimately harmless duel, someone else used their practices as a cover to commit murder.

As always, Castle throws himself into the world, enjoying his visit there. He also discovers the fun of (accidentally) threatening Alexis's new boyfriend with an antique gun, reverting to a simpler, more wild-west time. Before episode end, Castle is trying out a Steampunk-style robotic arm, a cutting-edge piece of Steampunk tech far more beautifully crafted than the knock-offs at costume shops.

> In short, "Punked" was perhaps the best first TV introduction to the mainstream world that the steampunk community could have hoped for. The general public can likewise watch with confidence that what they are being shown is an accurate and well-researched portrayal of the next big subculture that they, their friends or their kids will soon want to begin exploring. (Falksen)

Grey's Anatomy ("Anatomy of a Murder," 305)

> BECKETT: How much TV do you actually watch?
> CASTLE: Enough to know that this Nurse McClintock will probably be super-hot.
> MALE NURSE: Detective? You wanted to see me?
> CASTLE: And you are?
> MALE NURSE: Nurse McClintock.
> BECKETT: (*to Castle*) Care to revise your theory?
> CASTLE: Not what I was expecting, but no, I'll stand by it.

Obviously, Castle's knowledge of medicine comes from *Grey's Anatomy* (like *Castle*, also on ABC) and shows like it. The episode title, "Anatomy of a Murder," subtly references both *Grey's Anatomy* and the 1959 motion picture *Anatomy of a Murder*, a courtroom drama. Sarah Drew's actress even starred in "Nanny McDead" (102). Meanwhile, Castle and Beckett investigate the hospital in light-colored coats, symbolically entering the world. Beckett also reveals that the man she's dating is a cardiac surgeon, making Castle flare up with jealousy. Through it all, Castle's television view of hospitals continues:

> BECKETT: You know, with the state of health care and how stressful this can be for families and for patients, I'm surprised more medical professionals aren't killed every day.
> CASTLE: Yeah. Not to mention the betrayal, the lust, the bed hopping. (she gives him a look) I've watched enough medical dramas to know that doctors are notorious for sleeping with each other. I bet, as we speak, in this hospital, two doctors are in a break room doing it. And by it, I mean –

Castle, it turns out, isn't far off as Nurse McClintock has flirty relationships with everyone around him, so much that the female doctors will do him illicit favors. His alibi is just as colorful: "Okay, uh, I was … getting coffee with Imani. I mean, Dr. Phelps. No wait. At that time I was with Rhonda. Dr. Chimes." (Dr. Rhonda Chimes is in fact a shoutout to *Grey*'s creator, Shonda Rhimes.) Castle decides, "I knew my homicidal hospital love triangle theory had weight."

Likewise, 'Seriously? Seriously,' is a signature exchange on that show between main character Meredith and her colleagues, echoes in the episode:

> NURSE McCLINTOCK: Are you asking for my alibi? Seriously?
> BECKETT: Seriously.
> NURSE McCLINTOCK: Seriously?
> BECKETT: Seriously.
> NURSE McCLINTOCK: (to Castle) Seriously?
> CASTLE: Seriously!

Castle continues referring to Nurse McClintock as "McDreamy," a fan nickname for the character Derek

Shepherd on *Grey's Anatomy*. All the women's desperate love for Nurse Greg might be considered something of a parody. As the episode progresses, however, Castle notes: "Turns out, Greg isn't McDreamy or McSteamy. He's McSkeemy," as he's using his medical connections to rescue his girlfriend from prison by faking her death. His desperate love for this woman as they go on the run also echoes the medical show's drama and passion. The episode is more of a spoof or homage than exploration of the real medical world, but as such, it brings extra fun for the fans.

Male Escorts and Strippers ("Almost Famous," 306)

The dead cop they discover is actually a male stripper with tear-away pants and squirt gun of tequila. They trace him to the bachelorette party where he performed and see the salacious photos he took with the horny women. Esposito complains of them "Treating him like a piece of meat," while the bachelorette protests, "It's what he's paid for. He had fun, too."

As the detectives explore his life, they discover he was the acting student believed to have the most potential in his class, but his agent hadn't booked him any roles in a year. He soon became a stripper. As his agent tells them: "In addition to the private gigs, he also danced at a club called The Package Store couple nights a week. Most of those guys are juicing….People think woman are catty, but, uh, from what Derek said, those guys would make showgirls look like an afterschool special." Thus he paints a world of steroids and competition.

Beckett and Castle venture into yet another insular world, but his time Castle's the skeptic. "You know, ever since I've been following you, I've been dreaming of the day that you'd say, "Let's go to the strip club and get this dirt bag." I just never imagined it would feel like this." Beckett however dresses up and brings a stack of singles. It's a fake place, with a clichéd fireman strip show while crowds of women shout and grope. Backstage, "Hans von Manschaft" drops the fake German accent when he hears his rival has been murdered. Even Castle feels overwhelmed and calls on Beckett for rescue. Agent Lloyd Saunders tells Esposito, thinking he's come for an audition, "I'm already up to my ears in A-Rods. But, uh, your friend here...I got women requesting that skinny Twilight dude like crazy." With that, he tosses Ryan a G-string to his shock.

Rebecca Dalton, an elderly ex-model, was dating the victim, and her lawyer hired him for a scheme. This is certainly the sad tale of a young actor who failed to make it in New York and was exploited. But it spends too much time smirking with salaciousness, as it provides equal opportunity strippers for the female viewers (one assumes).

Bird Watchers and Bulb Changers ("Murder Most Fowl," 308)

Ryan notes, "Both parents are deceased, guy never married, has no children. It's like he barely existed." Their murder victim's nickname was Lightbulb Len, as it was his job to change the light bulbs in the stations and tunnels all over New York. He never missed work in twenty-two years and changed over a million bulbs. Meanwhile, his supervisor notes that they've never had a personal conversation.

> ARTHUR: The guy was one of the unsung heroes of this city. He saved a lot of lives.
> CASTLE: I'm sorry. I thought ... I thought he changed light bulbs.
> ARTHUR: Bad things happen in darkness, Mr. Castle. Dimly lit tunnels, darkened stairwells ... if Len heard about a blown bulb before shift end he would stay late on his own time to fix it. And of course there was his response to the Abe Lipschitz tragedy. 1989? An electrocution of a bulb changer at the Brighton Beach station? This is a circuit interrupter switch. Shuts down all the power inside a tunnel so that electrical maintenance could be performed safely. Down here it's called the Lenny Box, because it took a visionary like Len Levitt to design it and force the transit authority to install one in every station in this city.

He was an invisible man with an invisible job completely vital to New York's operation. Thus the conversation above waves to the quietest subcommunity of New York – the maintenance workers. His hobby, a quiet one for a quiet man, gives viewers another inside look into a very different insular world. The victim's place contains a parabolic microphone purchased by an insurance actuary named Byron H Singer.

> BECKETT: What did you see?
> BYRON: The two of them. Together. In the park. Like a pair of lovebirds. But he accused me of making the whole thing up. I mean, why would I make something like that up? Why would anybody?
> BECKETT: Mr. Singer, what exactly did you see in the park?
> BRYON: I saw enough. And believe me, I was pretty shocked to see them together. I knew I had to tell Len before somebody else did.
> CASTLE: Len must have been very angry when you told him.
> BRYON: Very angry and jealous. But I had followed them and found their secret spot. And I told him when and where to find them. I even lent him some of my equipment so he could spy on them himself.

Beckett and Castle spin a theory of jealous lovers, but they're completely wrong.

> BECKETT: Uh, who did you see in the park that night?
> BYRON: The red tailed hawks. There haven't been a nesting pair in the park for forty years.
> BECKETT: You ... mean this is about birds?
> BYRON: Not just birds. The red tailed hawks! Len oversees the log in the Central Park Boathouse where all the sightings are officially recorded. He refused to acknowledge my sighting. So I told him if he didn't believe me he should go out to the park and see for himself. They nest at dusk....I want this on the official record, I would never exaggerate or fabricate a bird sighting. It's unthinkable! They're there. And I saw them first.
> CASTLE: I'm putting that in the official record.

In fact, while bird watching, Len Levitt witnessed a

kidnapping and was killed so he wouldn't raise the alarm. Thus the story quickly leaves his tiny worlds far behind. However, at the climax, Beckett and Castle manage to save the kidnapped child because of his "Lenny Box" invention, emphasizing even small contributions and their power to reshape the world.

The X-Files ("Close Encounters of the Murderous Kind," 309)

Castle is clearly an *X-Files* fan, as he whistles the theme song several times when they struggle to explain mysterious events. In fact, Rob Bowman, who directed thirty-three episodes of *The X-Files* and the movie (*The X-Files: Fight the Future*) is a featured director and executive producer. David Amann is a recurring writer for both shows. For an added joke, actor Lance Henriksen, who guest stars as the abduction therapist, was actually in the film *Close Encounters of the Third Kind* in 1977. The episode title is clearly an homage.

The story begins with spooky music and dark lighting. The victim, Marie, is dead from explosive decompression – as if she went to outer space. She was an astrophysicist who had just called a friend in SETI (The Search for Extraterrestrial Intelligence) to describe a life-changing event. Castle, of course, is hooked.

> CASTLE: Check this out. She was reading *Taken By The Fourth Kind*. A book on alien abductions.
> BECKETT: So what's your theory, Castle? That she was abducted and then killed by aliens?
> CASTLE: Well... a story that makes more sense is ... alien abduction gone wrong. One that ends with Marie accidently being blasted out of the airlock of the alien spaceship.

As they discover an experimental chamber that could cause explosive decompression, as well as competitive workplace colleagues, Castle is undeterred.

> CASTLE: You know what would be a better story?

BECKETT: Hmm? (he holds up the book *Taken By The Fourth Kind*) We have an earthbound solution to this mystery and you are disappointed. I get it. But that? Really?
CASTLE: C'mon. Marie said she had a life changing event. What could be more life changing than being beamed up by this guy? (he holds the book up again)
BECKETT: C'mon Castle, we all know that there are no such things as alien abductions.
CASTLE: Yet most abductees report the same experiences. The white light, the memory flashes.
BECKETT: That's because they all read the same books so of course they describe the same event. The dark, lonely road, the bright light out of nowhere, memories of being poked and prodded.
CASTLE: I believe the word you're looking for is "probed." And then of course there's the alien implant that's used to track the abductees.

When Lanie Parish, the medical examiner, finds a strange mineral up the victim's nose, Castle knows it's an implant. Castle's comments about the aliens being grey, not green, Beckett dying her hair red and calling him "Mulder," shape-shifting aliens who only look human, and the Chinese spy he calls the "cigarette smoking man" are all *X-Files* nods. When Castle finds out the latter was Chinese, he adds, "Maybe she was killed by an alien. Just an illegal alien." Likewise, Beckett's comment about the real truth being out there is a reference to the show's tagline, which was "the truth is out there."

The previous week, Marie had discovered anomalous sub microwave bursts on her radio telescope. The signal was coming from somewhere nearby, with a repetitive pattern. She had a photo of what looked like an alien ship. More mystifyingly, she was losing time, blanking out on four hours of her life. When Castle hears that she was also having flashbacks of "A white room, a blurry face, questioning her," he's convinced.

Just as Beckett announces, "When this is all said and done, it will all come down to where and how she was killed. And I bet it will have nothing to do with secret agents or massive government conspiracies," government spooks clear out Marie's office.

Soon after, Castle and Beckett find themselves on a dark road. Terrifyingly, their car and phones stop working and a bright light shines overhead. They're taken somewhere strange, interrogated, and returned to their car with strange marks on their necks. Of course, it's the men in black, sent by the government to protect their secrets in another *X-Files* nod. The radio telescope anomalies and photos are Chinese spy equipment.

When they find the spooks, Castle gets fannish as always, insisting, "Where are the predator drones? The black helicopters? All those SWAT teams repelling down on ropes?" He stops a man from taking cyanide only to discover it's actually gum. The story ends with them telling Beckett something confidential, and Castle is stuck guessing whether this is about the Loch Ness Monster or thought control.

Stage Magicians ("Poof! You're Dead," 312)

Magician Zalman Drake is found in his own water tank, smothered by rabbit fur amid mystical music. Castle and Beckett both speak glowingly of his magic shop, bringing their own fannishness to bear:

> CASTLE: The murder is here? At Drake's Magic Shop?
> BECKETT: Yep.
> CASTLE: I've been coming here since I was thirteen years old. This place is a paradise for boys. Whoopee cushions, magic tricks, fake vomit.
> BECKETT: It's not just for boys, Castle. My grandfather was an amateur magician and I used to come here every Sunday afternoon when I was that age, too.
> CASTLE: I never pegged you for a magic fan. You know any good tricks?
> BECKETT I do this one thing. With ice cubes.

Castle nearly swallows his tongue. This time, Lanie is the skeptic, noting, "You know, it is beyond me why people think this is entertaining. I see a guy hanging upside down in a water tank, I think, 'you are a fool'."

Castle, insisting on his geek cred, retorts, "You know, the milk cans and the water torture tank, they were real game changers in the magic world. They were the first presentation of real life and death consequences. As the magician held his breath, so did the audience."

As the case unfolds, they visit practitioners from a street magician to popular showman Tobias Strange "the Johnny Depp of magic," who made a Ferrari disappear on the Vegas stage. Castle and Beckett arrive in time to see him escape a box of knives. Showing his own fannishness for someone behind the scenes, Strange describes Zalman as the heart of the community and a brilliant engineer.

They finally track down Zalman's workshop, where they must press a brick to enter. Magic paraphernalia of all sorts crowds the room, and the door shuts dramatically behind them. There's a sparkly chandelier and clap on lights. Beckett says, "Wow, Castle. My grandfather would have loved this place. Look, he has a guillotine. And an iron maiden! He even had a zig zag box. You know, you would have liked my grandfather. In fact, you remind me of him a little." Suddenly, Zalman steps out of the iron maiden. Castle delightedly calls it the "best trick ever!" but it's soon revealed that the man was Zalman's identical twin. Describing a mental connection with his brother, he hurried into the city to find him. Though he doesn't know what his brother was working on, he too describes the passion and engineering genius necessary for sleight of hand.

Castle notes, "In every magic story, there's an unexpected twist where things aren't always what they seem. It's an obligation of the genre." Finally Zalman's assistant explains, "He said this was his greatest magic trick ever. Said he was getting paid a fortune…to get away with murder." They discover Zalman was indeed doing an enormous trick – helping a billionaire fake his death and vanish. Beckett notes, "I mean, it's brilliant really. Magicians are masters at misdirection. If they can manipulate audiences, they can manipulate witnesses. They could even make people testify to things that never happened." The billionaire in turn killed him to silence him. Castle and Beckett solve the case through their knowledge of theatrics. Then, building on this, Castle uses his own celebrity status to realize that the billionaire hasn't left town:

> BECKETT: Castle, this is crazy.
> CASTLE: Crazy, but in character. Look at the kind of guy Christian Dahl was, how he loved the limelight, his fascination with life after death. You think a guy like that is going to miss the opportunity to attend his own funeral?
> BECKETT: Would you?
> CASTLE: Not a chance.

Once he's in custody, Beckett has Zalman's identical twin and Tobias Strange rig a creepy illusion of Zalman to startle Dahl into confessing. Beckett gleefully delivers her line, "Alakazam, jackass." As she and Castle pull small illusions, they both celebrate this life of mystery and fun.

As always, the B plot reflects the mystery. Other bits of misdirection in the episode include Esposito and Lanie's attempts to hide their romance and Castle's attempts to divert people from his own failing romance with Gina.

> CASTLE: No, nothing is all. Everything is fine. Everything is … just fine. It's ordinary. Problem is, I don't want ordinary. I want –
> MARTHA: Magic.
> CASTLE: Yeah. You know what the problem is? We just aren't in love. Neither one of us wants to admit … organophosphates.
> MARTHA is confused by the turn of conversation.
> CASTLE: It wasn't a nerve agent. It was jet oil. Zalman was at an airport.
> MARTHA: What? I –
> CASTLE: I gotta go.
> CASTLE leaves hurriedly.
> MARTHA: Now you see him, now you don't.

Soap Opera Stars ("One Life to Lose," 318)

MANDY BRONSON (as Angela Cannon): Joseph, this is the last time we can do this.
LANCE HASTINGS (as Joseph Fox): What are you talking about?
MANDY BRONSON (as Angela Cannon): I'm going back to my husband.
LANCE HASTINGS (as Joseph Fox): Alfonso?
MANDY BRONSON (as Angela Cannon): I'm sorry.
LANCE HASTINGS (as Joseph Fox): Angie, baby, what about us?
[A door closes.]
MANDY BRONSON (as Angela Cannon): Oh, my god. Oh, my god, that's him .He's home early.
ALFONSO: Angela, are you upstairs?
MANDY BRONSON (as Angela Cannon): Hide in the closet. Mi bello!

As they continue acting their scene, Lance opens the closet and a body drops out with an axe in the back. To their shock the body is real – it's their writer Sarah Cutler. The soap opera has turned deadly.

Some of the crew think her death by fire axe in the back is symbolic, as her first act as writer was to kill off the show's matriarch of thirty years.

CASTLE: Or maybe Sarah discovered that Greek billionaire Mikos had invented a machine that could cause blizzards that would plunge the entire world into an ice age.
BECKETT: Really? You're gonna go with an evil weather machine?
CASTLE: It already happened. On *General Hospital*. Look, bear in mind, we're entering into a world of epic drama with larger than life characters, each one teaming with twisted secrets and personal intrigue. It stands to reason that the motive for this murder will be worthy of a soap opera.
BECKETT: Castle, even in a world of epic drama, the motives are usually quite ordinary.
[They turn a corner and see the victim with the bright red fire axe in her back.]

CASTLE: Now, does that look ordinary to you? The victim
with an axe in her back on the set of her own show. Odds
are, the killer walks amongst us on this very soundstage.

Of course, Lance and Mandy hate each other offscreen.
Still the actors' lives resemble a soap as Sarah and her
husband are separated, and his alibi for her murder is sleeping
with Mandy. As Castle describes her dramatically, "Home
wrecking diva engaged in a tour d'affair with the victim's
husband. She fled their illicit love nest after a mysterious e-
mail from Sarah on the eve of her murder." In fact, she
promptly slept with a producer to keep her character alive.

Meanwhile, Sarah's mother gave her up for adoption and
only found her again as an adult. Castle protests that she's
clearly "a gold digging opportunist who's insinuated herself
back into her daughter's life because she's in need of a heart
transplant and Sarah is the only compatible donor." Beckett
retorts, "Sure, maybe on Temptation Lane. Not in the real
world." As it turns out, the mother is a fake in another
shocking twist. Castle's mother recalls similar insanity while
she was briefly on the show:

MARTHA: [Lance Hastings] was my love interest 30 years
ago. On screen. And off. After my character married his
character, Joseph Fox, she was kidnapped, buried alive,
trapped in a cave with bears, uh, kidnapped again, and held
hostage in the sewers of Paris.
BECKETT: How long were you on the show?
MARTHA: Three weeks.

Beyond all these scandals, someone betrayed Sarah.
Martha tells Castle, "Betrayal is a way of life on a soap opera.
And, let me tell you, Temptation Lane is like this seething
cauldron of sordidness, and treachery, and naked ambition.
And do you know which people are the most manipulative
and devious?" He decides he does – it's the writers. One of
them, as it turns out, is the murderer. Castle himself tries soap
writing to catch the murderer in the act, solving the case, as
usual, by fully plunging into their world.

The soap episode nods to Nathan Fillion's past roles, as his first real role was Dr. Joey Buchanan on *One Life to Live* in 1995 (repeated in 2007). The title is obviously an homage, and the episode brings in real daytime soap stars like Cameron Mathison. Fillion describes soap fans as the most obsessed in some ways, unable to separate him from his character ("Murder They Wrote). He adds, "I love running into actors who say 'Oh yeah, I did a soap.' I say 'Tell me which one!' It's like being a member of a secret society" (Nussbaum).

During their investigation, the detectives meet a truly obsessed fan who lives with her parents and is attempting to save the character Sarah's doomed through a massive Twitter and mail campaign.

> BECKETT: I mean, you saw how obsessive she was. She invests in these fictional relationships. She cares if Angela's gonna get back together with Alfonso, if Marguerite's gonna survive her cancer scare –
> CASTLE: Oh, my god.
> BECKETT: What?
> CASTLE: You watch *Temptation Lane.*

Thus Beckett is revealed as a fan herself. Another major nod to fandom itself appears as Beckett gives a dictionary definition of shipping as "a person who invests in the relationships of a show" along with the Portmanteau Couple Name of "Fox Can." In the same episode, Castle decides Esposito and Lanie should be "Esplanie." "Which is perfect, because they're always esplaining things!" Real life shippers of this couple have used the term ever since. Castle also uses the official fandom term Caskett to refer to himself and Beckett.

Law & Order ("Law and Murder" 319)

While ex-con Otis Williams is on trial for killing a pretty blonde socialite, Joe Mcusic, a jury member, drops dead from cyanide poisoning in the middle of court. The episode is set in the courtroom, showing the trial part of the crime that ordinarily occurs offscreen after Beckett's arrests.

"Law and Murder" is an homage to the classic police procedural and its terribly popular version *Law and Order,* with several spinoffs. The original *Law & Order* ran for 20 seasons on NBC. The first half of each episode involves solving the crime and the second, prosecuting the criminal. Thus most of the time in this episode is spent in the precinct eliminating the most obvious suspects – the victim's brother, an ex-con from the halfway house he ran. These of course are common procedural killers. "Statistically, most poisoners are women," Castle notes, buying into all the stereotypes.

Suspects are drawn from the nature of the courtroom: The defendant's cousin Wardell Williams tries to tamper with the jury and even brings Mcusic a cup of coffee, but tests reveal that victim was poisoned before this. Mcusic did have one shady secret – he sent two grand to the court clerk to buy his way onto the jury and she acquiesced.

Racism is a motivation here as the DA is eager to convict the Black car thief rather than the victim's influential brother. Mcusic's attempt to strive for real justice led to his death. Frequently the system is corrupted, in a plot point highlighted in this episode, but Beckett and her friends attempt to set it all right.

Pizza Restaurants ("Slice of Death," 320)

The numerous "Ray's" pizza joints in NYC (Original, Famous, Famous Original, etc.) are renamed to "Nick's" (Terrific, Authentic, Authentic Terrific, etc.) on *Castle.* The pizza places are a fundamental part of the New York lifestyle. After finding a body in a pizza oven, Montgomery says, "Authentic Nicks's. Oh, thank God. My wife loves Terrific Nick's. I didn't have the heart to tell her now it came in full-bodied flavor."

Branding is everything, as none are really named Nick:

CASTLE: You must be Authentic Nick.
RALPH: The one and only.

BECKETT: Nick? I have the proprietor listed as Ralph
Carbone.
RALPH: Yeah, that's me. Everybody calls me Nick.
BECKETT: Why?
RALPH: Because that's what everybody calls me.

Terrific Nick and Terrific Authentic Nick (not actually
named Nick) own nearby pizza shops. Of course, this, like
many others, is a merciless, insular world. All the Nicks pull
pranks on each other, leaking rumors and plotting to steal
ovens. Ralph Carbone, who insists he's the real Nick, adds,
"Weeks ago, one of them stuck a gallon of soap into my
secret sauce. Cost me a whole day of returned pies. Now
look, I may or may not have retaliated, but if I did, them
puttin' a cadaver in my oven, that's uhh them retaliatin'
back."

Castle notes, "Competition to be the best in New York?
Clear animosity? Carbone's said they'd broken in before."

Ryan adds, "He's right, you know? Pizza's a serious
business in this town." It is indeed, and the episode shows
the sordid side of their world. Of course, one has mob
connections, one has fat free pizza that's full of fat. And one
is dealing heroin. With all this underbelly to the business,
viewers might want to think again before ordering a slice.

Competitive Swimming ("The Dead Pool," 321)

The victim, a champion swimmer from the wrong side of
town with a single mom, is found poisoned with chlorine and
drowned. As his coach describes him:

Couldn't keep that kid out of the pool. Two weeks ago, he
got food poisoning right before a meet. Sick as a dog, just
puking his guts out. I told him to withdraw, but he toughed it
out. Won all his events. That was Zack. He was gonna be
the next Rob Tredwyck or Michael Phelps...He was a kid
from Bensonhurst, you know. It got him a partial
scholarship, but he lived on his own all the way out there
because it's all he could afford.

"Rocket" Rob Tredwyck, an image of where Zack will likely be in a few years, is covered in medals and sponsors. He's doing commercials for food and sports equipment, using his star power to make himself rich. "Most kids in this sport, they come from money," he notes.

However, it's a rough life, as Zack, unable to accept any funding while a student, steals cars to get by, and his silver-spoon rival Brian Morris takes specially-designed steroids to beat the tests, with an army of servants and lawyers to cover for him. As Zack's friend says, "SWM4GLD? Vanity plates? I mean, can you get anymore douchey? Brian's up in Greenwich with his own training pool, private coaches, whatever he needs. Meanwhile, Zack's stuck here boosting cars just so he can eat 'cause he can't take a nickel of outside money or else he's done." Zack devotes himself wholly to the sport, waking before dawn to get to school and swim. His rich kid rival is busy cheating the system by taking the drugs then faking an injury so he won't need to submit to drug testing. The very system invites corruption as the coaches build their reputations on the kids:

> COACH ROME: Brian's father came to me. He asked if there was anything more I could do. He said he'd donate millions to the program if that answer was yes.
> CASTLE: Yeah, but it wasn't just about the money, was it? Every coach knows he has to hitch his wagon to a star. In fact, you'd done it before with somebody very special.

It's the lifestyle, with its rivalries, secret steroids, and terrible pressure to excel, that kills Zack. This competition is anything but friendly.

LA ("To Love and Die in L.A," 322)

The title namesake, *To Live and Die in L.A.*, is a 1985 film about Secret Service on a mission. The show *Castle* is actually filmed in LA, so this episode simply stopped pretending they were in New York, taking characters to iconic Santa Monica Pier for the showdown. On arriving, Castle rents a flashy red

Ferrari convertible, stays in a very fancy four-star suite, and makes dinner reservations at Spago. His concierge at his preferred hotel can get anything for his spoiled guests.

> BECKETT: I'd like to start the investigation.
> CASTLE: We haven't even ordered room service yet.
> BECKETT: Castle, I'm not here for room service. I'm here for justice.
> CASTLE: Wow. In L.A. for all of a minute and already she's sprouting cheesy movie dialogue. Must be something in the air.

Of course, there's the fun meta moment when Castle and Beckett visit the Nikki Heat set and bring their real suspect into the fake interrogation room there. The extras and camera staff are the real ones from the show. Even the airplane from the airplane scenes appear on set. Castle does a fake interrogation there and finishes with the words "Welcome to LA" – this was as fake as everything else.

Beckett meanwhile is on vacation in a sense. She has no jurisdiction in California, so she starts having a little more fun. She dresses more casually and colorfully. She appears tanner. And most memorably, she entraps the villain who's "conducting business poolside" by making an amazing entrance in a revealing bathing suit. Gene Simmons, a star though one from the music industry, pops in for a fun cameo.

> CASTLE: This is so weird.
> Beckett: What?
> CASTLE: I've dressed up as him for Halloween.
> BECKETT: I did, too.

Beauty Pageants ("Pretty Dead," 323)

> CASTLE: "Death of a Beauty Queen." Scandalous.
> BECKETT: Yeah, I'm surprised it doesn't happen more often.

Twenty-one-year-old Amber Middleberry, Miss Illinois, is

found murdered and tangled in a lighting truss. Baron's All American Beauty Pageant has been rocked by the scandal. Meanwhile, Amber's father tells a typical story: "She started when she was nine. Little Miss Wholesome. I was against the idea at first but Amber's mom had a bug about it and uh, right after her mother died...I think it just helped her feel closer to her." He adds that the other girls loved her: "Even after she made it to the semi-finals everybody was hugging her and they were calling her the front runner and...this pageant, this one, was her dream." As Beckett reveals, she also has personal experience:

> BECKETT: Pageants aren't fairy tales. They're demanding, high pressure competitions that bring out the very best and the very worst in people.
> CASTLE: That is the voice of experience. Oh my God, you were a beauty queen!
> BECKETT: No. I had a roommate freshman year. Debbie Winaker. It was like living with Elle Woods on steroids.

Backstage, all is frenzy as moms lecture their daughters on slouching and contestants struggle to hide their physical flaws. Host Victor Baron adds that this is a reality show like many others: "We um, we film everything. The behind the scenes at the pageant. We like to catch the girls talking about each other. We let them confess their hopes and fears. You get the glamour but you also get the underbelly. People love the underbelly."

The young women do a great deal of preparation: Amber's coach trained her in her routine and interviews, and also oversaw stylists, makeup, clothing, violin lessons, and glamour shots. He adds, "Today's pageants are not just about beauty, they're about brains, talent, social issues, and what with the money and the exposure at stake...winning one of the majors can launch a career."

Of course, there's scandal and rivalry beneath. The visiting sitcom star is hitting on all the girls and the photographer also takes dirty pictures. One jealous girl stole

Amber's violin to ruin her talent portion. As the case breaks, Castle and Beckett discover Amber slept with Baron and blackmailed him for the questions she'd be asked, using this inside information to excel. Of course, all the concealed secrets led to the murder as everyone's chance at success was on the line.

Real-Life Superheroes ("Heroes and Villains," 402)

A mysterious costumed vigilante goes after the mob and then saves a young woman from a rapist, slicing the assailant in half with a sword. Castle of course is intrigued. He also seems to know lots about the business:

> CASTLE: Our killer is not crazy.
> BECKETT: He cut a man in two and he's running around wearing a superhero suit.
> CASTLE: I know costumes. That one is not commercial. He probably designed it himself, which means he's highly functional.

When Beckett asks for a real theory, Castle insists superheroes are real and dependent on their origin stories. He pulls up an online video of the Red Maroon, who operates out of Queens. However, as the hero clumsily crashes into bushes and gets beaten up by a mugger, he's humiliated.

> BECKETT: Wow. Impressive crime fighting skills. What do you think, mutant powers or years of training?
> CASTLE: Yes well, sometimes the runner stumbles. The point is, there is a subculture of real life superheroes that actually exists out there. People crusading for the public good.
> BECKETT: Yes and usually they get their asses kicked, just like this guy.

In fact, there are real-life superheroes crusading for the public good. This phenomenon of fandom, called "Real-life Superheroes" (RLSH) began spreading in the nineties and after, with heroes like Terrifica, who helps drunken women get home from bars safely, or Red Justice, "a substitute teacher from Woodside, Queens, who wears red boxer briefs over jeans, a red cape made from an old T-shirt and a sock with eyeholes to mask his identity" who urges teens to give up their seats on the subway to those in need (Lee). Both these New York heroes are possible inspirations for Lone Vengeance. They also belong to the group Superheroes Anonymous who met, masked in Times Square, as *The New York Times* reported. "We're not these crazy people," said one man, Geist, who traveled to New York from Minnesota. "We just have an unorthodox approach to doing good" (Lee).

Continuing to prove his case, Castle posts the vigilante's photo on the board, "juxtaposed with issues from my own Marvel collection," as he says. While he's apparently a Marvel expert, Beckett's well-read too:

> BECKETT: (pointing) You have *Avengers* #1?
> CASTLE: And there's more where that came from. You're welcome to peruse my issues anytime. (to everyone) Please note how the killer has drawn inspiration from costumes of other superheroes. For example, the color scheme evokes Spider-Man. The horned helmet, obviously an homage to Daredevil. The sword and scabbard, Deadpool. The high collar, just like Black Panther. Now, what do these characters all have in common?
> ESPOSITO: They're make-believe?
> BECKETT: They're driven by the death of a father figure or loved one.
> CASTLE: Exactly. I believe that our killer shares a similar backstory. Which is why he's been inspired by these characters' costumes. Furthermore, out of costume, these heroes tend to be ... unassuming. So, let's add mild mannered to our profile.
> GATES: Mr. Castle. So this is you working a homicide.

Castle appears completely ridiculous as he lets his love and enthusiasm for fictional superhero lore dictate the investigation. However, he makes a valid point as he adds, "Let me direct your attention to the golden belt worn by our masked vigilante. Based on the golden belt worn by Iron Man in only eleven original issues in 1963." Thus the vigilante, like Castle, is a true comic book connoisseur.

Less-than-coincidentally, this episode coincided with the actual Derrick Storm comic book release. "There's a definite connection between the TV show *Castle* and comic books. Fillion is a self-admitted comic geek, and on Monday's episode, the graphic novel factored into the plot of a case involving a vigilante dressed up as a superhero" (Truitt).

Castle and Beckett visit the comic book shop (where they find that the new Derrick Storm comic has arrived and Beckett has preordered it.) They also discuss their fantasies of being superheroes (Batman and Elektra respectively). As Beckett shows off her own nerd points, both wave to the audience of superhero aficionados. As always, Esposito refuses to play along, though Ryan is more open:

> RYAN: Ah. You gotta give him props for spirit, though, right? I mean, haven't you ever wanted to be a superhero? Going out there, prowling the city, knocking some heads?
> ESPOSITO: I do that now.

At the shop, the owner recognizes the costume from the fringe online comic *Sword of Lone Vengeance*. Castle reads it all (of course) only to discover the comic echoes an event in real life but only after it happened. Presumably the author, Sean Elt, knows the real vigilante and is using him as a model. His name is an anagram for Marvel creator Stan Lee and when the detectives track him down, he lies and insists he's the superhero…but only to protect the real Lone Vengeance, whom he loves. She's finally revealed as an NYPD detective, moonlighting:

> HASTINGS: My father owned a dry cleaners in the neighborhood. He got held up, by some junkie probably. Shot dead over eighty bucks. The day after I buried him I applied to the Academy.
> BECKETT: So then you decided to take the law into your own hands. Being a cop wasn't enough?

HASTINGS: Someone killed my dad. Nothing will ever be
enough. But doing what I do makes me feel better.

However, a mobster made his own costume and bisected
the victim, letting the irritating vigilante take the blame.
Beckett finally convinces Hastings to retire and seek
vengeance through the legal system.

The real superheroes interviewed by *The New York Times*
were "locals and out-of-towners, most were in uniform (don't
dare call them costumes) and all said they were serious about
helping make their respective communities cleaner, safer and
kinder places" (Lee). As the episode reveals, there are three
sides to the real-life superheroes – one is the tough,
committed Lone Vengeance who's honestly cleaning up the
streets (though anonymously and illegally). Another is the
mobster impersonating Lone Vengeance to get personal
vengeance. The last is hapless wannabes like Red Maroon,
hoping to imitate Lone Vengeance but only coming across
ass rather pathetic dreamers. This, unfortunately, is the
majority of the community:

BECKETT: Aren't you Lone Vengeance?
CHAD: Not the real one.
CASTLE: The real one being the comic book character?
CHAD: Comic book characters aren't real, okay?
CASTLE looks to BECKETT. She gives him a smirk.
    . . .
CHAD: No one knows. And he's a legend in the superhero
community. I dreamed of being him when I was Red
Maroon.
CASTLE: Protector of all, beholden to none?
CHAD: You've heard of me.
BECKETT: We saw the purse-snatching video.
His face drops.
CHAD: Yeah. That. Ugh. That hit the web and pretty much
turned Red Maroon into a joke. Those were dark days. I
was about ready to hang up my tights for good. Then I
decided to seek out Lone Vengeance's council.
CASTLE: What did he say?
CHAD: To stay the hell away from him. But that – that only
steeled my resolve. I mean, I made this costume. I got a

sword. I was about to go out on patrol when you guys busted in.

Thus the episode doesn't wholeheartedly celebrate the superhero community – there are more hapless clowns than real heroes. Castle and Beckett get in their Derrick Storm product placement as well as many shout-outs to Marvel (owned of course by Disney/ABC) but don't fully immerse themselves in the life.

Cryogenics ("Head Case," 403)

Head Case begins with a pan down from space, crashing into earth like an asteroid. It ushers Castle and his friends into the science-fiction looking world of a cryogenics lab, complete with frozen bodies. "Does anyone else have the sudden urge to run to the streets screaming 'they're here'?" Castle asks. The body is stolen, and they finally trace it to those who collected it:

> TECH 2: He was already dead when we arrived to pick him up. We work for Passageway, a cryonics company.
> CASTLE: Cryonics. That explains the room of human popsicles.
> ...
> TECH 1: They all have contracts with us. We cryo-preserve them.
> CASTLE: To be brought back to life in a science fiction future where death has a cure.

While Castle and Beckett are sympathetic about Steampunk and soap opera shipping, Castle's definition here certainly sounds less than credible, even to him. For possibly the first time on the show, he doesn't suggest he's a believer.

The lab owner, Dr. Ari Weiss, insists he's fulfilling the murdered man's dying wish by snatching his body without calling the police, but he comes off something of an irrational dreamer, as he insists (contrary to scientific fact) that the brain is still working in the dead body and finally concedes that they only need to preserve the head because "By the time the technology exists to revive Hamilton, we'll surely be able to regenerate our bodies." The victim's wife is another dreamer:

> CYNTHIA: If preservation is discontinued he's going to be gone forever.
> BECKETT: (gently) Well with all due respect, he already is gone forever.
> PHILIP BOYD: Lester would dispute that. He and I had been colleagues at Hudson for twenty years now and uh, he's a true believer. For him, the keys to life extension, to reversing death itself, were within reach, so he would never give up his chance at revival.
> CYNTHIA: Do you know why he chose to focus on life extension? We fell madly in love with each other. He told me that one lifetime together wasn't enough. He wanted more. So do I.

The victim's friend steals his head (in its freezer case) leading to a chase through the city and lowering the story to a farce, with Castle shaking the case and making quips like "talk about a header!"

In another gamble at eternal life, the victim was working on the Ambrosia Project, a pharmaceutical implant that caused the body to produce young cells instead of aging ones. He hoped it would extend human lifespan by ten years. While no one he knows seems interested in being cryogenically frozen, Castle asks several people about life prolongation. Martha tells him, "Oh, I don't know. Make you feel better, live longer...hell, I'd give it a try." Beckett disagrees, insisting it's the knowledge one's days are numbered that gives people a push.

While many cases involve the cutthroat competitive nature of the world leading to the murder, in this case, the wife committed it, secure in starry-eyed fashion that they will reunite in the future. She appears pathetically naïve, committing murder based on this unproven theory. She kills herself, either compounding the tragedy or preparing for a new life in the barely-imaginable future, depending which side of the argument one believes.

Ghost Hunters ("Demons," 406)

The episode begins in the interior of a haunted house with ornate architecture and sheet-covered furniture. Jack Sinclair, ghost hunter, walks in and checks the time. His monitoring device beeps faster and he reports, "Living room, 9:03PM. EMF level spiking off the chart." The door slams shut. The lights flicker, then shut off completely. He calls, "Hello? Is anyone there?" Then "Mercy ... I can see it. Mercy." Then he is killed.

Across New York, Castle and Alexis are watching a horror film, with Castle apparently using her as a shield against flesh eating zombies. The phone rings, and Castle has his new case.

> CASTLE: (on seeing the van) The Ghost Wranglers are here? Okay, that's why I love these guys. The body's not even cold, they're already tracking down the ghost.
> BECKETT: Why doesn't it surprise me that you actually watch that ridiculous show?
> CASTLE: Ridiculously awesome. Jack Sinclar is hands down America's most accomplished ghost hunter.
> BECKETT: Um ... Castle... Jack Sinclar is the name of our victim.
> CASTLE: And the hunter becomes the hunted.

Inside, Castle and his friends find a chilling scene. The victim had locked himself alone in the room, after a thorough check. Mysteriously, his throat was slit with the blood spraying everywhere...as if the killer was insubstantial. Of course, the mansion is haunted. Since 1898 there have been eight killings, "starting with the original owner, Robert Pettigrew, strangled, 1903, all the way to Melanie Benton, hacked to pieces, 1991." The killer is said to be a demon. In clichéd fashion, the owners describe thinking the history of the house was silly, then discovering "Lights going off, strange noises, doors slamming." The living room is trashed with "Tables flipped over, books ripped apart, pictures smashed."

BECKETT: You'll see, Castle. This'll turn out like every
other murder investigation. Once we find out more about
our victim's life, the details surrounding his death,
everything will be explained.
RYAN: Um... maybe not everything. I was reviewing the
footage shot inside the house tonight looking for signs
someone else was there, a shadow, a reflection,
something. Instead, I found uh ... well, you better see for
yourself...watch the tripod in the background.

He zooms in on the tripod, which after a second moves
across the floor, seemingly on its own. More details emerge
about the victim, who grew up terrified of the house, then
asked a felon to photograph the living room, the very room
where he died soon after. He had terrifying dreams of the
house, and another ghost hunter reports that these weren't
dreams but suppressed memories resurfacing. Mercy
LaGrande adds, "He said the face was blurred but getting
clearer. I told him if he returned to the room where it
happened, it might all come back to him."

As Castle discovers the room has a spy hole, things
become far less paranormal. However, when he and Beckett
investigate, the door to the room suddenly slams. The lights
flicker and go out. Beckett's flashlight dies. Castle nervously
observes, "This is the same sequence of events that preceded
Jack Sinclair's murder." As they break into a secret room,
they find a magnetic field generator which may have knocked
out the camera and moved the tripod. They are creeped out
repeatedly by rats, and then they discover a skeleton. At last,
they lay a trap for the murderer with ghosthunter cameras
and mention that they will be exploring the secret passage.
The murderer comes to clean up his mess and is caught.
Castle, of course, remains a believer, even after the case is
solved:

BECKETT: C'mon Castle. Even you have to admit
everything, every haunting, every death, everything even
remotely connected to paranormal activity in the McClaren
house can be explained by that passageway.

> CASTLE: I don't know. What about last night, when we were in the living room? How about the door? The light? The candle?
> BECKETT: Old wiring, drafty house.
> CASTLE: Well maybe it was something more. Think about it. If you hadn't gone looking for the draft that blew out the candle you would have never found the passageway or Matt Benton's body.
> BECKETT: Spell it out for those of us that are … paranormally impaired.
> CASTLE: Maybe someone wanted us to find that passageway. Maybe Jack Sinclair's ghost was helping solve his own murder.

To add to the humor, the actor who plays Azazel on *Supernatural* appears, only to add that the idea of demons is ridiculous. The title screen has Halloween music as well. It's a spooky episode and celebration of ghost hunting, but it also suggests the possibility of real paranormal activity.

Dog Shows ("An Embarrassment of Bitches," 413)

"An Embarrassment of Bitches" features a very famous woman with "no discernible talent," who carries a dog with her wherever she goes. Kay Cappuccio is an obvious homage to Kim Kardashian (and to a degree Paris Hilton). The line "Who will be this year's best in show" seems to nod to the mockumentary of that name, which emphasizes the silliness of dog shows.

> ESPOSITO: The victim is Franciscio Pilar, judge of the dog show. We found him here in his dressing room. He still had cash on him, plus his wallet, phone, and a key card of some kind.
> BECKETT: Is the cause of death what it looks like?
> LANIE: Yep. Someone put a leash around his neck and pulled.

He apparently had no family or outside life, only his beloved German shepherd, Royal. As the show organizer adds, "he got along with dogs a lot better than their owners."

Another insular world begins.

It's revealed that there's big money in dog shows, as the victim is accused of fixing them. There's a great deal of tension surrounding them. Ryan notes, "One of the losing contestants just filed this appeal of Francisco's decision, a guy named David Hernand. They said he was so angry that the vein in his forehead was visibly throbbing. Apparently, dog shows are this guy's whole life." Added to this is the ridiculousness of Dr. Patty Barker, dog psychologist. "Well, I am a canine therapist. It'd be pretty crazy for me to treat people," she notes. Beckett stops calling her "doctor" after the revelation. Dr. Barker lies on the floor to speak with her patient:

> DR. PATTY BARKER: Royal, look at me. I know. I know you're hurt. You're confused. You're dealing with abandonment issues. Oh. There's a lot to break through here. This could take some time.
> CASTLE: Tell me…did Francisco ever observe you during your sessions?
> DR. PATTY BARKER: No. He waited outside. Why?
> CASTLE: No reason.

It's finally revealed that this frivolous hobby was covering a far more serious one – training drug-sniffing dogs for US customs. Thus dog shows are abandoned as silly and light, basically harmless but honestly nothing to kill over.

Noir ("The Blue Butterfly" 414)

The episode opens in the 1940's Pennybaker Club as Lanie's actress sings period music. A gardenia sits behind her ear a la Ella Fitzgerald. Private Eye Joe Flynn (Nathan Fillion) is drinking at the bar and insists he's looking for a dame. The classic hardboiled film has begun.

In modern times, a treasure seeker is found dead in the club. The noir story is actually a diary left in his things that Castle was reading:

CASTLE: Uh, this diary in Stan's stuff. It's also from the '40s. It sounds like it belonged to a private eye. Listen to this. "Usually the wives turn on the waterworks when shown pictures of their husbands stepping out, but not this dame. She wanted payback. So what's worse? That I pitched woo with a client, or that I billed her for services rendered after?"
BECKETT: Cute.
CASTLE: Cute? I mean, this guy sounds like a hard boiled PI right out of a Raymond Chandler novel. I wonder why Stan had this.

As he reads, he imagines himself as the detective as Kate as his great love. Ryan and Esposito are the goons working for a mobster, and his mother and daughter are his secretary and client. This gives all the actors a chance to stretch, with new accents and '40s attitudes. The 1940s scenes are sepia-tinted with over-narration in Fillion's best noir accent. The credits share the episode's slow saxophone music, setting the scene.

The 1940s story follows the classic pattern as a country girl named Sally enlists Joe Flynn to find her sister Vera, and hard-drinking, cynical Joe tracks her to the bar but suddenly falls in love. Of course there's a catch: "This dame was trouble on two legs. I kept telling myself to look away. She was with Tom Dempsey, for crying out loud, the most ruthless mob boss New York has even given birth to." He's given her a blue butterfly diamond necklace that's worth a million dollars and said to be cursed. Meanwhile, his goons rough up Joe and forbid him to see Vera.

In modern times, Castle throws himself into the story, accidentally describing Vera as "Kate" and narrating aloud. On finding Joe and Vera were murdered, he notes in forties style, "Damn it, Joe. You old sap. Dizzy with a dame and got yourself cooked." Adding to the audience winks, Ryan calls Castle "Mr. Bogart."

When Castle and Beckett visit, witnesses are playing Louie Armstrong's "I Can't Give You Anything But Love" on an old phonograph, adding to the forties color. Talking to this elderly couple, allegedly a bartender from the time and his wife, Castle and Beckett gradually realize these are Vera and Joe, who escaped and found themselves a happy ending. They hid the blue butterfly forever, deciding not to continue living under its curse. In the process, the client, Sally, who was in fact a young liar seeking a vicious revenge, and her husband were killed in their place. The story ends with Joe and Vera kissing against the background of the burning car, able to put the past behind them and be together forever.

Dancing with the Stars ("A Dance with Death," 418)

The show *Castle* was a lead-in to *Dancing with the Stars*. Thus this episode seems a particular homage and audience wink. In 2009, Fillion and Katic appeared on it to promote their show. Fillion, being interviewed, was asked: "On the April 12 Leno/Conan-inspired episode of *Castle* ["The Late Shaft"] Tom Bergeron plays a murdered talk-show host. Is that payback for him pointing you out in the audience at *Dancing With the Stars?*"

Fillion replied, "Heck, no, I'm not upset about that. That's a bonus. He's a classy guy, so now I have an opportunity to return the favor. So far, he's been lying on a slab. He's very funny dead. I've said, 'You know what, I've seen a lot of your work. This is some of your best'" (Bierly).

Of course, this meant Bergeron wasn't available for the actual *Dancing with the Stars* episode (namechanged to *A Night of Dance*). This one begins with the stressful nature of the business as the judges make cutting comments, much as they did on *American Idol*.

> BRAD MELVILLE: Hey, hey, hey! Good evening America! It's dance off time and tonight's theme is latin. As always, tonight's challengers were handpicked by the judges. (to the judges) Max, are you looking forward to watching these two rumba?
> MAX: I'm looking forward to Santino redeeming himself for his samba inspired solo dance last week. Pathetic.
> The audience gasps and boos.

PIERRE DUBOIS: It was like a terrible dream my dog would
have after eating the leftovers of my Brazillian dinner.

Of course, reality TV is all about taking on a persona.
Adrianne Curry, former contestant on *America's Next Top
Model*, gives advice to potential contestants that they find a
persona like "drama queen" or "girl next door": "Just be
yourself, and if being yourself isn't interesting, make up a
character…Everyone loves the bitch. Everyone loves the
underdog. Everyone loves the diva" (Robinson 229). As host
Brad adds, "You know our semifinalists. Our matchup is
Santino versus Odette. Can the arrogant bad boy best
America's sweetheart?" Lanie, a fan, describes Odette as "an
heiress raised by her rich grandpa, a party girl headed down
the wrong path, then a brush with death made her wake up
and change her bad girl ways," the perfect appealing story.
However, she's the murder victim.

Of course, the competition is real, and the cruel nature of
it, with stars "eliminated" each week amid nasty comments
from the judges, leads to misery:

MAX: Well you have to understand. All the contestants are
cast on this show to tell their unique, yet familiar stories.
Odette was the poor little rich girl and Eddie was the kid
from the wrong side of the tracks. We cast Eddie to bring
the drama. Eddie brought the drama, and not just for the
cameras. He was furious when we sent him packing and we
all got an earful about it.
PAM: Oh, he was so rude.
PIERRE: I had to call security.
BECKETT: Was he threatening?
MAX: Let's just say that I was relieved when we was gone.
Ironic really.
CASTLE: How so?
MAX: Well, according to the rules, when a contestant is
unable to continue the last eliminated dancer returns to take
his or her place.
CASTLE: And that dancer is Eddie Gordon.

As Eddie says in his exit video, "Let me tell you
something about Miss sweet and innocent Odette. She threw

me under the bus tonight. She blew off rehearsals all week, then messed up her footwork, and blames it on me. Well where I'm from we know what to do with lying bitches like that." He mimes shooting a gun toward the camera, making himself a suspect. However, this was more mouthing off for the camera, as he was expected to do. As often happens on *Castle*, the murderer comes from outside the little world, only slipping into it to commit the deadly crime.

Among the NYPD, there are fans of the show, but more interestingly, Lanie dreamed of being on it:

> RYAN: I gotta say Dr. Parish, I never figured you for a fan of *A Night of Dance*.
> LANIE: I'm not ... exactly. It's just ... when I was young, more than anything I wanted to be a prima ballerina. If I wasn't dancing I was thinking about dancing.
> CASTLE: So what happened?
> LANIE: The girls came around when I was 13. (she gestures to her chest) Not that many top heavy ballerinas out there.

Nely Galan, creator of *The Swan*, explains, "Ultimately, the stars of reality TV are real people. I find it fascinating, because we spend so many years idolizing celebrities, and now real people get a shot at it" (Robinson 85). This is the dream – to become an instant star. As Lanie explains, speaking for the audience, many girls, including herself, dream of dancing on TV and thrill to see the underdogs get their chance.

Zombie Walks ("Undead Again," 422)

The vampire community already appeared, but now the show tackles zombies, the fun horror monster gaining popularity in fiction and cosplay. Shows like *iZombie* and books like *Beautiful Creatures* emphasize the growing popularity of this trope. In the episode, a professor of anthropology suggests, "Our fascination with zombies is a cultural phenomenon. A commentary on the inner numbness of modern life." This is a common response to the ancient fascination and new popularity of the genre.

The victim is found severely beaten at 4 AM, with a brutal bite mark on his arm. Nearby, Esposito finds a torn-off cuff from an old-fashioned shirt from the 1870s. As Castle insists, a zombie appears to be the culprit.

He's not the only one who thinks so, as they apprehend a suspect:

> CHARLIE: No, no, no. Stay back. Stay away from me!
> BECKETT: Listen, we just gotta ask you a few questions.
> CHARLIE: You need to leave! You need to leave right now! It's not safe.
> He's chained to the radiator.
> CASTLE: Relax, Charlie. Relax. We're cops.
> CHARLIE: (relaxes slightly) You're a cop?
> BECKETT: Yeah.
> CHARLIE: Is that your gun?
> BECKETT: Yeah?
> CHARLIE: You need to shoot me. Do it now! (he braces himself) Do it! Do it!

When they take him in, he insists on staying in the police station in case he changes into one of the living undead. As he claims, he's been bitten and may transform. To Castle's surprise, Charlie reveals that a zombie really did attack him and then murdered the victim, "just wailing on him." As he adds, "I elbowed it in the head, but it didn't even slow down." He called 911, but no one there believed him, of course.

They investigate but find nothing. As Esposito notes, "Only in New York could some guy dress like a friggin' zombie and walk down the street unnoticed." However, the horror of the episode increases as, amid creepy music, a group of humans flee through the streets screaming. Shuffling zombies lurch behind them. Castle jumps. Beckett raises her gun and they ignore her.

> CASTLE: That's – that's a – that's a zombie horde.
> BECKETT: (unbelieving) There's no such thing as zombies.

CASTLE: I'm sure I don't have to tell you to aim for the head....Beckett! Behind us. We're surrounded. Oh jeez, oh jeez. You don't have enough bullets. It's ground zero for *World War Z.*
The zombies are getting closer.
CASTLE: Get behind me. We'll have to fight our way out. Uh ...
BECKETT: There's no way this is real. (NYPD! Stop moving, now!
They're closing in on Castle, close enough to touch him.
BECKETT: And stop pretending to be zombies!
The zombie horde slows slightly. The zombie that was leading the assault straightens.
PAUL: Hey, hey, hey, hey. Take it easy. We're just zombie walking here.

Paul defines zombie walking as "an amped up form of tag. We dress up like zombies and we chase the normals." Castle, delighted, switches from believer to fan as he gushes, "How did I not know about this?" Admiring a costume, he adds, "This is outstanding. Did you do this yourself?"

The discussion expands into fannishness, as Castle considers the matter from his inside perspective: "Being a fan of zombie lore, I get it. But what's the appeal of being a zombie? Like look at this guy. Who would want to be alive in a decayed, mindless state? Being a vampire, that I understand. That's the romantic route to immortality. The gentleman's monster, as it were." Beckett retorts that she'd rather be Van Helsing, the monster slayer.

The story bounces back to "real zombies" as the murderer's corpse in the M.E.'s office suddenly springs to life, just as Lanie's occasional substitute Sidney Perlmutter tells Castle, "There are no zombies." Disoriented, the man stumbles and runs for the door.

BECKETT: Castle, call for backup!
CASTLE: How – how do I -?
PERLMUTTER: 9. 9.
CASTLE: 9. (he presses the extension) Is there a police code for zombie on the loose?

69

Of course, there is a rational explanation. Some of the zombies voluntarily take this zombie drug scopolamine to enhance the experience. Perlmutter explains, "You'll basically do whatever you're told. It's like a date rape drug, except the victims remain conscious. And when the drug wears off, they'll have no recollection of what happened." Basically, its victims become zombies in truth…and one is ordered to commit murder by his human handler. He is the killer but not the one responsible.

When the real mastermind is too cool to admit his scheme, Castle borrows Kyle's costume to scare him into a confession. He succeeds, producing a truly terrifying spectacle. Of course, Castle is gleeful about wearing the makeup and asks to keep the costume longer. At episode end, as Beckett tries to confess her feelings, he's even still wearing it. Castle thus dips into the zombie community, enjoying cosplay and a chance to scare others. "This isn't over," he promises the camera, voice altered and creepy.

Weather Forecasters ("Cloudy with a Chance of Murder," 502)

"Well, that's the weather folks. Straight from my lips to your living room," reports glamourous Mandy Michaels. Meanwhile, Castle reports happily on being a fan of her "assets"…until she ends up murdered. Her station, WHNY, certainly sounds like "whiny." Of course, the staff aren't much better, as Castle notes that they may be a family but they're very dysfunctional.

The other weather girl, Rebecca Fog, got into a fight with the victim, giving her motive but also a valid grievance. Rebecca calls Mandy "a lazy, entitled, big-boobed bimbo" and adds, "Look, I'm a certified meteorologist. I have a brain. Mandy was just set dressing with cleavage. My forecasts were way more accurate than hers and people were starting to notice."

BECKETT: Except now that she's dead you get to trade in the 4AM shift for the coveted and lucrative evening news spot, right?
REBECCA: (laughs) Oh, please. I didn't need to kill her for that. I just needed to wait. She was already past her sell-by date.
CASTLE: Well according to Harvey, she still had a very loyal audience.
REBECCA: Sure, yeah. People who cared about how many buttons on her blouse were open. But at her age in hi-def, she was running out of buttons, fast.

The makeup lady notes, "When a woman hits mid-30s, those HD cameras can turn on you." Mandy was apparently friends with a pro athlete as they both realized their careers had expiration dates. Castle too appears overlit and artificial when he's a guest on the show, as he flirts and denies that he's dating Beckett or anyone else (driving Beckett nuts now that they've finally begun a relationship). However, Mandy appears to have been more than a beautiful bimbo. She discovered a company is releasing harmful chemicals into the skies of New Jersey and getting kids sick. Thus motivated, she began researching for a hard-hitting exposé, even endangering her own health to investigate. Further, she cared about the kids more than a big exclusive. Unfortunately, her coworker didn't agree:

MILES: She was a colleague and a friend. Why would I kill her?
CASTLE: Because she discovered an expose of a lifetime. A story that big has to be vetted by legal and that could take weeks, even months.
BECKETT: But Mandy couldn't wait that long. Not while kids were getting sick. So she decided to turn the findings over to the EPA.
CASTLE: At which point, you lose your big exclusive. Now when was the last time you had a big exclusive?
MILES: This is crazy. This is crazy. You – you think I killed someone for a story.

In fact he did, emphasizing, as often happens, the ruthless

nature of the business. Mandy was a decent person and a true journalist, so she was killed by a man who sought only a profit.

Rock Bands ("Swan Song," 504)

"The victim is James Swan, he's the lead guitarist of Holy Shemp. They must be Three Stooges fans. Based on lividity I'd say the time of death is between 12 and 2AM," Lanie explains. He was clobbered with a guitar, killing him instantly.

Endlessly on the road, the band describe their life as a fishbowl, all forced into each other's space for five years. Though as member Keith adds, "Hey, we looked out for James. He was a middle-class kid from Ohio. He didn't know what the hell he was getting into with this life." The life is indeed cheap and shallow. While investigating, the team meet a drugged-out groupie and her worried father. One of the band members alibies with a girl whose name he doesn't remember, but he caught their hours of hijinks on camera.

It's finally revealed that one of the band members was going to be replaced, giving him motive. Their uncertain existence was an even bigger push:

> ZEKE: Do you know what it's like to play all those crappy street fairs? Live on nothing but Ramen noodles? Live in a van for 14 months? And then he calls me to his trailer after the show and tells me that I'm out? I admit, I might not be the world's greatest bass player but –
> CASTLE: No, but you sure can handle a guitar.
> ZEKE: Oh c'mon, man! I didn't mean to kill him. We're finally about to hit it big and he want to Pete Best me? For some roadie? I just – (he tosses the chair aside) – I just lost it.

His unwillingness to give up the lifestyle and his volatile temper led to the star's death. As Castle phrases it, "He wasn't about to stay and they weren't about to let him play George Michael to their Andrew Ridgeley." Indeed, Castle makes many music references, including his comment that the victim has much in common with other young, dead musicians: "The 27 Club. Memberships include some of the greats. Jimi Hendrix, Jim Morrison, Janis Joplin. The list is extensive."

More interesting than the rock band, however, is the documentary being filmed around them as camera crew butt in everywhere. Gates is pressured to let them tape the case, and as expected, Castle loves it and Beckett hates it.

All the characters respond differently to being filmed in a documentary. Beckett seems to resent it the most, and the guys critique her performance. They by contrast tend to overact. Even Gates and Lanie fight for screentime, dressing up and finding excuses to step outside their offices. Castle loves the camera and directs his own clips, ordering music and screen angles. He says dramatically, "Don't you see? Everything we need to solve this murder is right there in that clip. (he snaps his fingers) Do a hard fade to black, musical sting." As always, he loves the business.

Murder, She Wrote ("Murder, He Wrote," 505)

Seeking romance, Beckett and Castle get away to Castle's house in the Hamptons, which Beckett admits is magical – gigantic and beautiful. However, she has qualms about how many girls Castle may have brought there.

As they start to take a romantic swim in his private pool, a weekender out from New Jersey staggers in and dies from a gunshot wound. This means dilettante Castle has the crime thrust upon him in a particular homage:

> CASTLE: Anyway, I need your guys' help. There has been a homicide out here in the Hamptons in my backyard.
> RYAN: Seriously, Castle? What, are you in an episode of *Murder, She Wrote*?
> CASTLE: More like Murder, He Wrote. But unfortunately, unlike Jessica Fletcher, the local police chief? Not a friend of mine and I think he might have the wrong guy. So, I need you guys to question the victim's wife in the city. Find out what she knows.

Murder, She Wrote was a show that followed mystery

novelist Jessica Fletcher who lived in Cabot Cove, a cozy coastal town in Maine, where a surprising number of murders and other crimes occurred despite the peacefulness of the location. In fact, the constant appearance of dead bodies in remote locations became known as "Cabot Cove syndrome." Castle, a mystery writer in a peaceful small town, certainly parallels her in this new homage.

On her own show, Jessica is always more perceptive than the official investigators, who promptly arrest the most likely suspect. In fact, the local police chief in the Hamptons arrests the drugged-out bum on the beach, since he has the victim's wallet. When Castle and Beckett try to investigate, they are promptly arrested for interfering with a police investigation. However, when the police chief realizes who Beckett is, he drops all the charges and asks for her help since he's never investigated a murder before. Like Jessica Fletcher, Castle and Beckett ask clever questions and make careful observations, down to the proper tying of a boat's mooring line, to find the real killer.

Of course the Hamptons is the New Yorkers' wealthy getaway spot, contrasting them with the ordinary year-round residents who run the shops and businesses there. "Meth. These rich kids have learned everything these days. Drug arrests? They've doubled in the last six months," the local police chief complains. On this theme, the killer gives a long speech about how much he hates wealthy visitors to the Hamptons like Castle who act like they're better than the locals. Castle's response is a defensive "I don't think I'm better than you!" but the murderer has already struck his blow for the sake of his community.

Firefly and Comic-Con ("The Final Frontier, 507)

If Fillion is more polite than most – with fans, costars, journalists – perhaps it's because he occupies a special place in Hollywood. It started back in 2002, when, thanks to a few key roles from the mind of Joss Whedon – Capt. Mal Reynolds in *Firefly* and its big-screen adaptation, *Serenity*;

an evil preacher in *Buffy the Vampire Slayer;* and a vain superhero in *Dr. Horrible's Sing-Along Blog* – Fillion began receiving A-list treatment from sci-fi fans, even if he wasn't quite an A-lister himself. And he was more than happy to play to that audience. "I think of *Galaxy Quest* and the plight of those pigeonholed actors who don't do anything except for conventions," he says. "To be pigeonholed as a Malcolm Reynolds? Uh, dream. Winning."

Nathan Fillion, a frequent quest at cons, gets to wave to Comic-Con and *Firefly* in the fifth season. Fillion describes scifi fans as smart and able to separate him from his roles but devoted to collecting everything – books, comics, and memorabilia ("Murder They Wrote"). Every product imaginable, of course, appears in the episode's convention, as do several science fiction stars:

> Jonathan Frakes (Commander Riker from *Star Trek: The Next Generation* and director of the episode) shakes Castle's hand. He's decked out in Castle fan-gear, down to his "I <3 Richard Castle" t-shirt.
> JONATHAN FRAKES: Thanks. I'm you're number one fan.
> CASTLE: Well, thanks for coming. (he watches him walk away) How far they fall.

The show opens in a view of a spaceship, then going within as its heroic Captain Max Renard struggles to save his gal-pal lieutenant as well as the universe. This is soon revealed to be the Fan Experience paid simulation for a *Star Trek/Firefly*-style show called *Nebula-9*. As Castle's signing his own comic books, he hears there was a murder inside the exhibit. Castle bursts out, "Shiny!" in a *Firefly* homage. Surprisingly, Beckett is the fan, not him:

> CASTLE: I'm sorry, but how is *Nebula-9* worthy of all this? I mean, they were canceled over a decade ago after 12 episodes. Which was 12 episodes too many. [An obvious *Firefly* reference]
> Her face falls.
> BECKETT: I thought you would be a fan.

> CASTLE: I'm a fan of good sci-fi. *Star Trek, Battlestar,* that
> Joss Whedon show. But *Nebula-9*? No, no. That's all phony
> melodrama and lifeless acting.
> They walk into the ship set. Both are visibly impressed.
> CASTLE: Okay, this is a cool ship. The show is still lame,
> but this is a cool ship.

There they meet Gabriel Winters, the actor who plays
Captain Max Renard. (His name parallels *Firefly*'s Captain
Malcolm Reynolds. His Lt. Chloe parallels Zoe, with
cannibalistic Kreavers as the Reavers.) Meanwhile, Winters is
actually played by Ed Quinn, from *Eureka*.

Science fiction easter eggs fill the episode. Characters
dressed like Fillion's old characters Caleb from *Buffy*, Malcom
Reynolds (*Firefly*), and Captain Hammer (*Dr. Horrible*) were
filmed asking Fillion if they knew him from somewhere, but
this scene was cut. Beckett and her old friend use the term
"Frakin'" from *Battlestar Galactica*. Nodding to *Star Trek*,
Fillion imitates Kirk and Picard and sits in the captain's chair.
Beckett quips on Dr. Manhattan. Even the lights and framing
in their interrogations suggest *Gattaca*. Ryan and Esposito
have their own discussion:

> ESPOSITO: Oh yeah, this is probably too lowbrow for you,
> huh? You're probably into that boring-ass, intellectual kind
> of sci-fi like *Gattaca* or *2001*. The Monolith? What the hell
> was that?
> RYAN: Don't ask me. I don't know. Swords and sorcery,
> that's more my thing. Like uh … *Lord of the Rings.*
> ESPOSITO: Yeah, I could probably see you as an elf. Or a
> hobbit.

Armin Shimmerman (*Buffy, Star Trek: DS9*) guest stars as
a collectables maker, wearing a "Han Shot First" shirt and
selling a *Firefly* laser pistol. Magneto and Deadpool walk past,
and Captain America's image appears behind Fillion's signing.
Since ABC, Marvel, Star Wars, and Disney work together,
this isn't surprising product placement. Lone Vengeance
appears as well. Getting into the spirit, Frakes imitates
Captain Picard on the commentary and discusses his familiar

return to *Trek*. The title obviously echoes *Star Trek* as well. On *Nebula-9*, the captain is very James T Kirk. His crew all wear spandex, with the women in *Star Trek*-style miniskirts. The polished, militaristic bridge is more *Battlestar Galactica* or *Trek* than rough and tumble *Firefly*.

The convention experience is highlighted as well. Alexis tries cosplaying as a scantily-clad bounty hunter. Other fans eagerly throw themselves into their roles, refusing to speak English. A few characters hook up at the con each year. And other fans fall in love through their fannishness:

> AUDREY: It's just so awful. She's been my best friend since high school. She introduced me to Davis. She's the reason we're together.
> DAVIS: We bonded over *Nebula-9*. We all loved the show, so when Annabelle started the fanclub we helped out and it just kinda took off from there.

These fans have been making new *Nebula-9* webisodes, as fans are doing for *Star Trek* and other projects in real life. In a further easter egg, Audrey and Davis are played by the actors from *Alphas* and *The Last 10 Seconds of Lost*.

Castle is delighted for the first time when he hears the victim was killed by a phaser, or at least a high intensity laser beam. "A real sci-fi murder at a sci-fi convention. This keeps getting better," he cheers.

The episode looks at the larger world around a show, from the fans desperate to revive the series and keeping the world alive through fansites, to the aging actor working the con circuit. Another actress is desperate to shake off the association, as a few are in real life. There's huge money available as well, in the film rights and tie-in products. There are also the loving cosplayers like Beckett. As she finally tells Castle:

> You're right, okay? It was a stupid show. It was cheesy and melodramatic. (she sits in the captain's chair) I mean, a handful of academy students are on a mission and suddenly the Earth is destroyed and they're all that's left of

> humanity? I completely understand why you hated it. But Castle, I also understand why people loved it. Why Annabelle loved it. It was about leaving home for the first time. About searching for your identity and making a difference. I loved dressing up like Lieutenant Chloe. She didn't care what anybody thought about her. And I kinda did, at that time. I mean, she was a scientist and a warrior and that was all in spite of the way she looked. It was like I could be anything and I didn't have to choose. So don't make fun, okay?

She's certainly speaking in the fans' voice, and ends the episode convincing Castle to join her in a *Nebula 9* marathon, though she weirds him out by cosplaying with a Kreaver mask over her Lt. Chloe outfit. The show ends panning out to space above as William Shatner performs "Ideal Woman" in voiceover. The convention celebration is complete.

Professional Santas ("Secret Santa," 509)

Santa is killed, having apparently fallen from the sky, with no plane in sight. His only ID reads Kris Kringle, address North Pole, and his coat is stuffed with candy cane wrappers. All this mods to *Miracle on 34th Street* of course. Castle pipes up, "I'm sorry, are we overlooking the obvious here? He hit some turbulence and slipped out of his sleigh and fell to his doom."

The team find themselves visiting the Santa base of operations, on New York's Canal Street. The place is decked out in lights and decorations. "Wow. Someone takes Christmas seriously," Beckett says. The receptionist, who greets them with a cheerful "Merry Christmas," explains that their suspect is teaching a class. On asking what the business does, she adds, "We make magic." She escorts them to a room stuffed with Santas.

> DAVID DUNNE: Again!
> SANTAS: Ho ho ho!
> DUNNE: Again!
> SANTAS: Ho ho ho!
> DUNNE: Once again, from the diaphragm!

SANTAS: Ho ho ho!
DUNNE: That's it.
CASTLE: Santa school?
BECKETT: And I bet you one Santa is missing.

This is a serious profession, mostly booking gigs through the Bells and Holly Agency. Beckett and Castle delve into the world of high-stakes Santas when Dunne admits to hating his coworker: As he explains, "Edmund took one of my best gigs. It was a print ad for Cartier. I was their go-to Santa. But this year they wanted to go more warm and cuddly. Look at me. I'm warm, I'm cuddly. But no, they chose Edmund, so yeah, I drank too much peppermint schnapps and went over to his place and popped off. I'm not proud of it. But that was all I did."

The man's next-door neighbors finally fill the team in on the real man behind the velvet suit:

TIM CABOT: Ed was a professional Santa. (he slides open a closet door to show them lots of Santa costumes)
CASTLE: Looks like he took his job pretty seriously.
BETH: Oh, he lived it, really. I mean, volunteering at the rec center and the shelter. He was always here for Tim and the kids. He even helped with our lawsuit.
CASTLE: He was a Santa and a lawyer?
BETH: No. We lost our house and he was just trying to help us out. He was like that.

Five years previous, Santa Ed was James Edmund Smith, a private equity manager at a big firm. However, Christmas night he was watching *It's a Wonderful Life* with his wife and suddenly walked out on her forever. The team discover that his firm ruined the life of a small family, whose father was killed by falling asleep at the wheel while trying to manage three jobs. Ed gave up his job and moved in beside them, working to improve their lives and finally steal the files they needed to win their case. Thus he was inspired to be Santa in order to make the world better and make amends where he could. "Gotta admire the guy. Sacrificed everything to redeem himself. It's too bad his past caught up with him," Castle says in a fitting epitaph. Beckett relinquishes her holiday tradition of working alone to come celebrate with the Castles, and they all have a merry Christmas together.

Girls Gone Wild ("Death Gone Crazy," 511)

Beau Randolph, creator of *College Girls Gone Crazy*, an obvious stand in for *Girls Gone Wild*, begins the story as a deeply troubled man. He appears to carry the weight of the world as he walks past billboards proclaiming how immoral he his and protest groups shouting, "Beau Randolph! You're a creep! You're a loser! You're scum! Your whole life adds up to nothing!" The COO, Gary, explains that Beau received death threats on a daily basis from "Moral crusaders. Angry boyfriends. Angry fathers. Women who had second thoughts about being in our videos." Over and over the point is made that appearing in those videos is a permanent stigma.

A children's program turns away Beau's money, considering him a smut peddler. He's finally strangled with a bra in the midst of his own party. A fellow smut-creator has killed him, eager to keep the cash flowing. Meanwhile, Randolph has actually tried to walk away from smut-peddling, to find himself a job with respect, and this is what got him killed.

In an interesting counterpoint, a director tries to compete by making *College Guys Gone Nuts*. Beckett stares for quite a while at the half-naked male dancers. Castle interjects, "We're not here about your dancers, Mr. Parrino" (he catches Beckett looking at one of the dancers, and glares) "Are we?" As he explains, horrified, that his own daughter is this age, he finds himself being the mature one of the partnership. In the episode, Alexis points out that her lively G-rated video blog is nothing as degrading and compromising as being on this show, though Castle makes logical points about the modern world's internet risks. Both sides of the issue are presented here, as Castle and Alexis consider the permanence of the internet and the fact that all videos released on it could endanger the reputation and safety of those in them.

VALERIE ESTELLE FRANKEL

Music Industry ("Under the Influence" 512)

This episode begins by emphasizing the fakeness and competitiveness of the industry. Regina Cane, a pop star many consider "over," is hosting a party for her new album, and a younger, newly popular star arrives.

> REPORTER: Regina, your new album *Fatal Impact* drops next week. What can you tell us about it?
> REGINA CANE: It's about love, heartbreak, and revenge. It's my best album yet.
> REPORTER: Oh my God, it's Josie Lang!
> Everyone rushes to see the new arrival.
> REGINA: What the hell is Josie Lang doing at my release party?
> PUBLICIST: Her album's out next week, too. Having both of you here gets us more press.
> REGINA: More press for who? Me or her?
> JOSIE: Regina! Thank you for the invite. You know, you're the reason I'm a pop star. I've been a fan ever since I was in grade school.

Regina, of course, has no choice but to smile politely at this zinger. Regina appears spoiled and rude as she complains bitterly about the DJ's service from her red and gold bed. On hearing she's dead, Regina simply adds a casual, "Great. Now I feel bad for complaining." Her extensive marble staircases and candelabra emphasize that she certainly hasn't suffered from her time making music.

The case follows twists and turns, but it's finally revealed that the DJ at the party was murdered because she discovered a crime: Regina has stolen her rival's album to leak it on the web and destroy her sales. The industry, worth multimillions and filled with cutthroats, is thus exposed for what it is. Of course, Regina's producers are not without blame:

> BECKETT: If your album didn't perform, your record label was going to drop you.
> REGINA: I've been with Harmony 360 for ten years. They love me.
> BECKETT: It's no secret that Josie Lang's eclipsed you.

81

> REGINA: Oh please. She's been around for 2 seconds.
> Give it a year. You won't even remember her name.
> CASTLE: It doesn't matter. Both your albums come out next
> week and she's going to crush you.
> BECKETT: Unless someone mysteriously leaks Josie's new
> album online.

This was her plan, and when she was thwarted in her ambitions, she added murder to the list.

The Real Housewives ("Reality Star Struck," 514)

The show *The Wives of Wall Street* stars Penelope, the fashion mogul; Margo, the cosmetics queen; Colette, home décor diva; and Hannah. The latter becomes Penelope's assistant, and then seduces her husband. After this, she ends up dead. The Castle team go in to investigate and discover the "reality" is all lies. All the women only care about getting more screentime to boost sales of their own products. Hannah's affair with Penelope's husband is faked for the cameras. Margo's son Stone and Colette's daughter Ashley become engaged and begin planning a wedding, but only to get screentime and finally their own spinoff. This show is clearly *The Real Housewives*, where women create their lucrative skincare lines or clothing, all while snipping at each other. The producer is equally conniving:

> PETER: Poor girl. Such a loss. She was ratings gold. You
> have to find who did this. The audience will want to know.
> CASTLE: Yeah, not to mention her family, the DA ...

The producer explains, when Hannah tries to express her trauma onscreen, "She's just milking it for the camera. They all do." Certainly, this is a staple of the genre. "Evoking emotion from the casting department is the name of the game, so do whatever you can to up the tearjerker factor," advises Matthew Robinson, author of *How to Get on Reality TV* (39).

In fact, Hannah, a small town girl, is miserable at how phony she has to act all the time. Stone, equally miserable, falls in love with her, and their romance causes her death. As the murderer, Stone's fiancée, protests, "I couldn't just let her steal my fiancé. Our spinoff was in final negotiations, for God's sakes." The creepy motto of the show is "Don't let anyone stop you from getting what you want," and the murderess doesn't.

Reality television itself is framed as being shallow and pointless but engrossing, as Castle gets sucked in and stays up all night watching (Beckett stops after a single episode). Gates too is a committed fan. There's also the corrupting influence – as Hannah's brother explains, her family hates what Hannah became on the show: "It was killing us. See the choices she made, the way she was living her life. All of it out there on national television. And that was before she started having the affair." As the show demands bad behavior and blow ups as the price for screentime, the characters behave worse and worse.

The Ring ("Scared to Death," 517)

As a victim watches the clock tick toward midnight, she calls 911 and cries, "The lights went out. It's coming for me. I'm gonna die." Val Butler dies, with the door locked and her couch pushed in front of it. Her body lies in a pose of horror, mouth frozen in a silent scream. For three days she had been acting strangely, refusing to return calls. Investigating her house with the team, Castle finds a DVD and hits play. Satanic images flash across the screen – a cross, fire, an abandoned house. Over it all plays a woman screaming and a creepy child's laugh. Finally a child says, "You saw. On midnight of the third day, you die." Castle realizes that Val died three days after watching it. He adds, already in true believer mode, "She died because she saw this disc. And now I saw it. Which means I'm next."

Another victim received the DVD and he too has died. While Ryan and Esposito refuse to watch, Beckett does, to Castle's horror. As well as being credulous, Castle is also terribly genre savvy. He explains:

CASTLE: The actual DVD will not kill me, Esposito. It will be the spirit inside the DVD. Just like in *The Ring*.
RYAN: Ooh, ooh, the one with the creepy, waterlogged little girl that crawls out of the TV. I didn't sleep for days after that movie.
BECKETT: Yes! Exactly! Thank you. That movie. It's fiction. It's a horror story in a book about urban legends.
RYAN: Yeah. I mean, because that's ... all it is, right? A legend.
CASTLE: Many legends are based in truth. I saw the video. At midnight in three days' time I will die.

He refuses to sleep with Beckett because "In every horror movie I've ever seen, having sex pretty much guarantees we will die. So for the safety of us both, I say we just…hold off." Other horror clichés surface as Castle and Beckett visit a suspect in a mental hospital in a scene reminiscent of *Silence of the Lambs*, in which they're told to stay away from the glass. When Castle can't sleep, certain he's doomed, he finally calls Wes Craven to pick his brain for surviving the curse.

CASTLE: The name Wes Craven is synonymous with horror. You've made a fortune
scaring the crap out of people. *My Soul to Take,* all the *Nightmare on Elm Streets* – terrifying.
WES CRAVEN: So you call me up in the middle of the night to join my fan club? What?
CASTLE: (sarcastically) Ha ha. No. I know that you've researched evil spirits who reach out from the beyond for all your films.
WES CRAVEN: Well, of course.
CASTLE: I was just wondering if you knew how to stop those pesky suckers.
WES CRAVEN: Is this you making your own movie? I mean, are you writing a horror screenplay?
CASTLE: Yes. I just thought I'd give you a little friendly competition. Just got a little writer's block is all.
WES CRAVEN: Okay, what's the story?
CASTLE: Um … ruggedly handsome hero and his notoriously practical lady friend watch a disc that's killing its viewers within three days.

WES CRAVEN: Really? You don't think that's a little derivative?
CASTLE: Yes ... but ... I am hoping to distinguish the ending. You know, make the third act a survival tale rather than a blood bath. I just can't figure out how to get my heroes out of this mess.
WES CRAVEN: So the key is always in the spirit's origin story. Once you have that you can start to figure out the spirit's weaknesses. If it's using the disc as its portal into our world, then–
CASTLE: Then the disc would contain clues as to the spirit's story. Wes, thank you! Thank you. Listen buddy, it's late. I gotta go.
CASTLE hangs up.
WES CRAVEN: Friendly competition my ass.

Castle sends the images to his social media followers for help, and they decide the building is the Brunswick Inn in Port Campbell. It turns out, in 2008 both victims stayed there, as they were witnesses in a serial killer's trial. However, that killer, Nigel Malloy, died in prison three years earlier. Adding to the creepiness, he insisted at his trial, "My victims gave me unique inside information into death. Into its secrets. Even when my body perishes my essence will continue on. I will continue on. You see, death is just the beginning." It appears he is attacking the witnesses from beyond the grave.

Through his horror, Castle continues his genre-savvy approach as they track the third victim.

CASTLE: Uh ... we're going to a cabin in the woods in the middle of nowhere.
BECKETT: Yeah, so?
CASTLE: So it's like the coed checking out the strange noise in the basement in a slasher flick. It's a recipe for disaster.

He's certain he won't survive, as he tells Beckett, "I don't think I need to tell you what kind of chances the comic relief guy has." In the dark, terrifying woods, they enter the rickety cabin as strange noises and movement emerge from the shadows outside. A horrific showdown ensues. They finally discover it isn't Nigel Malloy who wants revenge, but the daughter of a man falsely accused, who sat in terror for three days then killed himself. Now she's bringing the same fate on those who accused him. Shaken but still strong, Castle and Beckett manage to take the killer down.

Irish Mob ("The Wild Rover," 518)

> LANIE: Okay, remind me who are The Westies again.
> CASTLE: Irish Mafia out of Hell's Kitchen.
> BECKETT: They deal in cargo theft, counterfeiting, extortion.
> RYAN: And public urination on St Patrick's Day ("Sucker Punch," 213)

In "Sucker Punch" (213), the Westies are introduced as a rival gang to the Latin Kings – the Latin Kings deal drugs, but the Westies execute anyone found doing the same. Eventually the case gives Beckett one of her first leads on her mother's killer and this takes over the story.

Kevin Ryan once went undercover in the Irish mob and, by wearing a wire, got half of them arrested. In season five, he goes back in to get their Bible, "a list of transactions and contacts going back years." Central to the story is Ryan's ex, bartender Siobhan, who's desperate to get free of the mob. The FBI are willing to help her, but only for the Bible – otherwise the mob boss Bobby S. will kill her. Heart torn by the damsel in distress, Ryan goes back in. The story is also a clear homage to *The Departed*, with Ryan reviving his old undercover alias to bring down the mob. There are also parallels to Hitchcock's *Suspicion*, in which Ingrid Bergman's character goes undercover on behalf of the feds to discover whether her ex-lover is a Nazi collaborator.

The Irish mob is a bit clichéd, as Bobby S. asks Ryan, "So, what? You're the wild rover from the song? Returning with gold in great store, is that it?" and references the Prodigal Son from the Bible. Clearly his knowledge of popular culture comes from Sunday School as well as Irish folksongs. Meanwhile, Bobby's tough second in command Liam and his wife are framing Bobby for murder so Liam can take over. As they operate out of a pub, they take Ryan to the docks in menacing, traditional mob fashion to kill him. Loyalty is everything in their den, but Siobhan is the only laudable character, and she's struggling to get out. With his alias permanently burned, Ryan ends his adventure with relief that it's over and that he won't have to return.

Rear Window ("The Lives of Others," 519)

The celebrated Hitchcock film *Rear Window* clearly inspired the Castle episode. After breaking his leg in the former, professional photographer L. B. "Jeff" Jefferies (James Stewart) is confined to a wheelchair in his apartment. Gazing out his rear window with binoculars, he gets to know the neighbors. One night, Jeffries hears a woman scream "Don't!" and smash of broken glass. Later, he sees the man Thorwald making repeated trips and cleaning a large knife and handsaw. His wife has disappeared. There's also a heavy trunk Thorwald has moving men haul away. Jeff discusses these observations with his girlfriend Lisa Fremont (Grace Kelly) as he sinks into obsession with his theory that Thorwald murdered his wife. The episode has several homages, as Castle's friends make film quips and Beckett, in a Grace-Kelly-style gown, perches in Castle's lap.

"Hmm. You must be bored. You've actually gone *Rear Window*," Ryan notes. Trapped in his own wheelchair and getting stir-crazy, with only a pair of binoculars for company, Castle witnesses a similarly disturbing sight. When he sees one of the neighbors cheating, he's amused, but when he sees the boyfriend pull a knife and head into the curtained bedroom, he's horrified. Over and over he tries to get the detectives to investigate, but each time, they find nothing. Each time, of course, they grow more convinced Castle is paranoid. Nathan Fillion says, "It's a bit of a tough go when your friends or the people you rely on deny you your credibility. So he's miffed" (Mitovich, "Castle Episode 100").

The commentators describe Castle doing an excellent job as the ordinary man in extraordinary circumstances.

> CASTLE: I'm not crazy.
> BECKETT: No. But you do have a vivid imagination. (she caresses his neck) And you've been stuck inside for two weeks. What were you doing looking out the window anyway?
> CASTLE: I was –
> BECKETT: Bored? So you saw what you wanted to see? (he's silent) When did you take your last painkiller?
> CASTLE: I was not hallucinating.
> BECKETT: C'mon, Castle. You're here with a broken leg, binoculars, seeing a Rear Window scenario playing across the way. I mean, what are the odds?
> CASTLE: (sad, low) Astronomical.
> BECKETT: All right. I'm going to make us some dinner and then get you to bed.

Marlowe explains, "What we wanted to deliver is something that was classic Castle-and-Beckett, something that felt like it could have played in [the] first season or now. And we were really excited to have found it" (Mitovich, "Castle Episode 100"). Castle is back on his wacky theories – chasing the most unlikely of all.

"There are a lot of references and callbacks for the hardcore *Castle* fans," shares series creator Andrew W. Marlowe. "We've peppered it with little pings from earlier episodes" (Mitovich, "Castle Episode 100"). Creators Andrew W. Marlowe and Terri Edda Miller make a cameo appearance as the couple in the building across from Castle's loft arguing over laptops, in a nod to Hitchcock making cameos in his own films. They even look like the writers they are, as Castle observes dismissively. The featurette "Martha's Master Class" on the DVD shows the episode's backstory as Beckett's dialogue appears along with Martha's notes for the performance.

There are subtle references to other Hitchcock films including *Rebecca* (the victim's name is DeWinter), *Suspicion* (the female victim married a charming man and then became terrified of her husband's true intentions), *Rope* (with two conspirators plotting and executing a murder, then planting the evidence in front of the authorities to throw them off their trail), and *Shadow of a Doubt* (the crime takes place in the family's home garage). Thriller music sets the scene as Castle watches each moment play out.

In *Rear Window*, Jeffries enlists the police to search the neighbor's house, but when they find nothing, he grows more desperate. His girlfriend Lisa finally climbs the fire escape to Thorwald's apartment and sneaks in, only to have Thorwald grab her. The police intervene and save her. When Thorwald comes to Jeffries' place for a final showdown, Jeffries sets off his camera flashbulbs, temporarily blinding Thorwald. Nonetheless, Thorwald hurls Jeffries from the window and breaks his other leg before he can be caught.

When Castle bursts across to save Beckett, he finds his friends have played a hoax on him and there's really a birthday party for him. After struggling through his initial shock, he calls it, "Without a doubt ... the greatest birthday gift of my life!" This is of course a celebratory party and April Fool's Day joke within the course of the show. This birthday gift was in fact foreshadowed in "Reality Star Struck" (514), where Castle thinks the "complex case where nothing makes sense" might be his Valentine's Day gift from Beckett. Beckett even uses this prank to solve the real murder she's investigating, a murder that was also staged.

Saved by the Bell ("Need to Know," 603)

Charlie Reynolds was an actor, once the star of the 90s TV comedy *2 Cool for School* where he played lovable nerd Dewey Hancock. In this *Saved by the Bell* stand-in, he's basically Screech, adding the suspenders of Urkel and the flip-up sunglasses of Dwayne Wayne.

His body is found hanging from the hook of a construction crane, and Castle makes a crack about a "Former child star literally getting the hook."

> MARTHA: Oh, how awful. I did a guest spot on that show.
> CASTLE: It was a simpler time, when Dewey's catchphrase "hubba hubba" passed as sparkling dialogue.

Ryan was a big fan of the addictive children's show, though Esposito quickly denies ever watching.

Their first suspect is Reynolds' old agent. The team go down the wrong path with her when they discover she has a creepy shrine to her favorite actor as Castle predicts.

> GERALDINE: After the show was canceled, the phone stopped ringing. Most agents would have dumped his ass, but me? I stuck with him. (she turns back to the TV) Oh, this is the scene. This is where history was made.
> CHARLIE (AS DEWEY): Hey Lisa!
> LISA stops walking and turns back to him. He flips the lenses in his glasses up and looks her over.
> CHARLIE (AS DEWEY): Hubba hubba!
> RYAN and GERALDINE laugh along with the laugh track.
> RYAN claps his hands.
> CASTLE (to RYAN): Timeless gem, really?
> RYAN: That was a very...nuanced...performance.

Castle gets his hands on a copy of the movie script for the actors' big reunion. It's called *2 Cool For School: Those Who Can't, Teach*. He describes the storyline, "Dewey and Marco are back at Bayview High as faculty. Dewey is the brainy science teacher and Marco's reliving his glory days as the football coach." There's much bitterness under the surface of the reunion film as Ryan discovers producer Hank Harper "has faced numerous charges of embezzling money from the films that he's worked on."

It's finally reveled that Charlie Reynolds was leaving, and thus was killed by his onscreen rival (who resembles Slater from *Saved by the Bell*) who feared the loss of the film when he had little left of his career to salvage. As often happens on *Castle*, the pressure of this microcosm world leads to the murder.

Time Travel ("Time Will Tell," 605)

A woman is murdered with no apparent motive. However, a strange man was hanging around her and then fled the murder scene. Esposito reports, "A couple of nights ago Shauna filed a harassment complaint. Apparently three days ago a guy confronted Shauna on her way home from work. Said the lives of half the people on the planet were at stake." He was put on a 72 hour psych hold and just released.

They watch tapes of him in the psych ward insisting, "Shauna Taylor! All I know is 12:58. That is all they told me. That is how it starts and if I am not there to stop it we are all dead. Do you understand me? Dead! Somebody has to let me out of here. All right? Listen to me! I need to save her!" The team catches him in Shauna's apartment, but he pleads to be released, insisting a billion people could die. He finally tells Beckett and Castle his story: He's from the future, 2035 to be precise. His name is Simon Doyle.

> SIMON: Look. After the bloody energy wars of 2031 we finally managed to cultivate new sources of power.
> CASTLE: Energy wars?
> SIMON: Yeah, neofacists come to power and try to control the world's energy supply for a select few. Don't worry. We defeat them. Turns out, one of these new sources of power is a tachyon generator. It lets us open doors in the time stream continuum allowing us to travel back in time. But of course, because of the possibility of abuse it was tightly regulated and kept secret from the public.

He adds that he's a temporal anthropologist who travels back in time to study culturally significant eras. "Ancient Egypt, Middle Ages…man, I've been in Nazi Germany." Genre-savvy Castle asks about the butterfly effect, but Doyle tells him small changes to history tend to even out over time. This time, however, someone unauthorized traveled back to fundamentally change history. It's a mystery why Shauna is significant.

Esposito nods to the most popular time travel television show by calling the suspect's strange gadget "Doctor Who's sonic screwdriver." Esposito also sarcastically suggests the suspect's story is derivative of *Twelve Monkeys* and *The Terminator*. 1995's *Twelve Monkeys* follows a time traveler from the post-apocalyptic future who comes to present day to locate and eradicate the source of a deadly plague before it wipes out everyone. In *The Terminator*, a future criminal travels back to wipe out humanity's future savior, or rather, his mother before he's born.

It turns out, as with *Terminator*, that it isn't Shauna but her relations. The criminal was seeking her brother, whom he tortures in order to find a twenty-one-year-old student at Hudson getting his post-doc in theoretical physics named Paul Deschile. Recognizing his name from history, Doyle realizes he is the target:

> The energy wars, all right? I told you about the other side. A group of fascists. They were worse than the Nazis. They were slaughtering people by the tens of thousands, okay? They were winning. Until Deschile. He and his team, they – they created an energy shield, okay? It was able to stop their weapons. It completely turned the tide. (he slams his hands on her desk) Detective, listen to me! Ward is still out there, obviously fighting for the fascists. They trying to win the war by rewriting history! And if he kills Deschile there will be no energy shield. And without that energy shield we lose that war! Ward's going to kill Deschile and that is why billions of people die!

The criminal is Garrett Ward. Ryan adds, "Until six years ago, no criminal record. In fact, until six years ago, no record at all. No DMV, no military, nothing....Whoever he is, his record begins when he was arrested for bringing a backpack bomb into a global energy conference here in Manhattan." The team remain skeptical of course. Nonetheless, they catch the murderer before he can kill Deschile. Either they have saved the future or, as Beckett notes, at least saved an innocent life. The episode ends with Beckett spilling coffee on the original of the letter the criminal from the future used to track Paul Deschile, then discovering it perfectly matches the stained copy he had. The time loop is closed. For science fiction fans this time travel story comes out plausible, even clichéd. Castle continues believing throughout, though he tells no one the time traveler basically vanishes in front of him. Castle is even left with the man's scanner. The show also keeps some deniability, as Ryan discovers Ward and Doyle were cellmates in a psychiatric facility. Nonetheless, there's a terribly plausible look into the future for Castle.

Doyle gives Castle a glimpse, quoting his book jackets as saying, "Richard Castle lives in New York with his wife, Senator Beckett, and their three children." Though he doesn't go into details about the craziness of their future, he adds that Castle's "serious literature" is "so much better" than his mysteries. Beckett considers becoming senator only a year later, suggesting she still may when the time is right.

The Da Vinci Code ("Get a Clue," 606)

"A posed body, mysterious medieval symbols, and now a murderous monk. It's a real life *Da Vinci Code*," Castle crows.

> BECKETT: Do we have any idea who this guy is?
> CASTLE: I'll tell you who he is. He's part of a brotherhood of assassins, chosen to guard an ancient secret.
> BECKETT: Castle –
> CASTLE: Stalking a woman obsessed with medieval symbols? This is what the evidence suggests.
> BECKETT: (to RYAN) Can we get a closer look at his face?
> RYAN: No, he never turns his head.
> BECKETT: Wait, zoom in on his scalp. (RYAN does) There. Do you see that?
> CASTLE: Ritual markings. Left by some unholy initiation.

Lanie reports that the victim was stabbed with a saber, and the plot thickens. Just before her death, Susannah Richland developed a sudden interest in occult symbols and medieval history. She was researching ancient symbols, and a Freemason one was written on her hand. Esposito notes that "Castle might be right about this *Da Vinci Code* thing" since

Susannah called Professor Jason Byford at Hudson University, expert in ancient languages and symbology. In fact, symbology is not a real discipline – it was borrowed straight from Dan Brown's character. "Just like Tom Hanks in the movie. It's not a baroque plot. It's a best-seller plot," Castle smirks. Masonic symbols appear in several of Brown's books, and his *The Lost Symbol* tracks them through the secrets of the American founding fathers. *National Treasure*, a popular film in this genre, does the same.

The victim also had a handwritten letter from the ancient mason Theodore Rose, a friend of George Washington. When Castle finds it, he adds, "They're not riddles. They're clues. Clues leading to some great Masonic treasure. And this last line could be why she was murdered. (he points and reads) My Latin is pretty rusty, but I think that means, 'peril and woe to him who follows this path with the dark heart.'" As they follow the clues they find themselves unraveling complex clues based in esoteric myth, history, and symbol, as do the characters in these books and films.

CASTLE: Theodore Rose's letter. There's that one clue in Latin. Uh ... (he pulls out a photocopy of the letter) ... "the world turns between the heavens and ash heap". In Latin the word for ash heap also means altar. The heavens are depicted in that stained glass.
BECKETT: And the altar is right underneath it.
CASTLE: So the clues led her to this chapel. But why?
...
CASTLE: Listen to this. (he reads) "For Gods and men alike doth lame Hephaestus strike." I know what that means. I know where that is!
BECKETT: You do?
CASTLE: Yeah. Hephaestus was the Greek God of blacksmiths. His forge was in Mount Etna. There's a blacksmith shop right here in lower Manhattan called Etna's Forge. It's been there since the 1700s. I know because I was there with ... Alexis. It was a field trip. Third grade. But that's – that's gotta be it.

They reach the next place, and to their surprise, a masked man with a sword attacks. Castle of course revels in the drama.

> MASKED MAN: You have trespassed into secrets beyond your understanding. You will pay with your life.
> CASTLE: Okay, okay. But before you kill me, there's one thing you should know.
> MASKED MAN: And what is that?
> CASTLE: I am *really* good at this.

Castle snatches a sword and wins their duel, and the man offers him the next clue. However, when Castle and Beckett move to arrest him, the man appears confused and admits it's all a scavenger hunt. The letter was handwritten in modern times for the contestants. The clues are based on old carved symbols that are really scattered around the historic buildings, but the treasure hunt has been invented by the New York Historical Society, with a prize of $2500 – probably not worth killing for.

Despite his disappointment, Castle rallies when he realizes the ancient puzzle is real: He insists, "Burns told us that he based the game on some of the writings of Theodore Rose. Now, what if Rose's clues were real and actually lead somewhere? What if Susannah figured that out?" He places the symbols side by side on the murder board and shows how they all line up when he adds the extra one Susannah drew on her hand, which she found at the chapel the night she was killed.

They finally find the treasure, a thousand half-dimes minted in 1792, worth over a million dollars each. Of course, Castle and Beckett are trapped in the dark (in the tradition of all the works in this genre) and must struggle to escape. Castle also sticks a hand into a stone carving and screams, *National Treasure* style.

Nolan Burns, who created the contest, reveals that he found the real Freemason letter but couldn't solve the treasure hunt, so he gathered players. One of those players,

Susannah, solved the case and was killed for the money. It's a fun homage to the treasure hunt stories, with Castle, of course, finding the prize.

Miley Cyrus ("Limelight," 611)

Beloved teen pop star Mandy Sutton is killed at 22. She parallels Miley Cyrus, the child actor gone sexy and adult, with a touch of Lindsey Lohan's drinking and rehab cycles. As Castle describes her, "Alexis used to love her kid's show, Mandy Melody. She was a regular teen by day and a crime fighting pop star by night and nobody recognized her at school because she wore glasses." This is the plot of Disney's *Hannah Montana*, of course, in which Miley Cyrus played dual roles of ordinary schoolgirl Miley Stewart by day and famous recording artist Hannah Montana by night. This Disney show (2006-2011) has 200 million viewers across the world at its height. It spawned several movies and a host of children's toys and merchandise.

However, the beloved teen icon grew up, in life and on the episode. As Mandy's mother notes, "A lot of people dislike her, who she became. Provocative clothes and dancing. They just wanted her to be Mandy Melody forever." She tells stories of threatening letters, of paparazzi mobs and stalkers, and worse of drinking and drugs.

> MARILYN: But the last few months, Mandy had been doing pretty great. She'd stayed clean since her last stint in rehab. She even met a guy while she was doing her community service. Zach. He builds houses for the poor. And then a couple nights ago she went to a club for someone's birthday and ... (she trails off) She got drunk and she started making out with an old boyfriend.
> KELLY: And someone took a picture. It hit all the gossip sites. When Zach saw ...
> MARILYN: It was too much for him. They got into a big fight and he left her.

The story twists when the victim is discovered to not be Mandy, but Claire Samuels, 25, an aspiring actress and

Mandy's decoy, They find Mandy in a hotel room, with the spreading red stain only wine from overindulging. The hungover Mandy can only describe her decoy's murder as "pretty harsh" and adds that she was rarely in contact with her decoy. When Castle tells her she may have been the intended target, all she says is "Oh. Yeah. That does make more sense. Okay."

> BECKETT: So um, do you know if anyone would have wanted to hurt you? Do you have any enemies?
> MANDY: The press. But they wouldn't hurt me. Without me who would they write all those bad things about?
> BECKETT: Okay, well, the last two days when you were out socializing did you have any fights or did you upset anyone?
> MANDY: (shrugs) Probably. (BECKETT waits) I'm a little hazy on the details.

The blitzed out star seems apathetic to her double's murder and the potential for her own. Beckett and her team decide to keep the world thinking Mandy is dead, for her own safety. However, her mother callously asks how long, adding, "She starts a tour next week, and as her manager I can't imagine that it's going to help ticket sales if everyone thinks she's dead." Thus the star's life with little maternal feeling is highlighted. Meanwhile, Alexis walks into the room, describing her shock at the celebrity's death: "But then she grew up and, whoa. I mean, how does that happen? How does someone become such a hot mess?" Alexis asks, not realizing Mandy is there. Despite their rocky start, they later open up and speak to each other about their inner turmoil:

> MANDY: It happens when you're not looking.
> ALEXIS: Excuse me?
> MANDY: Before, you asked how it happens? How someone becomes like me? It happens when you're not looking and by the time you realize it, it's already who you are. Like the car crash on the side of the road everybody stops and watches.

ALEXIS: That doesn't mean that's who you have to be. You can always change.
MANDY: Turns out I don't do change so well. But you steal a police car and you set it on fire? I'm your girl. Or if you find the greatest guy in the world, fall madly in love, and then mess it up by hooking up with my dirtbag ex? (she shrugs) That I can do.

Mandy adds, "If I don't drink then I start to feel. And I don't like what I feel. I wish I had those glasses from Mandy Melody and I'd just put them on and ... disappear."

Alexis empathizes, since as she puts it, "Because right now I wish I could disappear from my life, too." Thus both girls explore their disassociation and disappointment at the way their lives have turned out.

It's finally revealed that the photo of Mandy kissing her ex was staged, as someone paid off the double to ruin Mandy's life and get her into all the tabloids. To Mandy's horror, this person is her mother.

MANDY: Wait a minute. Wait. You did this to break me up with Zach? He was the best thing that ever happened to me. He was going to take me away from all of this.
MARILYN: That's right. Away from everything we'd worked for. Your tour. Your career. He was going to cost you missions.
MANDY: You mean cost you millions.
MARILYN: And for what?
MANDY: A chance to be normal?
MARILYN: (scoffs) Normal. You're special. Zach didn't understand that. And neither did Claire.
MANDY: So you killed her?
MARILYN: She was going to tell you what I'd done. She was going to make you hate me. And I couldn't let her drive a wedge between us. I couldn't.

The pain of Mandy's life is central as stalkers and media all want her to be unhappy and interesting. Through it all is a young woman striving for normalcy, emphasized by her bond with Alexis.

Vogue ("Dressed to Kill," 614)

Ella Hayes, 26, assistant to the editor of *Modern Fashion,* is killed. Her boss, designer Matilda King, parallels Anna Wintour, the infamously demanding and eccentric real life editor-in-chief of *Vogue.* (Her aloof and tyrannical personality as she insists on tasks her assistants have no time to complete has earned her the nickname "Nuclear Wintour.") With her trademark pageboy bob and sunglasses, she's nearly an identical match. She also echoes the editor in *The Devil Wears Prada* as she makes vicious demands. Of course, this bestselling book (later a film) was written by Wintour's former personal assistant, Lauren Weisberger. In the episode, Castle briefly mentions this.

> CASTLE: Seriously? You've never heard of Matilda King?
> ESPOSITO: I'm betting that most real men haven't.
> CASTLE: Yes. If by real you mean uninformed.
> ESPOSITO: Whatever.
> CASTLE: Matilda King is a legend in the fashion industry.
> BECKETT: Or infamous. Depends on your point of view.
> CASTLE: Yes, former assistants of hers have written books about how tough she is. A dragon lady that chews people up and spits them out.
> ESPOSITO: Does she also strangle them? Because that's how Lanie said our vic died.

In fact, she was strangled with a blue alpaca scarf that was the magazine's holiday gift to its employees. Even the victim had one. When they arrive at the magazine office, Beckett observes this is "the big leagues for anyone who wants to work in fashion." In fact, Matilda remembers Beckett from her time as a model, to Castle's surprise. Matilda notes, "I offered her a spread in the January '99 issue. Nicole Kidman was on the cover. And you passed. To date you're the only person to tell me no."

They discover a high-stress environment where Ella had just been fired for messing up appointments. Further, her phone is bugged. Castle notes, "Still, wire taps, threats from mysterious men, murder. Whatever's going on here, it's bigger than fashion." In fact, the fashion world is bigger than he thought. *Couture Chic* magazine, competitor to *Modern Fashion*, tried to have Ella spy for them. They note that Ella found out something. "Something that will ruin *Modern Fashion*, take down the whole operation." Matilda King, who bugs her employees' houses, may have overheard the call.

Matilda's own job is at stake, and, as with *The Devil Wears Prada*, she's not portrayed completely unsympathetically. She also gets a word in for the value of fashion. As she insists, "For 57 years women have been purchasing this magazine for the fashion!...Whenever they've had a bad day at work, or at home, they've come to us. We are their escape. We are their fantasy. It's the clothing that stitches it all together. That's what matters!" In a sweet scene, she gives Kate a Cinderella moment: She has Kate try on an enchanting silver and crystal wedding dress for a shoot, and then sends it to her as a gift, describing how lovely she looked in it.

Sabotage and plagiarism enter the story as one employee tries to bring down the angry diva and another steals Ella's designs. Ella is in a position to reveal the truth, so her killer takes her out of the picture so he can launch his own clothing line in the surprisingly high-stakes business.

Carrie ("Smells Like Teen Spirit," 615)

BECKETT: I bet that principal must have *hated* you.
CASTLE: I'm wonder if 'hate' is a strong enough word; Principal Dunham had to hire a crane to get that cow off the roof. But I'm sure that old battle-axe has long since retired. Put out to pasture, so to speak.
DUNHAM: [From behind] Is that a bovine reference, Mr. Rodgers?
[Castle jumps up, startled]
CASTLE: Principal Dunham. You're, uh... still here.
DUNHAM: And sadly, you have returned.

In high school, Castle was expelled for the prank, as he was the scholarship kid with no connections. Castle returns there when Madison, the head of the mean girls, is murdered by the abused, invisible teen Jordan who appears to have telekinesis. The mean girl was video-chatting with her friends Kris and Hillary when they watched her get flung up to the ceiling and murdered.

As Beckett and Castle learn, a mysterious incident happened in the school cafeteria a week before. As they watch a cellphone recording, Jordan bumps into Madison and drops her tray. Then she appears to get angry. Around them, chairs shake and move by themselves. They slide down to menace Madison, Kris, and Hillary and crash into the walls beside them. Everyone screams, while Jordan stares at her hands. Castle says, "The outcast. The mean girls. The rage that erupts in a telekinetic attack. This is a real life *Carrie*." Castle even mentions that "Stephen" will love hearing about this case.

Jordan was a scholarship foster child, bullied by the mean girls. Like Carrie, she had every motivation. In Jordan's room, Ryan finds a stack of *X-Men* comics, books like *Telekinesis Unleashed, Developing Telekinetic Powers,* and *Telekinesis for Beginners* and a copy of Stephen King's *Carrie.* On discovering this, Castle says (in heavy-handed fashion by this point), "Clearly Jordan had powers and was trying to understand them. This is exactly like the movie *Carrie*." As one of Madison's friends notes, Jordan is certainly the culprit based on her previous stunt. "It was if some invisible force threw Madison around the room like a ragdoll."

They track Jordan's movements to the lab of Dr. Rampinel, who teaches biophysics at MIT and also conducts research in telekinesis. As they discover, he's harboring a frightened Jordan, who's convinced she's out of control. "I got so angry and stuff just started flying around the cafeteria. And then I wished for Madison to be dead and the next thing I knew she was. It had to be me, right?" she asks.

When they charge in and arrest her, objects are hurtling all around her. However, her best friend reveals that he is responsible, though not in the way gullible Castle thinks.

LUCAS: You wouldn't understand. Most people don't.
That's why I've learned to hide what I am.
CASTLE: Telekinetic.
LUCAS: (scoffs) What? No. Smart. You know, people don't
like it when you're smart and you do things people don't
understand. I mean, all that stuff that you saw? I rigged.
CASTLE: Rigged? But you – chairs moved. The tables –
LUCAS: Right. Special effects are kind of my hobby. It's
pretty amazing what you can do with some fishing wire and
magnets. And people are pretty gullible.

He staged the cafeteria event, and then spoiled Madison found out and blackmailed him into helping her with a robbery. The top of the social clique was stealing from the local rich families, and she knew she could get the nerdy scholarship kid expelled. (This appears a shout-out to the film *The Bling Ring*). She also made a prank video to spook her friend. As she told Lucas, "She is so going to freak when she sees this. She'll think your psycho sweetheart is coming for her next." However the friend murdered her and used the video to cover her crime by making witnesses believe they were watching the murder live. As a third friend notes nastily about the murderer, "She is captain of the cheer squad. She knows her way to the top of the pyramid." Thus the cruelty of high school culture is explored.

Investigating, Castle finds himself nostalgic for the time gone, and tells Beckett, "Yeah. It's strange, going back. Everything seems smaller, yet unchanged. I mean, the hallways are the same, the principal is the same. The same banners for school dances." The episode ends with Jordan and Lucas happily together at the dance, their own star-crossed, geeky love made right, while Beckett and Castle make up for their own missed proms.

Ninjas ("The Way of the Ninja," 618)

This episode is named for a popular arcade game and teases Castle's knowledge of movie trivia as well as his credulousness. Jade Yamata, a visiting Japanese woman, is suddenly hit in the chest with a knife and dies. She was a dancer at the New York Ballet Conservatory, or at least that was her cover. Near the place where she died, the find a shrine with a dagger and red altar cloth. As they explore, a figure dressed as a ninja whisks the dagger from Castle's hand and rushes away in a puff of smoke. Castle is of course thrilled by this development.

> CASTLE: Our killer is a ninja.
> BECKETT: Or he is just an athletic person with a hooded tracksuit.
> CASTLE: Yeah, that disappeared in a puff of smoke.
> BECKETT: Yes, which I could do if I had a smoke bomb.

Consulate officer Amaya Tagamai tells them the shrine is built to honor Izanami, Shinto goddess of creation and death, though having it is not an obsession with murder but a common way to honor one's ancestors. She also tells Castle there are no such things as ninjas anymore.

> CASTLE: What does she know, anyway? I bet she's never even seen *Ninja 3: The Domination*.
> BECKETT: Yeah, no. I mean, she only comes from the country that created the mythology.
> CASTLE: Which does not make her an expert! Our victim was killed ninja-style, by a killer who had some sort of mysterious shrine.

They discover Jade was calling a tea warehouse each night, but when they arrive, they discover it's a Japanese hostess bar, at which attractive women seduce the businessmen and serve them alcohol. Castle adds, "They flirt, they get you to buy drinks, just keep things generally fun." While visiting, Ryan finds himself singing karaoke while Esposito orders expensive drinks and both try (badly) to fit into this world.

Jade appears to have worked there. Each night she flirted with a regular client, financier Michio Saito, and appeared to be targeting him for her own purpose. The night she died, she was working a private party at his house. As Jade's friend adds, "Something happened at the party last night. One of the girls said Mr. Saito found Jade going through his things. He hit the roof and had his people throw her out."

After getting kicked out of the club for being police, the team stands on the street. Suddenly, a throwing star impales Castle's phone. A figure dressed in black appears behind them, swords drawn. However, a second black-clad figure intervenes to save Castle. The first avoids Esposito's bullets and the second vanishes instantly.

> GATES: Now there are two ninjas?
> ESPOSITO: Captain, I know it sounds crazy –
> GATES: You bet it sounds crazy. One attacks you, the other saves your life? It makes no sense.
> CASTLE: Unless they are rivals in an ancient feud. Two warring clans. One committed to the path of darkness, the other sworn to follow the path of light.
> GATES: This is not a ninja movie, Mr. Castle. This is a murder investigation.

As they soon learn, Saito is apparently part of the Yakuza (transnational organized crime syndicates). "He's high up on the chain of the Uzumi clan out of Okinawa. His legitimate businesses are just suspected fronts for money laundering, drug trafficking, and extortion." He also has a display case of fifteenth-century ninja stars.

The team also discover Amaya Tagamai is an imposter. Jade's background too was fabricated. Her father was a building contractor who had a run in with the local Yakuza. The Yakuza retaliated by stabbing the parents then blowing up his house, scarring the daughter. Rumor had it at the time that the family was murdered by the Green Dragon, "a secret ninja enforcer of the Yakuza." Castle decides, "So this is a classic revenge story. Jade was hunting down the man who killed her family." Saito is clearly the Green Dragon.

The team finds the consulate officer, really an undercover police officer and Jade's sister Saya Ozu. She tells them, "If the Green Dragon knew who I was he would kill me. I tried to put what happened to my family behind me. But Jade? She could not let it go. She made it her mission to find out who he was. It's why she came to New York." The shrine was Jade's, with a replica of the dagger that killed her parents.

They confront Saito, but he's killed by one ninja, and once again a second ninja intervenes to save them. The pair fight. They are finally revealed to be Saito's American lieutenant and Saya. After the case is wrapped, Saya assures Castle, "There are no more ninjas, Mr. Castle. I am merely a practitioner of their martial arts. But I'm very, very good." Castle is left with his fantasy debunked once more.

Seventies Cop Shows (That '70s Show," 620)

"That 70's Show" has an unlikely premise – that to jog a senile mobster's memory the entire precinct must disguise themselves as being stuck in the 1970s. Still, the cast manages to have lots of fun. Mobster Vince Bianchi is dug out of cement printed with the date 1978 – the first iconic image shown onscreen. Every study of the old case brings them back to the long-vanished time, to Castle's glee.

> BOYLE: Mickey "the Blade" Carcano, Louie "the Lip" Maneri. Both wanted to muscle in on Bianchi's territory, so they had motive.
> CASTLE: It's like being transported to a bygone era. Mickey the Blade? Louie the Lip? Where are these guys now?
> BECKETT: Probably under concrete.

The victim's assistant, Harold Leone, knew much about the case, but apparently chose to lose himself in the seventies as a coping mechanism for his friend's death. He was "Vince's advisor. His consigliere," in another old-fashioned term. When they go see him, he's watching an old episode of *All in the Family* on an old TV. His living room looks like it's straight out of the 1970s with brown wallpaper, LO/VE clock, and so on. His suit is bright and garish.

Esposito and Ryan watch video of cops of the time and dress as them – they end up basically being a *Starsky & Hutch* parody. Esposito quickly becomes a fan of the period:

ESPOSITO: By starting with this documentary I found on these two NYPD badasses from back in the day. (he points at the screen) Snookie Watts and Ray Price. Check out Snookie's move right here.
They watch as SNOOKIE slides across the hood of their car.
NARRATOR (on screen): Snookie, you and Ray have made quite a name for yourselves in the anti-crime units.
SNOOKIE (on screen): You better believe it, baby. Stopping crime one skell at a time.
They high-five.
RAY (on screen): Right on, right on. See, when the bad guys see the old red rocket here? They know a serious head cracking is on the way.

Beckett tells Castle that the only 70s outfit Lanie has is her Foxy Brown Halloween costume. She looks stunning in it, and Esposito can't stop staring. She too throws herself into the role as she shoots down Leone's flirting. Beckett is more skeptical as she wears a striped shirt then a long vest and beads. First they make the morgue look seventies for Leone, and then they redecorate the entire precinct with Martha's help. Castle drives him there with vintage suit and police car. "Twelfth precinct. Let's boogie." Esposito and Ryan become Snookie and Ray. "Ah hah, that's us, baby. What it is," Esposito adds. A truly fun moment is watching Esposito slide off the hood of the *Starsky & Hutch*-style car, turning cool into clumsy. Ryan too discovers he likes it: "I tell you, these clothes? That car? I feel invincible, man. Like Ray Price, kicking ass and taking names 70s style. I get it now, baby."

However, Leone is unconvinced and Captain Gates returns early (with the words "Mr. Castle, what on earth possessed you to turn my precinct into the set of *Kojak*?!") Ryan and Esposito in their Starsky and Hutch roles take him to Glitterati, a seventies nightclub that's recently been reborn as vintage. It's filled with period costumes, neon lights, dancing, and music of course.

Despite the fun the characters are having, a downside appears to the seventies as Ryan quips about police brutality.

Leone makes sexist comments towards Beckett especially, calling her "cupcake" and ignoring her to talk to Castle. Of course, the greatest flaw in the past is that Leone and Bianchi had to hide their love for each other. The final scene at the disco with Harold dancing alone and paying homage to Vince during "Last Dance" is sweet and memorable, a fond farewell to a bygone age.

Competitive Skateboarders ("Law & Boarder," 621)

The episode begins with teen skateboarding champion Logan Moore racing across the city around three in the morning with a guy on a motorcycle chasing him.

> CASTLE: Sounds like a scene from an action movie.
> ESPOSITO: Yeah. I know. Especially when the biker started shooting and Logan crashed through that window right there.

After growing up on the wrong side of the tracks and making something of himself, he returned to New York for the New York Street Sport Festival down by Chelsea Piers...or so he claimed. However, as he mailed burglary tools to a friend and bought an old camcorder, there appeared to be more going on.

Skateboarding and the festival are explored as motives for murder. One suspect, Manny Castro, was a top pro who'd threatened to kill him. Esposito explains, "Six months ago Logan showed him up in an event in Los Angeles and then beat him two more times after that. Tension got super high between the two of them." However, Castro insists, "I talk a lot of trash. The fans go nuts for it. It's all part of the show." The competition is actually quite friendly.

The motive for murder goes back to Logan's days on the street as a young boarder and his need to find justice for a friend's death. His mother explains:

> He was a scrawny little kid from the neighborhood a couple
> years younger than Logan. He and some of the other kids
> in the neighborhood used to call themselves the Bronx
> skate crew. None of them had much of a home life so
> they'd just ride around on their boards all day long and get
> into places they shouldn't. But Jay was the one Logan
> might be even better than he was.

Thus skateboarding is emphasized as a sport for kids and teens, with the murderer a fellow teen about to turn twenty-one. The team arrests him at his birthday party, before he can receive his trust fund and destroy all evidence of his crime.

The episode features BMX bikers and skateboarders doing practice runs on ramps, pulling colorful tricks for the camera. As this is a more dangerous sport than usual, Castle doesn't get into it as he normally does. Beckett, however, seems to have a background in this:

> BECKETT: Whoa! Nice tail whip.
> CASTLE: Oh. So you know the lingo? Any extreme sports
> in your history I've yet to hear about?
> BECKETT: Well, I mean, I think catching killers is pretty
> extreme.

Her past in this arena is left for another time, however.

Second Grade Classroom ("Child's Play," 704)

An ice cream man is shot, with a closed cabinet suggesting a witness who hid within. More interestingly, the witness dropped a permission slip from a local elementary school. After the kids offer no leads during interviews, Castle infiltrates one of his most foreign worlds of all – second grade.

> DANIELS: In cases like this, a child is often more likely to
> open up to somebody who's not an authority figure: a
> classmate, a friend.
> BECKETT: So...basically we're looking for someone who
> won't intimidate them. An adult presence, in the classroom,
> that eight-year-olds will view as a peer. Someone that they
> can consider one of their own?

In Castle goes. "Being 90% kid myself I have an ability to get into the minds of children," he insists, and has them all write stories. "It can be about a little boy or a little girl, just like you. It can be as silly or as scary as you want it to be." While in class, he makes faces at kids (forbidden in the classroom) and protests "he started it!" The kids laugh at him because his pants are wet and throw erasers at his head. They take his wallet and spill marbles on the ground so he slips. "Uh, no breakthroughs yet, but the good news is um…it looks like they've accepted me as one of their own," he reports. He plays green army men with one kid and dresses as a fairy to join another kid's tea party. When the latter child, Emily, complains she's being bullied, he helps her though it doesn't connect to his case. He tells her:

> CASTLE: Emily, do you know why people do mean things? Because it makes them feel strong. Really though, you and me? We're the strong ones. We just keep our strength inside. So sometimes we forget it's there.
> EMILY: Like sometimes I forget I have gum in my pocket.
> CASTLE: Exactly. So, next time Jason does something mean, you just use that strength and just let it go. When he sees he can't upset you, he'll stop bothering you. Okay?

Unfortunately, Emily takes this as advice to punch Jason in the nose. As Castle is thrown out, however, one of the kids slips a drawing of an ice cream truck in his pocket and the witness is discovered. Castle discovers the truth of the story and lays a trap for the killer. When the villain chases them to the classroom, Castle defeats him by hurling marbles on the floor and knocking him down, using his new training in the kiddie lifestyle. The Alexis plot has her hovering overprotectively over her father, making him bag lunches and demanding, "Dad, what took you so long? School ended hours ago." He ends their story reminding her that he's back from his disappearance at the start of the season and can be the adult once more.

Instagram ("Meme is Murder," 705)

A celebrity is murdered...at least a celebrity of the digital age.

> RYAN: Uh ... Abby was a celebrity?
> CARLOS: She was huge on social media.
> ESPOSITO: So was she an actress or a singer or what?
> CARLOS: No, she posted pics on Snappamatic. You know, the photo sharing app? Snappamatic reviews, she called them.
> ESPOSITO: And that got her personal appearances?
> CARLOS: Yeah, and sponsors, too. Especially when she had half a million followers.

The killer not only texted her menacing photos but uploaded her picture after she died. Using the identity Netslayer, he shares it on Snappamatic, a site like Instagram, with the caption, "This star's 15 seconds are over."

> ESPOSITO: He kills her and then posts her picture. Why would he do that?
> CASTLE: Tear down the victim? Add insult to injury? "This star's 15 seconds are over." Maybe that's why he killed Abby, because she's a web celebrity.
> RYAN: Or he wants to become one himself.
> CASTLE: Abby did have half a million followers. Killing her would give him an instant high profile.
> BECKETT: Or he could just be using social media to hide his true motives for killing her. Either way, maybe these photos can help us find him.

In fact, Snappamatic is completely anonymous, aiding the killer to gain notoriety safely. This of course is a real problem with cyber bullying. He takes things to the next level by posting taunting messages and collages of clues for the police. Next, he kills one of the teens featured in "The Spoiled Brats of Snappamatic" article, about rich kids who post pictures of their extravagant lifestyles. Once more, being celebrities has led to the teens' deaths. He also posts a picture of Castle and Beckett smiling over coffee that makes them look uninvested in solving the crime.

> BECKETT: This is why I hate social media. Once something is out there you have control. People can take a private moment and create their own context. I mean, we weren't even investigating the murder yet and they made us look like we were bad cops. Or worse. Like we didn't care.
> CASTLE: Come on, Beckett, it's the internet. No one's going to take that picture seriously.
> BECKETT: 1PP did.
> CASTLE: Look. It's going to blow over, okay? With millions of items being posted every minute this is but a blip on the net continuum.
> BECKETT: You know the problem with anonymity? There's no accountability. It empowers cowards to become bullies, just like this guy.

Once they identify him, they discover the murderer was cyber-bullied himself. As the cop in charge at the time explains, "He was taking a shower when this meathead football player, Tim Witherspoon, stole his clothes. Now, this had happened to Lane his whole life, but this time he went ballistic. There he was, buck naked, screaming at Witherspoon in the locker room." Witherspoon filmed it and posted it on MySpace. After, hateful emails barraged him and cyber-bullying laws weren't prepared to prosecute the teens who'd started it.

It's later revealed that he broke into the victims' houses and cars by photographing their keys and making copies on his digital printer. "Welcome to the future," Ryan says grimly. As Lane continues killing, he gains thousands of followers. At last they find him and bring him in only to discover he's kidnapped the creators of Snappamatic. He has them wired to enough electricity to kill them and posted live video, urging his followers to vote for which one should live. In interrogation, he appears fearless, having gotten what he wanted, as he tells Beckett: "A legacy. The internet is permanent. The Netslayer will live forever. I'll be mentioned in the same breath as Mason and the Zodiac and…if I commit a murder while in police custody, while looking you in the eye, I could argue I did them one better. And there's nothing you can do to stop me." They solve the crime, not with cyber tools but by Beckett shaming the murderer into revealing too much, telling him, "And you're always going to be the victim. You think that hiding behind a user name and killing is going to change that? That won't get you respect. You're always going to be the same pathetic loser that you always were."

During the themed episode, the others get into the internet spirit. Ryan reveals that he runs a blog called The Ryan Report. "It's the musings of a homicide detective." But it's Castle's online commercial for his new book *Raging Heat* that comes out funniest. It ends up not being serious as he'd expected, but a music video of spliced outtakes, as he crashes into bookshelves and calls himself Crichard Rastle over and over in looped video. The news that it's gotten a million hits and will help sell his books only adds to his humiliation. The net has done its damage once more.

It's a Wonderful Life ("Time of our Lives," 706)

Castle and Beckett, disappointed they missed their wedding, begin considering what-ifs. She jokes that without Castle's distracting her, she would probably be captain of her own precinct.

> CASTLE: Okay. (he thinks) Had I not been bewitched by you I think by now I'd be working on my second Pulitzer.
> BECKETT: So we're bad for each other, huh?
> CASTLE: The worst.
> They kiss.
> BECKETT: (teasingly) Guess we'd both be better off if we'd never met.

Castle even nods to the film, quipping, "It's like *It's A Wonderful Life*. Every time your phone rings a victim gets their wings." On the other hand, since Castle and Beckett don't *really* believe they'd be better apart, the plot has a major hole. Likewise, after so many debunked magical scenarios, many fans were annoyed by the actual fantasy of this one.

On the case, Castle picks up a magical Incan amulet and is transported to an alternate reality where he and Beckett did not meet. He assisted another detective on their episode one case. He decides his own fantasy is responsible. "I was thinking maybe I wasn't good for her. Maybe Beckett would be happier if we had never met. That's what changed. That's where I am. In a world where we never met. It's like the last six years didn't happen."

This Beckett is captain of the precinct, but also cold and aloof. She's single and gives up easily on pursuing their case to the end. Worst of all, without Castle, she never solved her mother's murder. She's also unhappy:

> CASTLE: So, youngest woman to ever make captain. That's impressive.
> BECKETT: It's not all that it's cracked up to be.
> CASTLE: No?
> BECKETT: No, and if you really are basing a character on me then she's going to be boring.
> CASTLE: Oh, I doubt you could ever be boring.
> BECKETT: Well, my life mostly consists of paperwork and politics.
> CASTLE: Ah, you miss the streets.
> BECKETT: Um ... (she forces a smile) ... truthfully, I don't think I was meant to be a homicide detective.

Lanie and Esposito are hostile toward each other and Ryan never married Jenny. Castle is dating someone he's only known for two weeks. Alexis moved to LA. When he asks her why they fell apart, she replies, "You gave up. You read all those terrible reviews on your magnum opus and you couldn't move past it and I couldn't stick around and watch. But you know what? Now I think I understand it." She adds that her own life "seems so small and pointless," though Castle manages to convince them both that everything they do makes a difference.

As Alexis explains, Castle finally did give up mysteries and write the great American novel, but it was terrible. About the only one whose life improved is Martha, who became a more active and serious actress to bail out her son:

> MARTHA: Oh, Richard. We have talked about this. Now
> that we share the mortgage, it is our place. And since you
> have lost most of your life savings –
> CASTLE: Whoa. Wha – lost my savings? How?
> MARTHA: You invested poorly. Mostly blondes and
> racehorses. And it's not as if your great American novel
> here flying off the shelves.
> CASTLE: *Finite Laughter*? I did not write this. This ... (he
> opens the book and reads) "Babcock was a small man. A
> small man with large dreams and one of those dreams was
> Betty." (he startles) This is awful!

As happens in plots of this nature, Castle learns his lesson and says, "I'm going to take my own advice. I know why the universe sent me to this world. So the most important day of our lives got screwed up. Big deal. She's better off with me and I'm better off with her." When alt-world Beckett is shot at, he takes the bullet for her and dies, only to wake in his own reality. There, he seizes on the lesson and marries Beckett immediately. He also tells Martha she should take the latest audition, because she has the potential to excel.

Westerns ("Once Upon a Time in the West," 707)

The title is straight from a popular Western, and the episode uses every cliché. When a woman's poisoned on vacation, Castle and Beckett head to Arizona. Though Beckett seems uninterested, Gates sends them out to investigate. "Saddle up, honey, because we are honeymooning out west," Castle beams. The place, Diamondback Old West Ranch, is "a living history resort where both staff and guest dress in old west attire and engage in cowboy activities." Every western cliché follows – with Western themed credits, they arrive on a stagecoach. "It's like we rolled right into a John Ford movie," Castle smiles. There's also a *Bonanza*-style flaming map. They both quickly change into ranch clothes with cowboy hats. "Whoa. This is like, three fantasies coming true all at once," Castle says on seeing his bride. He buys six-shooters for himself and Beckett at the gift shop. Throwing himself into the fun, he learns harmonica and checks out the saloon while sending Beckett off to hogtying.

Of course, being Castle, he often fumbles the tropes. On entering the salon, Castle has the doors bounce back and hit him in the chest. He tries ordering a drink cowboy style, and finally chokes on it:

> BARTENDER: What'll it be, fella?
> CASTLE: I'll take a cough and varnish.
> BARTENDER: Some what?
> CASTLE: You know, a gut warmer. Face burner. Nose paint? Cowboy cocktail? What do you all call whiskey here?
> BARTENDER: Whiskey.

He plays poker, which is interrupted by the required gunfight at high noon. He gets thrown out of the bar, but adds that it was at his request as he covers for their investigation.

Snooping around, the pair discover the victim, Whitney, was tracing a legend of stolen gold from 1893. This is a popular legend around the ranch as the bartender tells them: "Them Peacock Boys, they outrun a whole squad of soldiers by traversing Dead Man's Gorge. Two days later they was gunned down just outside of Phoenix. But the gold was gone."

On her visit, Whitney stole dynamite and rode a horse to the Yavapai reservation, to ask about translating a map. Beckett and Castle follow her trail (complete with horses and a wagon) to ask the same question ("Seriously? You're rolling up to the reservation dressed like extras from a Gene Autry movie? That's some real cultural insensitivity" the tribal elder mock-scolds.) Then Beckett and Castle camp out under the stars. All is getting romantic until a snake winds around Castle's boot. Kate shoots at it but startles the horses. In Western tradition, they have a long, dusty walk back to the ranch.

> GRADY: Your horses came back hours ago. What happened up there?
> CASTLE: (sighs) We met a namesake of your ranch.
> GRADY: Oh… rattler. Yeah. Well, why don't you mosey on over to the cantina and strap on a feedbag and get some fresh jitter juice in you?
> BECKETT: Yeah, I think we'll do that.
> CASTLE: Yeah, just as soon as we get on some fresh union suits.

In fact, Beckett dons a black leather cowboy outfit that has Castle mesmerized. When they find the killer, the Western genre takes over and he and Castle both finger their firearms. However, before he can shoot Castle, Beckett arrives out of nowhere to win the duel. She ends the episode by lassoing Castle in a white corseted dress, telling him she's gotten a few days off so they can have a honeymoon after all. The End appears in western lettering as they share a final kiss. All in all, it remains a fun romp, even while being the obvious "western" episode for the series.

Action Stars ("Last Action Hero," 709)

The camera pans down on a theater marquee for *Last Action Hero* to the body nearby. This is Lance Delorca, star of the film. Castle describes him as "one of the biggest action heroes of the 1980s and a huge role model for my youth." As Castle adds, "He's the star of all the *Hard Kill* movies. Ex-Navy Seal Zen master Rico Cruz? With the catch phrase 'Time to hit Cruz control'?" He reveals that growing up, those films were how he got his male bonding time. Now, however, his hero has been quietly strangled.

> BECKETT: A garrote? Who would use one of those?
> ESPOSITO: Special forces will sometimes, when they want to kill quietly.
> CASTLE: The bigger question is how they got the drop on Lance Delorca.
> RYAN: Uh, Lance played an action hero, Castle. Doesn't mean he was one.
> CASTLE: Au contraire, mon frère. Lance was born in Spain

where, before he became an actor, he was a member of the
CNI, the Spanish Intelligence Agency. He was black ops.
This man was a lethal weapon.
BECKETT: Yeah, well .... Not lethal enough.

This is not the only way where the film comes to life.
Serafina, the mixed martial arts star, is actually quite gifted.
Parallels of Dolph Lundgren and Zhang Ziyi appear among
the cast. The films' villain is ruthless drug lord El Jefe, played
by Henry Booth, who later becomes a drug lord in truth.
"Apparently he spent so much time with drug dealers,
researching his roles, that he actually became one," Beckett
adds. Further, Lance married his film love interest, the
scantily dressed archeologist.

Castle is a big fan of the latter and gushes, "She's coming
here? I had her poster on my wall for like – (off Beckett's
judgmental look) – about a minute." He even asks her to
autograph it when they bring her in as a suspect. Meanwhile,
Ryan's fannishness appears as he tries catchphrases for
himself. Esposito begs him to stop.

It's finally revealed that Lance stayed in town secretly and
checked into a seedy motel with the name Rico Cruz, his
character from *Hard Kill*. Attacked by four thugs, he actually
takes them all down.

BROCK: So you .. .you're a pretty big fan, huh?
CASTLE: Of *Hard Kill*? Ah ... I was an average, ordinary
fan. Not like I had the *Hard Kill* pajamas.
CASTLE laughs. BROCK gives him a look and his smile
fades.
BROCK: Say, the gang and I are going out for drinks later
tonight. How's you like to come with us?
CASTLE freezes. He'd love to go with them.
BROCK: Castle? (CASTLE doesn't move) Hey.

The aging action heroes discover Lance successfully
planted a bug in a drug den, and they pile into a van to collect
it, bringing Castle along. They all wear their costumes, and
Brock tells him such lines as, "Son, we came straight from

hell. Let's roll" and "We're The Indestructables. Tense up, guys. It's show time." After costuming Castle in a sleeveless shirt and bandana headband, they march into combat all in a row, in darkness. Suddenly, an explosion lights them from behind. (Castle turns, startled, subverting the moment.) As Castle joins in their caper, the show uses all the movie tropes – as the characters recite their plan, it's acted out in split-screen, with action music. As always, something goes wrong and they call in with cheesy code names to abort.

As it turns out, Lance was killed trying to step up and truly be an action hero.

> TREY: I wanted to make my own way. Not have Brock Harmon come to the rescue.
> CASTLE: But Lance found out. He tried to buy out Booth. Pay your ransom, just like Rico Cruz did in *Hard Kill*.
> TREY: And I begged him not to. This wasn't some movie. I knew that Booth wasn't going to let me go and Lance couldn't just walk in there with a bag of money and fix things. But suddenly he wanted to be a hero. I told him he was going to get us both killed.

He dies saving a young man who needs him, and Castle and Beckett celebrate his life by watching his film.

The Mob ("Bad Santa," 710)

> RYAN: I wonder why the Carlucci's would kill their own doctor.
> CASTLE: Maybe he saw something he shouldn't have? Let the wrong mobster die on his table?

Castle investigates the killing of a mob doctor, explaining that his mob friend Dino is a genuinely nice guy. However, when the detectives arrest his right-hand man, Dino must tell Castle that the man is innocent, as he was pulling a mob job. He decides that as the writer is outside the law, he must be the one to solve the case. He adds: "I need you to prove Christopher's innocence and find Eric's killer. Hey, nobody connected is going to talk to the cops. But if I vouch for you it'll give you access no cop has ever gotten." Dino inducts Castle into the mob and tells him to investigate solo in "an offer you can't refuse." They take the blood oath, Omertà. Now one of them, he takes the case, investigating from within.

Castle finally catches the killer, but is ejected permanently from the police department for doing so. Gates tells him, "As he was being transferred to central booking, Detective McBride was shot and killed by unknown assailants. The DA learned that you were cooperating with members of organized crime in your investigation. People that might have wanted McBride dead. This doesn't look good. Especially for you. I am so sorry, Mr. Castle, but the DA spoke to the mayor and you are no longer permitted to work with the NYPD." Playing mobster means he's barred from playing cop.

Dino's clichéd accent from *Godfather* and his daughter's embarking on a Romeo-and-Juliet romance with a rival gang's member, all make this classic television mob. They talk like they're Fat Tony's friends on *The Simpsons:*

> DINO: Um ... I do not recognize this person.
> BECKETT: Mr. Scarpella, we've connected Dr. Mercer to a surgical suite paid for by your organization.
> CASTLE: Dino, we know Eric worked for you, but who would want to do this to him? Can you help us out?
> DINO: Sadly I have no help to offer. But please, stay. Enjoy yourselves. It's on the house.

However, some genuine feeling appears as Dino levels with Castle about his conflict in wanting his cousin's son to make a life outside "the family," and his difficulties when his daughter falls for a rival gang member. Dino ends the story owing Castle a substantial favor.

Telenovelas and Hardboiled Detectives
("Private Eye Caramba!" 712)

As a young woman races through the street to pound on

her own door and be suddenly dragged offscreen, the story is all prepped for a hardboiled tale. The victim, Anahita Menendez, plays a beautiful neurosurgeon on *Santos Desesperadas,* Desperate Saints. Thus the story delves into both genres, laying them side by side.

Esposito insists through the episode that it's his aunt that's a telenovela fan. In fact, he was happily describing Chiquitas as early as "One Life to Lose" (318) when he tells Castle, "I used to watch it growing up with my grandmother. Bro, there was this one episode where Gabriella discovered that her husband was sleeping with her evil twin sister Teresita. Only to later find out that she had multiple personality disorder."

He watches, rapt, as they film the show. Like soap operas, it's far-fetched melodrama with enormous amounts of emotion and revelation. Beckett describes it as "Sultry tempestuous men and women and over-the-top acting." The stars film their scene in the bedroom, him with his shirt open to the waist and her in gorgeous fluffy lingerie.

> SOFIA DEL CORDOVA: She's half your age! You are the mayor and my husband. This torrid affair will ruin us both. And what if she talks?
> MANUEL VILLALOBOS: It was a moment of weakness. Please forgive me, my love. Besides, that girl won't live to tell another soul. I'm making sure of it myself. Tonight ... on the yacht!

After hearing of the murder, Manuel even tries to comfort her with emotionally bland lines from an episode.

Meanwhile, Sophia Del Cordova insists the murdered woman had borrowed her diamond purse and enlists Castle to track it down. When she enters his office, another genre entirely appears, as Castle, bored, is narrating his day in a noir style:

> CASTLE: It was 11 in the morning. My phone was quieter than a dead church mouse. My head hurt after hitting the sauce like there was no tomorrow. For all I knew, there was

no tomorrow. I was about to pour a smile in my coffee, have a little hair of the dog that bit me when she walked in.
SOFIA: Señor Castle. I'm looking for a private investigator.

Castle begins doing legwork and shaking down leads – the old-fashioned way, as Beckett won't help him. She does stop by his office however and he turns on the genre charm.

BECKETT: Ready to get out of here? Call it a night?
CASTLE: Whoa, what's the rush, doll? Why don't you stick around a while, give those stems of yours a rest?
BECKETT (playing along): Could I? I'm all alone, and this is my first time in the big, scary city.
CASTLE: Spare me the tell-tale, precious. A dame like you, you got an angle.
BECKETT: You're pretty quick for a gumshoe.
CASTLE: Come on, spill the story. Time is money, and I got none of either.
BECKETT: All right, I'll give it to you straight. I'm just a girl, looking for a private dick. (grabs him)
CASTLE: Whoah! Then your search is over, sweetheart.

In noir fashion, Castle's client ends up turning on him. When he finds her purse, he discovers it's a knockoff and realizes she's actually seeking the USB drive within. She turns a tiny pistol on him and reveals she's been lying all along to use the clueless P.I. for her own aims.

The two worlds converge when Sofia reveals her real mission: to create the first Latin American, female driven television network. She adds that Anahita came to her "because she needed someone with star power who knew the business. But we had to keep everything secret. If anyone had found out we were trying to leave *Santos Desesperadas* and the very network that created us, it would endanger the deal." In fact, the head of the show bugged Anahita's trailer (in another genre mashup) and suddenly lashed out and killed her for betraying and abandoning him. He was overwhelmed by passion – fitting for the telenovelas episode. The women still get to realize their dream and another case is solved.

BECKETT: So, how does it feel to have your first satisfied customer?
CASTLE: I want to satisfy another one.
BECKETT: Oh, I think that can be arranged.
CASTLE: As the sun set on the mean streets of the naked city, I could feel my luck was about to change. The killer was caught, my case was closed, and hanging on my arm was the dame of my dreams.
BECKETT: Are you going to be doing that all night?
CASTLE: Not if it hurts my chances.

Vertigo ("I, Witness," 713)

Castle's PI client turns up dead and he's sure he witnessed her husband murdering her. However, some of the events appear staged for his viewing. He decides "This whole thing, it's a work of fiction. It's a – it's a Hitchcock movie with me cast as the witness. I'm Jimmy Stewart in *Vertigo*."

In this film, a husband pays a woman to impersonate his "possessed" wife and attempt suicide on a bell tower (which Jimmy Stewart is too paralyzed by heights to climb). He fakes the suicide by throwing the body of his wife from the bell tower, leaving Jimmy Stewart with a personally terrifying mystery to solve.

CASTLE: There's no way Eva is really dead. In a classic Hitchcock-ian twist, it won't be her body. Mark my words.
BECKETT: Then who did we pull out of the river?
CASTLE: Someone who could pass for Eva.
BECKETT: Okay, we'll run her prints. That should clear up whether it's Eva or not.
CASTLE: Except her prints will be altered. Her face, unrecognizable. All part of Eva's plan to commit the perfect crime. You'll see.
...
BECKETT: (sighs) If Eva is a part of this setup then why is she in the morgue?
CASTLE: Because, in classic Hitchcock fashion, her co-conspirator doubled crossed her.

As always, Beckett is the skeptic. She tells him, "Listen to me. Eva was your friend. She came here, to this very office,

VALERIE ESTELLE FRANKEL

and asked for your help and now she's dead and you feel responsible and that can make you see ghosts." It's revealed at last that Eva staged her own murder in front of Castle to frame her cheating husband. The husband Cole unexpectedly hangs himself. The case is closed.

Castle however insists it's far too neat, so someone else must have killed them both. Cole had high levels of sedatives in his blood. Shockingly, the real culprit is the lawyer who's been hidden in plain sight – she takes revenge for Cole murdering his first wife by framing him for murdering the second. When Eva gets cold feet, the lawyer must make both murders real. This number of twists and turns is indeed Hitchcockian, with Castle's insistence on being taken seriously for what he's witnessed nodding back to his *Rear Window* episode. Both times, a huge twist has ended the tale.

Space Program ("The Wrong Stuff," 716)

The title spoofs on the famous film about the race to the moon, *The Right Stuff*. When a murder takes place inside a Mars simulator, the detectives, especially Castle, must go where no man has gone before. "One small step for man, one giant murder for mankind," Castle insists. He thinks investigating in a space suit is the coolest thing ever, as shown by his gleeful grin. He walks slowly, as the music from *2001: A Space Odyssey* plays.

The Mars simulation is filled with astronauts who got in because they were the best of the best. They are completely driven, and they and their boss refuse to shut down the program. The millionaire in charge is a clear parallel for wealthy dreamer Elon Musk in the real world. He insists the mission to Mars is "this generation's space race" and their simulation can't be compromised, so Beckett and Castle don spacesuits to investigate from within.

The suspects are furious pros rejected from the program, all of whom contemplate sabotaging the program that doesn't want them. One performs espionage in return for a pilot's slot in the competitor's program. As soon appears, however, things within the program were less solid than they appeared as hyper-competitiveness was all. One bad seed could ruin the mission, and there was definitely one trapped in their self-contained bubble. MIRA, the project computer, is their "sixth team member." Castle calls her "a bit 2001." She appears a space-age version of Siri, clever and helpful. However, Castle and the team finally find themselves in a *2001: A Space Odyssey* death trap, when her mission parameters are threatened. Thus the evil computer and the astronauts locked together cause the murder.

Obviously, Castle loves space, and he also pulls in his science fiction expertise. He does a Kirk impression. He adds, "There goes my *Rise of the Machines* theory" and "Is it just me, or does this remind you of *Alien?*" He also worries they're being attacked by a Xenomorph who's impregnated Beckett. She decides they'll need to have a talk about biology and soon.

Personal Injury Lawyers ("Habeas Corpse," 719)

The Savannah Hammer and the Pitbull both are colorful characters from television commercials, both rather juvenile looking. The latter is murdered, beginning their case, and the team quotes his memorable commercial.

> CASTLE: Yeah. Richie "The Pitbull" Falco. Come on. You've seen the ads. A guy's head on a dog's body. (mimicking) "You in an accident? Take the law by the tail."
> LANIE: "And get a bite at the settlement you deserve."
> BECKETT: "I'll make the law – "
> LANIE, BECKETT, ESPOSITO, CASTLE (together): "- your bitch."
> RYAN looks lost.
> ESPOSITO: "El tipo tambièn habla español."

His ex-wife reveals that he was corporate law and *Harvard Law Review*, until he self-destructed. Now he's a personal injury lawyer trying to help the little guy.

> BECKETT: Yeah, well, there's always going to be people looking for a quick settlement and plenty of opportunistic bottom feeders like Richie ready to help them cash in.
> ANNIE: He didn't have a girlfriend. I kept hoping. Look, I – I know what you guys are thinking. Personal injury lawyers are gutter rats, right? But Richie was different. He really cared. He thought the law was there to protect everyone and not just corporations who could afford it. And his clients, they loved him for it.

It's slowly revealed that his big law firm once represented Modesto Car Company, who had been negligent. As the little guy, he was determined to make things right karmically and sue them on behalf of his dead and injured clients.

However, his competitor The Savannah Hammer was far less scrupulous. He tells the police, "Why? Because he couldn't see that that dummy was a gold mine. And all he wanted was justice? You're as naïve as he was." Thus one man can try to make a difference, but the job itself can be a corrupting influence. Especially personal injury law.

Saturday Night Live ("Dead from New York," 722)

Sid Ross, the creator of *Saturday Night Tonight* and many films, is suddenly killed, thrown down the elevator shaft at the SNT studios with his body left there. *Saturday Night Tonight* is obviously *Saturday Night Live*, with its title is a pun on its catchphrase, "Live from New York."

Inside their world is one of egos and a tyrannical dictator, while all the writers and actors would stay literally until sunup polishing the sketches. Beckett and Castle discover that a drug kingpin originally bankrolled the show. "So a show that brought joy, laughter, and Judge Booty to people everywhere may have been built on drug money."

"Yeah, I know. It sounds like one of their comedy sketches, right?" Ryan says.

Urkel arrives to play the brilliant but goofy cast member Mickey Franks, an Eddie Murphy type whom Castle loves.

Franks loses it and has psychotic outbursts in which he threatens to kill Sid. When they haul him in for questioning, he insists on involving his lawyer, a puppet he's manipulating. However, when pushed, he admits he's not mad, just trying to be let out of his oppressive contract.

> MICKEY: I'm an actor, okay. I am an actor that's tied to a long term contract that's uh ... not exactly covering his expenses.
> CASTLE: Are you saying you were trying to get fired?
> MICKEY: I'm saying, Sid controlled my career. Because of him I'm missing out on major movie roles. That's why I attacked you guys. I figured if you 51-50'ed me on a Bellevue psych hold he'd finally cut me loose.

Ryan throws himself into the world, mentioning he's a big fan and trying to treat his partnership with Esposito like the SNT sponsored improvisation class he took in college. Esposito is annoyed. Meanwhile, Castle and Beckett are both big fans:

> CASTLE: Are these cast photos from all thirty five seasons of the show?
> CHAD: Yep. Every performer who has ever been on SNT.
> BECKETT: Oh, I love him. He played Fluffy the Space Puppy. That was my favorite.
> CASTLE: You know, the majority of this nation's comedy was born in the mind of these geniuses. (he spots a poster of the current writers) Except for this season. Those guys suck.
> BECKETT: Yeah, they were terrible.
> CASTLE: Oh, this guy! Ned what's-his-name. Played uh, Doctor Finger. (he waves a finger in the air and then, in a German accent) "I'm sorry, sir. It's necessary I probe you." (off her unamused look) How can you not like Doctor Finger?

Also, Carly Rae Jepsen guest-stars, and Castle turns crazily fannish, telling her "I'm Rick – I'm Rick. This is Kate. We're huge fans" and "Um, Carly, quick question. That one song, um, 'Call Me Maybe,' what did you mean by the lyric 'it's —'" While she sings, he swing dances with Beckett, enjoying the song.

Of course, their fannishness grows even more self-referential when they stumble on a sketch of themselves as model/policewoman and writer, both rather incompetent.

> VALENTINE: Detective, I have no idea what you're talking about.
> TINA: Look, buddy. I'm a cop and a model so I know when someone's lying to me. And when their outfit is clashing. Now stand back! This could be dangerous.
> VALENTINE: Don't worry, my experience writing crime novels has prepared me for danger. Plus, I have my vest.
> He grabs a Kevlar vest that has "RIGHTER" written on it. CASTLE laughs.
> TINA: Look out, bad guys! Here we come!
> TINA tries to kick in the door but her high heel gets stuck in the door.
> TINA: Oh. Oh, model cop down. I broke a heel.
> LIZ: And scene! Great job, guys.
> BECKETT: Okay, well, I don't know whether we should be flattered or offended.
> CASTLE: Who cares? Danny Valentine's playing me!

Valentine flirts with Beckett, and she's rather star-struck. As he's the one playing Castle, there's a circle of self-reference here. Similarly, Tina begins following Beckett around and copying her mannerisms, leaving Castle to stare.

At episode end, the pair burst into the sketch of themselves on live TV to arrest the criminal as the audience applauds. To cap it off, their friends critique their performance:

> ESPOSITO: Beckett, that was a badass takedown tonight on that show. It was strong yet ... sexy.
> RYAN: Yeah, Beckett. The camera really loves you.
> BECKETT (laughing): You guys, shut up, both of you.
> CASTLE: What about me, guys? How did I look?
> ESPOSITO: Like you should stick to writing.

CASTLE ♥ FANDOM

Just for the Fans: Easter Eggs

The Show Waves to being Fictional

> Real-life writers Stephen J. Cannell, James Patterson, Dennis Lehane, and Michael Connelly treat Castle as one of them, emphasizing that he's a "real" mystery writer. The creator decided to create the circle of mystery writers around the poker table so "That it would help legitimize him and make him seem more real to the audience." From there he decided to have the writers help him and say "if I were writing the story..." and solve it a far different way than the cops' strategies ("Murder They Wrote").

> Often, Detective Beckett can be seen drinking from a coffee mug that reads "Innocent Bystander."

> Castle's mother, an actress, has much to offer on acting, parts, and throwing oneself into roles, an ironic discussion for all the actors onscreen to have.

ALEXIS: I couldn't sleep. I thought the case was over.
CASTLE: Oh, it is. Wrapped up all nice and neat.
ALEXIS: That's a good thing, right?
CASTLE: In a book, that's a good thing. In real life, nothing is that neat. What's got you still up? ("Tick Tick Tick," 217)

SHAW: His manifesto?
CASTLE: His manuscript.
BECKETT: "Dead Heat"?
CASTLE: "Heat examined the bullets, each of them perfectly engraved with a letter. She rearranged them like a scrabble tiles until they spelled her name."
BECKETT: A book? All of this over a damn book.
SHAW: (Holds another manuscript) He was writing about his murders long before Nikki Heat. "Night Terrors." Looks it's about killing prostitutes in Seattle.

...

> SHAW: Writing is probably a symptom of his psychosis, like taking a trophy. He both memorializes the deed and distances himself from it by turning fact into fiction. And then along comes Nikki Heat... Tailor-made for his psychosis – one part fact, one part fiction, just like him. Who better for him to challenge? ("Boom," 218)

➘ They discover the killer doesn't just imitate Castle's books – he writes his own then makes them come alive. The killer tells Beckett, "This is your story, Nikki, not hers. She's just an extra. The showdown only works if it's between you and me. Come to the Battery Park Ferry Terminal at midnight tonight, Nikki" ("Boom," 218).

➘ The soap opera episode ("One Life to Lose," 318) has several fakeouts as something appears real but is actually actors performing a scene. Castle writes a script and uses it to catch the killer, in the *Hamlet*, play within a play, style.

➘ When Castle and Beckett visit the Nikki Heat set, they interrogate their suspect on the set. The extras and camera staff there are the real ones from the show ("To Love and Die in L.A," 322). They also meet the actors playing their cop friends.

> BECKETT: Aren't you Lone Vengeance?
> CHAD: Not the real one.
> CASTLE: The real one being the comic book character?
> CHAD: Comic book characters aren't real, okay?
> CASTLE looks to BECKETT. She gives him a smirk.
> ("Heroes and Villains," 402)

> BECKETT: And what could explain the picture suddenly going out like that?
> LULU: I don't know. It's never happened before.
> CASTLE: Well, there was that last episode of *The Sopranos*. ("Demons," 406)

By comparing "real life" to television, Castle emphasizes his own show is made up.

↘ Beckett says, "I don't really watch reality television, Ms. Cappuccio. Would you like to know why? ...Because I usually find that it's not all that real. And I don't like things or people who present fiction as truth. In fact, I find it to be a waste of time" ("An Embarrassment of Bitches," 413).

↘ Castle notes after he reads about Joe and Vera's first meeting, "The Blue Butterfly! It's a necklace! That's why Stan was killed? Why am I narrating?" ("The Blue Butterfly," 414).

> CASTLE: And it happened backstage, right upstairs. They were stealing a moment together, which was dangerous, because she was Dempsey's girl. As they stared into each other's eyes, Kate's heart quickened...
> BECKETT: Did you just say Kate? Are you picturing the PI as you and me as the gangster's moll?
> CASTLE: What? No. and I didn't say Kate, I said fate. Fate's heart quickened. I was being poetic. ("The Blue Butterfly," 414)

> CASTLE: That whole, uh, sinking car thing? Much cooler in movies than in real life.
> BECKETT: And for the record, I prefer watching spy thrillers to being in them.
> ("Linchpin," 416)

↘ Sophia, Clara Strike's inspiration, tells Castle, "You're sorry? We are on the next 9/11 or worse. This isn't one of your damn books, Rick. This is real life and when things go bad you just can't rewrite the ending like you did with us" ("Linchpin," 416).

> CASTLE: No. (shakes his head) This is not the perfect murder. Can't be.
> BECKETT: It happens.
> CASTLE: Not to me. Not unless I've written it. No, we're just missing something. ("Undead Again," 422)

> CASTLE: This whole thing. The fake IDs, the dossiers, Luvania, the banking minister. It's all part of a game.

HANS: Come on. You're breaking the fourth wall here. ("A Deadly Game," 224)

➤ Martha says, "Oh, Richard, Richard. For a man who makes his living with words you sure have a hell of a time finding them when it counts. Darling, let me give you word of advice, alright? From someone who's better than halfway through the movie, don't waste another minute of it" ("Rise," 401).

➤ "This doesn't even seem real. Like some kind of show," Castle says, watching the exchange for Alexis on a screen ("Hunt," 516).

➤ Castle enjoys the documentary being made of their investigation and even directs the action: "Don't you see? Everything we need to solve this murder is right there in that clip. (he snaps his fingers) Do a hard fade to black, musical sting" ("Swan Song," 504)

➤ While most episodes nod to the fans, "The Final Frontier," (507) visits an actual convention.

➤ An actress puts on a terribly bad acting job on "The Final Frontier" (507). Castle participates with her but also makes observations on his own less-than-realistic life:

> CASTLE: Hmm. I'll tell you what. I'll forgive you your terrible taste if you … (he checks her out) … try on that Nebula-9 costume for me.
> BECKETT: In your dreams.
> CASTLE: Look at my life. My dreams come true. ("The Final Frontier," 507)

> CASTLE: How many murders do you think we've solved since we met?
> BECKETT: I don't know, uh, maybe a hundred or so?
> CASTLE: A hundred?
> BECKETT: Mm-hmm.
> CASTLE: Here's to a hundred more.

➤ This was said during the 100th episode of *Castle*. It aired on April 1, Richard Castle's birthdate. It even features an April Fool's Day joke on Castle and on the audience.

❧ The featurette "Martha's Master Class" on the DVD has Martha explaining how she directed all the scenes for Richard's birthday surprise.

❧ They indulge in bad acting in "That '70s Show," (620)

> RENO: I don't talk to no fuzz, pig.
> CASTLE: Well, you're going to talk to this pig – (he checks his script) – this fuzz.
> RENO: Yeah? Why's that, jive turkey?
> CASTLE: Because I'm about to make you one sweetass deal. (he drops character) My god, who wrote this.
> RENO: I did.
> CASTLE looks at him sheepishly.

❧ The mug shot of Louie "The Lip" Maneri is a picture of Nathan Fillion in disguise ("That '70s Show," 620).

> ESPOSITO: Oh, according to our witness, one Logan Moore, was hauling ass on a skateboard with a guy on a motorcycle chasing him.
> CASTLE: Sounds like a scene from an action movie.
> ESPOSITO: Yeah. I know. Especially when the biker started shooting and Logan crashed through that window right there. ("Law & Boarder," 621)

> CASTLE: It was a minor blow to my ego. After that I had to channel my inner Castle, but once I did ... nailed it.
> BECKETT: (dryly) Wow. You nailed playing yourself. That's impressive. ("Meme is Murder," 705)

❧ The team watch the action movies in the precinct and watch the filming as Beckett calls it "cheesy" and Castle "amazing" in "Last Action Hero" (709). The actors finally decide to be real action heroes and recruit Castle, their biggest fan.

❧ Alt-World episodes "The Blue Butterfly" (414), "That '70s Show" (620), "The Time of our Lives" (706), "Once Upon a Time in the West" (707), and a clip show "Still," (524) mix things up.

133

❯ Gushing over *Saturday Night Tonight*, Castle smiles, "You know, the majority of this nation's comedy was born in the mind of these geniuses. (he spots a poster of the current writers) Except for this season. Those guys suck." Beckett agrees ("Dead from New York," 722). There's a line about the terrible things actors get up to at the private entrance. More delightfully, Castle and Beckett stumble across a skit of themselves.

> VALENTINE: Detective, I have no idea what you're talking about.
> TINA: Look, buddy. I'm a cop and a model so I know when someone's lying to me. And when their outfit is clashing. Now stand back! This could be dangerous.
> VALENTINE: Don't worry, my experience writing crime novels has prepared me for danger. Plus, I have my vest. He grabs a Kevlar vest that has "RIGHTER" written on it.
> CASTLE laughs.
> TINA: Look out, bad guys! Here we come!
> TINA tries to kick in the door but her high heel gets stuck in the door.
> TINA: Oh. Oh, model cop down. I broke a heel.
> LIZ: And scene! Great job, guys.
> BECKETT: Okay, well, I don't know whether we should be flattered or offended.
> CASTLE: Who cares? Danny Valentine's playing me!

❯ Describing their case, Castle says, "This is not how the story was supposed to end" ("Hollander's Woods," 723).

❯ *Raging Heat* ends with the Afterword saying "First off, I am not Richard Castle," then adding that he's an editor standing in for the real Castle long enough to write the Afterword.

❯ Storm says, "There's no shame in having a ghostwriter" as "Some of the best books published every year are penned by talented writers whose identity the public will never know" (*Wild Storm* 76).

The Show Imitates the Books:

❭ Episode one has a copycat killer imitating several of Castle's early and obscure novels.

> CASTLE: The, uh, blood in the bowl? Most likely animal. Part of the ceremony. The pouch is an offering to the spirits, but I don't recognize the symbol.
> ESPOSITO: If you did, you'd be a suspect. So, how do you know about all this?
> CASTLE: Research for my sixth Derrick Storm novel.
> RYAN: *Unholy Storm*. ("Always Buy Retail," 106)

❭ *Unholy Storm* exists in comic book form, blending a short respectful look at voodoo (including the sacrifice ritual) with zombies, voodoo dolls, and violent revenge in New Orleans.

❭ Detective Ryan can often be seen carrying a copy of one of Castle's books.

❭ On hearing *Heat Wave*'s been optioned for film, the gang cast themselves ("Tick, Tick, Tick..." 217). Ryan wants James McAvoy, Espo wants Javier Bardem, Lanie wants Halle Berry and Castle wants Kate Beckinsale to play Nikki Heat.

❭ Calling Beckett to report a murder a man calls himself "a fan" and leaves her sneaky clues. "Does he realize she's a fictional character, not a real person?" Montgomery asks. This is ironic, as Beckett is in fact also fictional. The FBI summarize and read *Heat Wave* while Castle begs them to avoid spoilers. The killer than uses the text to send a message. "Severed digits, a secret code – This is like one of my books" ("Tick Tick Tick," 217).

❭ Shaw, the agent in charge when a serial killer obsesses over Nikki Heat, observes, "In the end, Dunn did actually face Nikki Heat. She is, after all, part you, part Castle" ("Boom," 218).

❭ During Castle's interview, Bobby Mann promoted the fact that *Heat Wave* would be coming out in paperback on

July 27, 2010. This was its actual release date ("The Late Shaft," 220).

❯ At one point in the episode, Castle suggests to Beckett that the two of them should have a signature line. He then pitches two: "She's armed, he's dangerous." and "A new chapter in crime solving." Both are promotional tag lines used for the show ("The Late Shaft," 220).

❯ Castle studied the Triple Killer for his novel *When It Comes to Slaughter* ("3XK," 306).

❯ A bouquet of red roses falls to the floor. A blonde aims her gun at a man with a hostage. The scene feels right for the one in which Castle was held hostage by the murderer of Beckett's mother, but the acting feels off.

> NATALIE RHODES: Game over and you lose, Tom! Drop it!
> "TOM": Put down the gun or I swear I'll blow his head off!
> NATALIE: You know I can't do that, Tom.
> "TOM": You think I'm kidding around here, Detective Heat?!
> NATALIE: No, I don't! I think you feel trapped and you're serious as hell, but right now I need you to think about the people who love you, and they need you to put down that gun—" ("Nikki Heat," 311)

❯ Castle freezes this scene on his television and complains, "I can't take it anymore. The character of Nikki Heat is a smart, complicated detective with, with enormous...depth, and then the studio goes and casts the bra-less co-ed and blood soaked t-shirt from Knife 2?" Natalie Rhodes, the actress, arrives at the precinct to shadow Beckett. As the episode continues, she steals more and more of Beckett's mannerisms, and finally wears a copy of her outfit. While Castle remarks he once had a fantasy like this, Beckett is horrified. Rhodes finally begins beating Beckett at effective investigation, at last talking the murderer down with her cheesy dialogue from the beginning. Meanwhile, as Rhodes ignores Castle, he at first struggles to come up with more interesting detective dialogue than Beckett has, then discovers to his surprise that Rhodes wants to sleep with him. She shoves him against the elevator wall and tells him, "You know the script is so much about the passion between Nikki and Rook. If I'm gonna play Nikki right, I gotta feel that heat."

- However, Castle refuses. He tells Beckett afterwards, "Oh. Well, a fictional character that I wrote, based on you, played by Natalie Rhodes? That's just...way too meta." Meanwhile, their many discussions of how actors throw themselves into roles and how to write dialogue emphasizes all of their roles as fictional characters.

- "So, we were just talking about our books becoming movies. Michael had *Lincoln Lawyer*, I had *Shutter Island*, Ricky has *Heat Wave*," Dennis Lehane says. At the poker game, they all heckle the new writer ("The Dead Pool," 321).

- The season three finale mentions the Derrick Storm graphic novels were coming. *Castle: Richard Castle's Deadly Storm* was published by Marvel Comics on September 28, 2011.

- Castle says, "It's easier in my books. The just are rewarded, the wicked are punished. Unfortunately real life isn't that easy" ("Knockout," 324).

- *Heat Rises* comes out onscreen in the episode after Montgomery's shooting. It is in fact the book about Montgomery's death, thinly adapted.

> BECKETT: I like the dedication.
> CASTLE: It seemed right.
> BECKETT: It must have been hard, writing that ending.
> CASTLE: Yeah. Yeah. Given the circumstances, yeah.
> ("Rise," 401)

- The Derrick Storm graphic novel comes out in real life and in the comic book episode "Heroes and Villains" (402). Beckett preorders a copy and discusses it with the owner. Bendis gleefully describes being asked to create "A Marvel Comics adaptation of Richard Castle the writer who doesn't exist novel of his character that doesn't exist," adding that such a thing has almost never been done ("Murder They Wrote").

> BECKETT: Well why would you tell a story when you don't know the ending?
> CASTLE: If you wanted a beginning, a middle, and an end I have 27 novels you can choose from. ("The Blue Butterfly," 414)

On the CIA mission of "Pandora" (415), they're locked in the trunk (imitating *Frozen Heat*) and Castle presses his CIA handler's panic button (from *A Bloody Storm*), nodding to moments in the thrillers. "Pandora" also introduces Sophia Turner.

> SOPHIA: Rick and I met when he was just beginning to do research on his first Derrick Storm novel. He wanted an up close and personal look at the life of a female CIA agent. (she looks at CASTLE) So I gave him one.
> BECKETT: You're Clara Strike? The Clara Strike from the Derrick Storm books?
> SOPHIA: I wouldn't say that I am Clara Strike, but I like to think that I inspired Rick in some small way.

Sophia tells Beckett and Castle that the CIA is forbidden to operate on US soil and they're already doing well with the case, so she needs them to work for her – precisely what Clara Strike says to Storm on their first meeting in an example of life imitating art (or rather fictional life imitating art). However, at the end, she's revealed as the traitor:

> BECKETT: Must be tough. Finding out that she's a traitor, especially after you based Clara Strike on her and all.
> CASTLE: Hmm… well, Clara started off as Sophia, but she ended up being more like you. You know, smart, fierce, kind. I think that was one of the reasons I was drawn to you. As a muse. ("Linchpin," 416)

Sophia, the inspiration for Clara Strike leafs through the Derrick Storm graphic novel in Castle's apartment.

> CASTLE: How – what're you – how did – how did you get in here?
> SOPHIA: I'm CIA. So they're turning them into graphic novels now?
> CASTLE: Yeah, um… first one did well so they're gonna do another. ("Linchpin," 416)

He's writing *Frozen Heat* and stuck on it in "Headhunters" (421). This is the book about Heat's mother's murder, and Beckett too is stuck in a holding pattern on her own mother's murder.

Castle is signing copies of his new graphic novel *Storm Season* at the convention on "The Final Frontier" (507).

Castle decides, "Maybe I'm not speaking the right language. (he tries again, this time with a trucker accent) Breaker, breaker. I got a mama bear and two joes who need a ride back to the bear cave." After, he adds, "I once had Derrick Storm beat up a trucker" ("After Hours," 508).

> CASTLE: When you were advising me on those last few Derrick Storm novels you mentioned a man that the French government would sometimes hire when they couldn't afford to take official action.
> GASTON: Ricky, I told you that in confidence.
> CASTLE: But he exists.
> GASTON: (pauses) It is one thing to write about these characters from the safety of your own desk. But men like this? They are not the kind of people you ever want to know. ("Hunt," 516).

Seeking Alexis, Castle meets the man in a church where they exchange cryptic countersigns, then the man takes Castle to his friend la taupe – the mole. He's blind but has prenatural senses for tracking through sound. All this including the codename of "mole" is full of spy clichés.

Jackson Hunt tells the story of giving Castle a copy of *Casino Royale* that made him want to be a writer. He adds that he's read Castle's novels and helped him with research ("Hunt," 516).

➤ Castle says of Alexis, "She left me alone for a couple of days so I could finish *Deadly Heat,* which, by the way, is both deadly and hot, thank you very much for asking" ("Watershed," 524).

➤ Castle is on a book tour for *Wild Storm* ("Veritas," 622)

➤ Castle is doing a commercial for his new book *Raging Heat* in "Meme is Murder" (705). Though it's turned into a silly music video, it is in fact a real commercial for a real product. Martha adds acting tips to complete the job.

➤ Returning from his disappearance at the start of season seven, Castle does a guest spot advertising his books but finds himself interrogated about where he's been.

➤ Castle comments, "I used a clue like this in one of my early Derrick Storm books. It's very unusual to find unrefined coal outside a coal-fired power plant" ("Time of our Lives," 705).

➤ In the alternate reality, Castle manages to take Beckett out by offering to tell her why he killed off Derrick Storm ("Time of our Lives," 705). She tells him she went to one of his book signings.

➤ Dino the mobster tells Castle, "Oh, man. You know I just finished you book, *Raging Heat*" ("Bad Santa," 710).

➤ Castle starts a PI business and tells Beckett, "And once I do become established, much like my Nikki Heat novels were inspired by you, my new series of PI novels will be inspired by me. I'll be my own muse" ("Private Eye Caramba!" 712).

➤ Castle becomes a PI in season seven just like Derrick Storm. He even finds himself investigating a cheating husband in "I, Witness" (713). In this episode like in *Deadly Storm,* his client is attacked while Castle/Storm trails the husband.

> CASTLE: Eva got cold feet. She wanted to come forward but you couldn't have that, not after all those years, after all that planning. So you decided that Eva's fake murder would have to become a real one. And killing Cole was just a way of tying up loose ends.

AUBREY: Wow. That's an exciting story, Mr. Castle. Maybe it will make a great book. But it doesn't make for much of a case. ("I, Witness," 713)

BECKETT: Patterson Syndrome?
CASTLE: Yeah. Every time I write a bestseller, Patterson writes, like, six. It's maddening, but comparing myself to him does not make me write any faster. ("Hong Kong Hustle," 717)

Castle compares two author photos of himself and considers why he became a writer during the course of "Hollander's Woods" (723). He ends the episode accepting the Poe's Pen Career Achievement Award, the biggest honor a mystery writer can get.

ESPOSITO: Castle, who's going to be your inspiration if Beckett becomes state senator?
LANIE: Yeah, you won't be able to follow her around anymore.
CASTLE: Oh, I don't know. Maybe I'll write a political thriller next. ("Hollander's Woods," 723)

The Books Imitate the Show

In another nod to the name's origin, Castle reveals he was born during "a howling thunderstorm on the first of April, shortly before midnight" (About the Author, *Deadly Storm*).

Characters in the Nikki Heat books include detectives Sean Raley and Miguel Ochoa, and gal-pal Lauren Parry the mortician. Margaret Rook is Jameson Rook's mother. Captain Montrose is killed in book three while fighting corruption, and the pencil-pusher Captain Irons takes over (in a nod to at least the name of Captain "Iron" Gates). All these except Irons parallel the personalities of Castle's friends.

Raley's nickname around the department is Sweet Tea – on the show, Ryan's nickname is actually Honey Milk, a drink he makes Jenny that the others heard about.

◥ In the series, Castle's judge friend is played by Dan Castellaneta, the voice of Homer Simpson. In the book, Jameson Rook's judge friend is named Horace Simpson. Nikki even expects him to say "D'oh!" when she beats him at a poker game.

◥ In the book he copies a show conversation:

> "But I hadn't seen this guy before. Or maybe it's his muscle. That is what you guys call them, muscle?
> "Sometimes," said Raley. "There's also goon."
> "Or thug," said Ochoa.
> "Thug's good," continued Raley. "So's badass."
> "Meat," from Ochoa, and the two detectives alternated euphemisms in rapid-fire succession.
> "Gangsta."
> "G."
> "Punk."
> "Bitch."
> "Gristle."
> "Knucks."
> "Ballbuster."
> "Bang-ah."
> "But muscle works," said Ochoa.
> "Gets it said," agreed Raley.
> Rook had out his Moleskine notebook and a pen. "I gotta get some of these down before I forget."
> "You do that," said Heat. "I'll be in with the ... miscreant."
> (*Heat Wave*, 57-58)

◥ Likewise, Rook's consultation with Casper the thief parallels the ex-thief he consults in "Home is Where the Heart Stops" (107).

◥ Beckett says that she sent her security detail home, nicely parallel to a similar scene in *Heat Wave* ("Tick Tick Tick," 217). In both, Castle goes to Beckett's house to protect her and she points a gun at him.

> CASTLE: Oh, no. I'm not leaving. I'm here to protect you.
> BECKETT: What, with your vast arsenal of rapier wit?
> CASTLE: There is a madman gunning for you because of me. I am not going to leave you alone. ("Tick Tick Tick," 217)

\ *Heat Wave* begins their romance. Nikki Heat uses the line "you have no idea," said between them at the beginning of the show and in their wedding vows (100).

\ *Naked Heat* has the team visit witnesses such as a pop star, celebrity chef, pro baseball player, talk show host, politician into S and M, Fat Tommy the Mobster, and a hotel concierge.

\ Rook tells Heat he loves her cast iron bathtub. "If the asteroid ever hits, this is where you should duck and cover" (*Naked Heat* 117). This nods to Beckett hiding there during the fire.

\ Rook has the snarky line after a big revelation, "If this were a TV show, this is where they'd go to a commercial" (*Naked Heat* 148).

\ *Naked Heat* is dedicated "To the real Nikki Heat, with gratitude."

\ Book three, *Heat Rises*, is Castle's adaptation of Montgomery's death. Beckett's mother is gone from the story, though it still features a police conspiracy and thugs who will murder anyone to get their hands on a tape that incriminates the top of the conspiracy, who's risen to wealth and power. The third book ends like the third season – only this time Rook is the one shot while Heat pleads with him to live.

\ *Heat Rises* opens with Rook returning to New York after a dangerous assignment across the world from Africa to Mexico. Heat's jealousy at seeing him hobnobbing with his agent at Le Cirque parallels Beckett's jealousy as Castle is featured dating in celebrity magazines early in season four. Meanwhile his excuse for not calling her is presumably something Castle wishes he could say about himself at the start of season three – he tells her that he never speaks to anyone when he returns from a trip:

> "The only explanation I can give may sound flimsy, but it's the truth. When I come off assignment, I have a routine. I

sleep like the dead and write like the devil, in seclusion. It's the way I've always done it. For years. But now—I realize something is different now. I'm not the only one involved."

✎ However, he realizes his inattention has hurt her. He tells her:

"Now, if I could take back the past twenty-four hours, I would, but I can't. What I can do, though, is say when I look at you now and see the hurt in you—the hurt I caused by being insensitive I see pain I never want to bring to you again." He let that sit there, then said, "Nikki, I apologize. I was wrong. And I am sorry." (*Heat Rises* 63)

✎ In book three, a short sequence as the officers debate Luigi's Original verses Legendary Luigi's Pizza (actually the original) nods back to the competing pizza places of the show (*Heat Rises* 168). Rook suggests a man in the hospital could die easily, adding, "I've heard of contract killers who dress like nurses and inject poison into the IV drip of their victims" (*Heat Rises* 251) the plot of "A Death in the Family" (110). Also, Rook's piece on Chechnya is optioned for film. Just before the climax, he infiltrates the old writers' pub called The Brass Harpoon and discovers the secret rooms under the floor, an obvious parallel for The Old Haunt.

✎ "Victoria St. Clair" (actually Rook) has written the romance novel *Castle of her Endless Longing*. Here seems to be a particular shout out, in more than the title, as a man, "handsome in a roguish way" offers "Lady Kate Sackett" a "ride along" (*Heat Rises* 301).

✎ The murdered priest of *Heat Rises* enjoyed mysteries, particularly "Cannell, Connelly, Lehane, Patterson" in something of an Easter egg. Nikki asks Rook at one point "Have you ever thought of writing crime fiction instead?" (202). He tells her he's "all about keeping it real."

BECKETT: Are you really asking for my number?
CASTLE: You show me yours, I'll show you mine.

> BECKETT: *(amused)* Men. You all wanna know, but you don't wanna know. Listen, every woman has her secrets, including Jenny. And sometimes, for the sake of a relationship, it is better *not* to share. ("Till Death Do Us Part," 411)

- This parallels a scene in *Frozen Heat* where Rook hint at wanting to know Heat's number of men she's slept with and she refuses to tell. She says, "Rook, are you seriously asking me my number? Because if you are, that's going to open a ginormous subject" (*Frozen Heat* 133).

- The body in a wheeled suitcase in *Frozen Heat* is from "The Mistress Always Spanks Twice." There's also a treasure hunter, a young biochemist who now competes in dog shows, an insurance investigator, and the sex goddesses phone line, all paralleling *Castle* episodes.

- Salena Kaye is a villain in *Frozen Heat* and *Deadly Heat*. Her name is similar to Catwoman's and to the ex-art thief on the show.

- Rook is famous for his pasta carbonara (*Frozen Heat* 184) like Castle is ("Pandora," 415).

- Rook can't decide which pizza he likes best: "Original Ray's, Famous Original Ray's, or Swear to God Folks, This Really, Really, Is Ray's" (*Frozen Heat* 42), referencing the many Rays of the show.

- Nikki forces Rook to wait in the car, as with early *Castle* episodes. He actually requests a bulletproof vest that says "WRITER" (*Frozen Heat* 45)

- Book four covers the murder of Heat's mother, as a second murder provides a break in the case. As with the show, there's a police cover up and information her mother had that everyone's struggling to find. Nikki finally discovers a code her mother left her (much like the final resolution of the television case) but as with the television case, she ends the book with her witnesses suddenly dead and her investigation stalled, even as it's blocked from above.

➘ The statue The Fist of Capitalism is on display (*Frozen Heat* 55).

➘ Rook insists he and Heat need a portmanteau name like Rooki or Nooki (*Frozen Heat* 54). This is definitely a nod to the "Caskett" fans.

➘ Nikki Heat sees a counselor in book four.

➘ They have dinner at Le Papillon Bleu (The Blue Butterfly) in Paris. Rook's spy contact in Paris handcuffs them together and stuffs them in a trunk before driving them out to the forest (*Frozen Heat* 172). Castle has a similar visit to Paris on the show, and gets stuffed in a trunk with Beckett. This echoes the episode "Boom" (218).

➘ Book five, *Deadly Heat*, begins with health inspector Roy Conklin's body in a pizza oven, certainly a show homage. An anchor from WHNY (From "Cloudy with a Chance of Murder," 502) is the second victim.

➘ Rook's big article on Nikki is called "Bringing Heat" (13), a parallel to the book titles. Nikki hates how much of her thought process he's shared with the public.

➘ There's talk of making a Nikki Heat movie. The comment even comes up that "Nathan [Fillion] would be perfect for casting, if he's available" (*Deadly Heat* 156)

➘ At the start of "Pandora" (415), Beckett and Castle identify a man who doesn't exist, who soon vanishes from lockup along with their evidence. They suddenly get bags thrust over their heads and emerge in a in an elevator that carries them deep underground.

> BECKETT: What is this place?
> CASTLE: Uh ... uh ... I don't know. I have no idea.
> SOPHIA TURNER: Rick Castle as a loss for words? That must be a first for you.
> CASTLE: Sophia Turner.
> SOPHIA: Hello, Rick. Welcome to the CIA.

➘ In *Deadly Heat*, Homeland Security pulls a similar kidnapping into their underground offices. There, to Rook's surprise, he meets an old girlfriend and current spy just as Castle does. Yardley Bell seduced him to go through his notes but also rescued him when he got captured. Most intriguingly, Rook's reason for dumping her was meeting Nikki (35-36).

➤ Rook snarks that Lauren might need to use a wooden stake on the operative always faking his death, nodding to "Vampire Weekend" (206) (*Deadly Heat* 142).

➤ Rook gets a WRITER vest.

➤ An act of terror bigger than 9/11 is planned and the culprit shops around for a Muslim extremist to deliver it (*Deadly Heat* 211). This echoes the episode "Countdown," (317). With the terror threat, Rook decoys his mother out of the city without telling her why (*Deadly Heat* 191).

➤ There's a plot to create a smallpox epidemic just to cure it and make millions. Rook rides up on a horse to save the day (a possible reference to his police horse stealing). When he boasts of saving the world unnoticed, Heat adds, "Maybe you, Batman, and Lone Vengeance should form a support group" (*Deadly Heat* 278). Lone Vengeance of course is an independent comic on the show.

➤ The serial killer of *Deadly Heat* targets Nikki Heat, providing an interesting parallel to "Tick Tick Tick" (217) in which the serial killer fixates on Beckett *as* Nikki Heat (202).

➤ "It's like a ghost came to visit you," one detective says (*Deadly Heat* 176). Another, Raley, calls himself clairvoyant and she offers to call him "the Great Ralini" (*Deadly Heat* 179). With a ghost episode, a magician episode, and a clairvoyant episode, the book seems to be providing easter eggs.

➤ Similarly, Rook quips that if they're partially brain dead they're zombies and proposes a toast to this (*Deadly Heat* 111).

➤ In *Deadly Heat,* the writer thanks Terri Edda Miller for being his heart – this is Marlowe's real life wife.

➘ In *Raging Heat*, Beckett is offered a promotion but realizes the travel will take her away from Rook. She thus keeps it a secret. She also finds an engagement ring receipt and worries about Rook's intentions through the book. After they fight about her job offer, he asks her to meet him at Tecumseh Playground where she finds him sitting on a swing. There he tells her, "I wanted to give you something that would symbolize our trust and cement it for the future" (186). However, he doesn't give her the ring but a bullet, showing the legwork he did after hours to prove himself to her. At book's end he insists on really proposing before he hears whether she accepted the job, and the book ends on the proposal. All this of course parallels the end of season five.

➘ The investigation takes them to the Hamptons, as in "Murder, He Wrote" (504). Detective Sergeant Inez Aguinaldo of Southhampton Village is happy to have Nikki's aid on the case, but she's strong and competent, unlike the Hampton's detective on the show. Meanwhile, Rook makes fancy reservations (on the show he needs reminding from his family) and takes Heat to see the scenic and aptly named Beckett's Neck. College kids apparently had a zombie party – a *Thriller* flash mob – on the beach there (39).

➘ Castle says in "Heartbreak Hotel" (408), "Well boys, I'm sorry. I'm sorry it had to come to this. I didn't want it to, but it looks like we have no choice. There is no other way. IBPWOC. (He gets lost looks from the others.) Impromptu bachelor party while on case!" In the Hamptons with Nikki Heat, Rook makes up similar acronyms.

➘

> ESPOSITO: Crystal Sky? That name's so fake it sounds like something out of one of your books.
> CASTLE: (chuckles) Right? (realizing) Whoa, whoa. What is that supposed to mean?
> ESPOSITO: What do you mean, what is that supposed to mean? Derrick Storm? Nikki Heat? Jameson Rook? Would

it kill you to name someone Gonzalez every once in a while? ("Watershed," 524)

➤ His following book indeed features Detective Inez Aguinaldo, suggesting he took Esposito's advice.

➤ Heat suspects that behind paid assassins and thugs is Commissioner Keith Gilbert, "billionaire, power broker, senatorial hopeful, and golf buddy with the mayor" (*Raging Heat* 283). After several failed attempts on the slippery politician, Nikki Heat finally arrests the commissioner as he campaigns at a rally, much as she does with Senator Bracken. Like Bracken, Commissioner Gilbert was building a political war chest with illegal activity, in this case human trafficking instead of Bracken's drugs. Both men had brutal hit men who killed all the loose ends that they could, though Beckett/Heat managed to escape them and bring them down, together with their employers.

➤ Rook loves his Comic-Con baseball cap (*Raging Heat* 18). He keeps having a vivid dream that Nikki is a senator, nodding to Beckett's future path (*Raging Heat* 34). They debate wiseass versus smartass (*Raging Heat* 44).

➤ In the Hamptons they call on an unnamed bestselling mystery writer who insists he's "Got Connelly, Nesbo, and Lehane waiting for me and Nick & Toni's, but that's all right. Good for humility" (*Raging Heat* 56). This is presumably Castle.

➤ Rook quips about an [illegal] alien falling to earth and insists his next article is writing itself (*Raging Heat* 60). Rook suspects chicken sacrifice and a voodoo connection.

➤ Rook insists, "I am all sleekness like the fabled ninja," nodding to the ninja episode (*Raging Heat* 65).

➤ "The Manhattan skyline set the low ceiling ablaze like a CGI special effect" (*Raging Heat* 215). Apparently they're on a television show now.

❯ Rook is trapped by his seatbelt in a sinking car at the climax of *Raging Heat*, and Heat shoots it free, as happens on the show.

❯ When they're a couple, Nikki Heat calls Rook "babe," as on the show.

❯ *Driving Heat* begins with Rook and Heat engaged (the opening of season six) and Heat now captain of the precinct on her first day of the job (the opening of season eight). Rook suggests they honeymoon on the ranch in Diamondback, Arizona (*Driving Heat* 295). It ends with Beckett and Castle getting married. She wears the silver lace gown from the show. As with the show, he's caught in a car fire, but this time he makes it to the wedding. Phrases "your partner in crime" and "the time of our lives" appear in both sets of wedding vows.

❯ *Driving Heat* begins with a murder on a ballfield (paralleling "Suicide Squeeze," 215). Soon enough, a criminal conspiracy to cover up a faulty car part appears ("Habeas Corpse," 719). Castle is found over several dead bodies ("A Deadly Affair," 301) and constant drone attacks threaten the heroes ("The Human Factor," 523). A plot where a man crashed into a woman's car, killing her, then covered it up also appears ("Once Upon a Crime," 417).

❯ When they lose internet, Rook suggests that they've become part of a seventies cop show. Ochoa wants to be Starsky and Hutch (*Driving Heat* 130). This nods to the seventies episode. Gruff ME Stu Linkletter appears. Rook considers becoming a P.I. (*Driving Heat* 91). Rook hums the five notes from *Close Enounters of the Third Kind*. They consult Backhouse, a professor at Hudson University. Rook's pen guy notes that he's not much of a mystery writer (*Driving Heat* 204). In the afterward to *Driving Heat*, Castle mentions he's just finished the Poe's Pen Award ceremony.

❯ The Derrick Storm comics become unbelievably meta, adding: "There're two Jake Palaces in the world: real and fictional. The real one is a hard-bitten, hard drinking detective who's sensitive to female needs." After he thwarted a presidential assassination (possibly by accident) the fictional version was based on him. This was "A lookalike actor whose previous claim to fame was a short-lived space opera. He now stars in the TV series 'Palace,' loosely based on Palace's life. Now in its fourth season. Plus there's books, even graphic novels" (*A Calm Before Storm*). Thus armed, the real Jake Palace becomes a billionaire detective to the stars.

\ Derrick Storm has an ex-girlfriend named Nicole – this may be a Nikki Heat reference (*Deadly Storm*).

\ Rook quips that if they're partially brain dead they're zombies and proposes a toast to this (*Deadly Heat* 111). This nods to the zombie episode of course.

\ Castle says in his award acceptance speech, "Kate. Seven years ago I thought I would never walk again and then you walked in the door and my whole world changed. You were right, you said I had no idea. But now I do. This is because of you, because of us. Always" ("Hollander's Woods," 723). The dedication of *Driving Heat* is the last line here.

\ Derrick Storm quips, "Do I look like a killer to you?" (*Deadly Storm*).

\ Derrick Storm, PI, is listed as Number Seven on Most Eligible Bachelors (*Storm Season*).

\ Storm compares Strike to a ninja, a quick show reference (*Storm Season*).

\ The Fear tells a quipping Storm he has "a knack for turn of phrase" and adds, "You should have become a novelist" (*A Calm Before Storm*).

\ Derrick Storm returns from death in *Storm Front* (2013), a novel dedicated to Richard Castle's father, presumably inspired by their partnership in "Hunt." Agent Kevin Bryan and Agent Javier Rodriguez join the team. Captain Roy Montgomery appears as a heroic plane captain. And

Storm meets Nikki Heat and Jameson Rook, in a delightful cameo.

↘ They consult Dr. Rodney Click, an economist who tells them his journal won't be confused with a page-turner and adds, "It's not like I'm Michael Connelly here" (*Storm Front* 107).

↘ One book's afterward, like most of them, notes:

> As ever, I am in the debt of the top professionals at the 12th Precinct who tolerate me still. Detective Kate Beckett has shown me the ropes of homicide investigation, not to mention how to make sense of songs. Her colleagues, Javier Esposito and Kevin Ryan, have welcomed me like the brothers I never had. And the late Captain Roy Montgomery, to whom this book is dedicated, was a great mentor to all who worked under him and an even greater man to all who knew him. Dr. Lanie Parish at the Office of Chief Medical Examiner has given me almost as many insights as she has eye rolls. I may be a pain in the ass sometimes, but-I do like to think I break up a day when you work in a refrigerated environment. (*Heat Rises* 303)

↘ In moment of wall-shattering, author Richard Castle thanks "Nathan, Stana, Seamus, Jon, Ruben, Molly, Susan, and Tamala" in his afterward to *Heat Rises* and the books that follow — these of course are the show's actors including Castle's. He adds, "You remain the embodiment of dreams that come true relentlessly and tirelessly. You always bring the heat." The final acknowledgement adds, "Finally, to the fans, please know how you are admired and honored. You are the reason for it all" (*Heat Rises* 304).

↘ *Storm Front* is dedicated "For my Father."

↘ Pi cameos in *Wild Storm* with "Muppet hair":

> Pi is the leader of the International Order of Fruitarians, a quasi-religious group that tries to convince people that fruit is the original diet of mankind – nutrition as God intended. Really, it's a cult. It slowly lures innocent college kids, especially unsuspecting young women, into its clutches and

then eventually brainwashes them into doing things like selling flowers at the airport.

- Storm decides, "A father would go to any lengths to protect his daughter from a monster like that" (24). Pi even gets killed off.

- In *Wild Storm*, a young woman on an archeological dig discovers a life-sized bust of the pharaoh Khufu ("Wrapped Up in Death," 219). Storm has read Alice Clark's *Mating Rituals: A Field Guide to Relationships* ("A Diamond is Forever" 614). He also references *2 Cool 4 School* ("Need to Know," 613).

- Having saved a plane, Captain Estes "was destined for a *Time* magazine cover, a book deal, even a guest appearance on a highly rated ABC television crime drama" (*Wild Storm* 8).

- For a book-book reference, a Jameson's Finch is a terribly lucky bird in Egypt. It was hunted nearly to extinction before Jameson Rook wore an exposé. "The Egyptians were so thrilled not to lose the bird, they officially renamed it Jameson's Finch in Mr. Rook's honor" (*Wild Storm* 197).

- There's a husband wife scientist team where the elderly man thinks longingly of his beloved wife. "She wasn't just his ghostwriter. She was his muse" in a Castle-Beckett parallel (*Wild Storm* 203).

- On August 20, 2014, ABC announced that the early development stage has begun on a television series centered on Derrick Storm. The series will be a CIA procedural written by Gregory Poirier will write and executive-produce with *Castle*'s Andrew Marlowe and Terri Miller.

- Castle (or someone in his voice) posts goofy pop culture and family related tweets at @WriteRCastle such as "Happy Birthday @NathanFillion: A man after my own face."

Other Shows Reference Castle

❖ The show's two stars appeared on 2009's *"Dancing with the Stars:* Round Five."

❖ Castle was a question on "Who Wants to Be a Millionaire: Episode #8.163" (2010)

❖ *"Scrubs:* Our Driving Issues" (2010) When Denise is looking for Drew, she asks a nurse if she has seen anyone who looks like a serial killer. Michael Mosley plays one on the show *Castle,* this may be a reference.

❖ On *"The Gates:* Digging the Dirt" (2010), Dylan tells Nick "No motive, no murder. At least that's what they say on *Castle.*"

❖ Vanessa calls Mike "Castle" in *"Last Man Standing:* Co-Ed Softball" (2011) when he figures out what she's talking about.

❖ Fillion and Katic appeared on *The Morning After* (2011-2012).

❖ A review by Richard Castle appears on Martin's book in *"Missing:* Tell Me No Lies" (2012).

❖ Neal says he spent 10 minutes talking to a homeless guy about *Castle* on *"Men at Work:* Devil's Threesome" (2012).

❖ Christina Applegate describes it as her favorite on *"The Tonight Show with Jay Leno:* Episode #21.13" (2012)

❖ On *"30 Rock:* Stride of Pride" (2012), Jenna says she is too old to party because she watches *Castle.*

❖ When Nathan Fillion visits *"Neil's Puppet Dreams:* Doctor's Office" (2012), Neil Patrick Harris says to Nathan Fillion, who plays the doctor, that "this place is a Castle."

❖ In *Much Ado About Nothing* (2012), Nathan Fillion plays the detective.

❖ The film *Percy Jackson: Sea of Monsters* (2013) sees Hermes (Nathan Fillion) says that he admires the way Percy and Annabeth finish each other's sentences. They're a future couple like himself and Beckett of course. He also mentions *Firefly* was the best show ever.

\ In "*Robot Chicken* DC Comics Special II: Villains in Paradise" (2014) a supervillain complains that his mother used up all his data watching *Castle* on Netflix. (Nathan Fillion guest-starred and played Green Lantern, among other characters.)

\ Danny's mom says she only watches "Castle" in "*The Mindy Project*: Annette Castellano Is My Nemesis" (2014)

\ It's namedropped in "*American Dad!*: The Kidney Stays in the Picture" (2012) and "*Mystery Girls*: Death Rose" (2014), It gets a mention in "*BoJack Horseman*: Live Fast, Diane Nguyen" (2014). The next year, in the episode "Still Broken, Bojack says, "You like Horsin' Around but how could you like 'Horsin' Around' but not like the horse? That's like watching 'Castle' but hating castles: I've never seen Castle"

\ In "*Red Band Society*: The Guilted Age" (2015), Kara tells Nurse Jackson: "Before you go home and watch 'Castle'..."

Fun with Credits and Theme Tune

Occasionally the episodes have done special opening credits. "Countdown"'s title sequence is simply the logo, unanimated and tinted blue, to avoid jarring the watchers (317). "Kick the Ballistics" (404) has the logo in normal colors, but silent, for the same reason. "Always" (423) has the logo slightly greener, without cheery music.

"Demons" (406) has a Halloween special version with spooky pipe organ and wolves howling. "The Blue Butterfly" (414) plays the tune in jazz style with a saxophone. "Swan Song" (507) features a rock version, and "Secret Santa" (509) a Christmas-themed version. The credits are extra loud and lit up for "Last Action Hero," (709) and Western for "Once Upon a Time in the West" (707).

In the cold open for "The Wild Rover" (518), a cake reads "Happy 99th!" and the title sequence for the following 100th episode "The Lives of Others" (519) has a few "100"s mixed in.

The theme tune has also cameoed on the show. In "Home is Where The Heart Stops" (107), Castle sits in the car and hums his own action-scene theme. When the bad guy shows up and drags Castle into a fistfight, he stops humming and the theme music starts playing over the scene. After the suspect is caught, he hums it again, only for Beckett to make him stop. When Castle walks into The Old Haunt in "Last Call" (310), the bar's piano player starts playing that action theme. Castle thanks the piano player for remembering and tips him. Castle uses the same musical sting to end a scene in "Swan Song" (507).

Castle Meets his Fans

❭ The first episode of course features Castle's book signing, Beckett's fannishness, and a copycat killer inspired by his books. It ends with Castle deciding to write the *Nikki Heat* books about Beckett.

❭ In "Boom" (218), he drinks out of a Richard Castle mug.

> CALDERON: Pleasure. (to CASTLE) And you, sir, need no introduction. I am a huge admirer of your fictions. Whenever I desire a taste of my old, grittier life I call upon your works. My favorite is Nikki Fuego.
> CASTLE: Nikki Fu-? Oh, you mean Nikki Heat.
> CALDERON: No, I mean Nikki Fuego. I only read the Spanish translations. Have you read you novels in Spanish?
> CASTLE: No.
> CALDERON: Oh, you should. Everything is better in Spanish. ("Anatomy of a Murder," 305).

❭ Frakes appears as Castle's biggest fan at the convention in "The Final Frontier" (507). Castle finds him ridiculous.

❭ In "Number One Fan" (604), Castle is brought onto a case because a young woman appears to have murdered her boyfriend then taken a bank full of hostages. "Hostage negotiators have been trying to talk to Emma, but she's demanding to speak to only you, Mr. Castle." She wants him to solve her case as he's the only one she trusts. As Castle adds to Beckett, "She's a fan. I know my fans. She won't hurt me." She also makes him prove it's him by playing fan trivia:

> EMMA: Okay, you say you're Richard Castle, you're going to have to prove it, all right? In the *Nikki Heat* series, what's Rook and Nikki's wine of choice?
> CASTLE: Sancerre.
> EMMA: In *Deadly Heat* what's Douglas Sandman's nickname?
> CASTLE: Bedbug Doug.
> EMMA: In *Storm Rising* what's Pierre DuBois's last words?
> CASTLE: Ah, trick question. Pierre was a Trappist monk. He took a vow of silence. He never spoke. Boom! Believe it's me now, Emma? Because I could play Richard Castle trivia with you all day. I will crush you.

Castle gushes over an action star only to be told to his delight, "The honor is mine. I've passed many an hour in the john reading your books" ("Last Action Hero," 709).

> LIZ BELL: Detective Kate Beckett! And you're Richard Castle. Hi, I'm Liz Bell, I'm the head writer for SNT and I absolutely adore you. (to BECKETT) And you, especially you.
> BECKETT: Wha – me? Really?
> LIZ: Oh, of course. I followed your career. I wanted to be a cop, but I ended up a writer. I know, it's pathetic.
> CASTLE: Excuse me? ("Dead from New York," 722)

The real Nathan Fillion enjoys Twitter. He explains:

> My father once said long distance relationships only work if you have a basis to work with. Over the telephone, everybody's in charge of their presentation. You never get to see them in an adverse situation. Or talking to a waiter, which is very important to me. I think Twitter is like that. You only get someone's presentation. I try to be—I'm often wry on my Twitter, but I try to be positive. Some people are just outright mean. And I just go: block. Block! (Nussbaum)

Castle Quotes Pop Culture

> CASTLE: Tell me something: do you ever have any fun? Let your hair down? Drop your top? A little "cops gone wild"?
> BECKETT: You do know that I'm wearing a gun? ("Flowers for your Grave," 101)

❧ Richard Castle's apartment is the same set as was used for the main character's apartment in the vampire detective show *Moonlight* (2007).

❧ Castle has a custom ringtone for calls from Beckett – a creepy pipe organ. At one point he says "I Hear Dead People" when it sounds.

> CASTLE: Style section. Anything I need to know?
> ALEXIS: The '70s are back.
> CASTLE: Hmm. They're like the Highlander, they just won't die. ("Hedge Fund Homeboys," 103)

❧ Castle's ringtone when his mother calls is Richard Wagner's "The Ride of the Valkyries" (which, for film buffs, evokes 1979's *Apocalypse Now*). ("Hell Hath No Fury, 104).

❧ "A Chill Goes through her Veins" (105) is the first time Castle and Alexis are seen playing laser tag, a game first started when Alexis was five years old.

❧ Castle calls his ex-wife Meredith "like Auntie Mame on meth" ("Always Buy Retail," 106).

❧ As Castle and Alexis are fencing, they both quote dialogue from *The Adventures of Robin Hood* (1938) ("Home is Where the Heart Stops," 107).

❧ Stuck in the car, Castle imitates Clint Eastwood: "This is Detective Castle to all Units. That's a negatory on the back-up. This dirtbag's all mine" ("Home Is Where the Heart Stops," 107)

❧ Upon seeing photos of the victim and her husband at a potential suspect's apartment, Castle says, "Look who's stalking." This is a play on the title of the 1989 movie, *Look Who's Talking*. ("Ghosts," 108).

Castle makes the statement, "I feel like Michael finding the gun taped behind the toilet" ("Little Girl Lost," 109). "Michael" is Michael Corleone, from the 1969 novel and the 1972 film "*The Godfather.*"

> ESPOSTIO: Wow, look at her. How can anyone do that to themselves?
> CASTLE: Right? It's like she escaped from the Island of Dr. Moreau.
> BECKETT: Come on guys, she's not an animal. She's a human being.
> CASTLE: Yeah, I know but...wait, are you being sincere, or quoting the Elephant Man? ("A Death in the Family," 110)

> CASTLE: My little girl- She's all grown-up.
> MARTHA: Yeah, well, at least one of you is. A severed head?
> CASTLE: Ooh, I was just getting started, too. I was gonna break into my Chris Waken. (Imitates Chris) Whoa. Tell me, little man... Have you ever been to prison? ("A Death in the Family," 110)

> BECKETT: Yeah, well, no one said that the feds were original.
> CASTLE: Yeah, next thing you'll tell me, they'll be pulling up in a black suburban with tinted windows.
> A black suburban with tinted windows pulls up.
> CASTLE: Oh, someone's been watching way too many Bruckheimer films. ("A Death in the Family," 110)

Castle is reading *Sweetheart* by Chelsea Cain while waiting for Alexis to get home ("A Death in the Family," 110).

As Beckett throws herself into an investigation with cup after cup of coffee, Castle tells her, "When I gave you that little speech last night, I really didn't mean for you to go all *Beautiful Mind* on me" ("A Death in the Family," 110).

Cosmopolitan magazine is doing a spread on Castle for the launch of *Heat Wave* ("Deep in Death," 201).

➤ Castle cries, "It's raining men!" ("Deep in Death," 201).

➤ At the crime scene, Castle says that he is reminded of the film, "Capricorn One" (1978). In the movie, astronauts are forced to act as though they have landed on Mars. ("Fool Me Once," 204)

> BECKETT: Who would go to the trouble of killing someone that way?
> CASTLE: Lycans. They've been at war with the vampires since Lucian was murdered in the fifteenth century.
> (Beckett rolls her eyes for the benefit of Ryan & Esposito)
> Again, this is just theory. ("Vampire Weekend, 206)

➤ Castle dresses as Edgar Allen Poe in "Vampire Weekend" (206). He later reveals his made-up middle name, Edgar, is an homage.

➤ Castle notes during the pop song murder "Famous Last Words" (207), "Death, she grows near? It's kind of like *Final Destination*, but in song form." and "Sometimes when we lose an artist we like, it's kind of like losing a friend. You know, I remember when John Lennon died, I didn't leave my room for a week."

> MARTHA: Oh, oh! That reminds me of sitting around with Lisa Olsen, trying to decode The Beatles' lyrics, spinning the record backwards and to see if, uh, "Paul was dead."
> CASTLE: And who could forget the countless hours I spent pondering the lyrics to Van Halen's "Hot for Teacher"? Mmm. ("Famous Last Words," 207)

➤ Castle begins the episode "Famous Last Words" (207) playing *Guitar Hero*.

> CASTLE: And he was pulling a Kevin Bacon in *Quicksilver* when all of-
> BECKETT: I'm sorry, a what?
> CASTLE: *Quicksilver*. [Beckett shakes her head] Kevin Bacon is a bike messenger who failed as a –
> BECKETT: [turns to Esposito] Esposito, take him to school. ("Kill the Messenger," 208)

❧ Castle announces, "Just another contestant on Who Wants to Marry an Amnesiac?" ("The Fifth Bullet, 211).

❧ When the amnesiac is saved by a copy of *Crime and Punishment*, Castle compliments his taste. As Castle adds later, "What I wouldn't give to read "The Cask of Amontillado" for the first time. Or any Stephen King. Ah. Silver lining. You get to read all my books for the first time again." ("The Fifth Bullet, 211)

> CASTLE: Whoa, no no wait, don't do that.
> BECKETT: What?
> CASTLE: Well, once you open it we'll know. Could be an alien corpse in there, Ark of the Covenant, or… Johnny Vong DVDs. ("Sucker Punch," 213)

> CASTLE: That was so cool just now.
> BECKETT: You like that?
> CASTLE: Yeah, it was very Miami Vice. ("Sucker Punch," 213)
> BECKETT: Whoever he's working for scares him a lot more than prison.
> CASTLE: There has to be a way to get it out of him. We could force him to watch Paris Hilton videos.
> BECKETT: You want be brought up on charges? ("Sucker Punch," 213)

> BECKETT: Montgomery's post-incident evaluation, you come off like Steven Segal.
> CASTLE: Should I be flattered or insulted?
> BECKETT: Both. ("Sucker Punch," 213)

❧ Castle suggests a loan shark "pulled a little *Untouchables* De Niro on his head" ("Suicide Squeeze," 215).

❧ "A .45 makes a pretty loud snap, crackle and pop," Castle says ("Tick Tick Tick," 217)..

❧ Another Castle moment of wisdom is, "A very wise woman once told me you can't blame Jodie Foster for John Hinckley. But you can blame her for 'Nim's Island'" ("Tick Tick Tick," 217).

> CASTLE: Hmm. Nicely played. However I do think you misjudged the relationship only slightly. (Takes a book from the shelf) "Eat, pray, love." Judging from the condition, I'd say she's read it more than once, meaning that she's a woman on the other side of a search for identity – a romantic, someone who wouldn't be satisfied with just a casual relationship.
> BECKETT: And who's to say that that book isn't his?
> Castle gives her a 'you-can't-be-serious' look.
> RYAN: Oh, I love that book. ("Wrapped Up in Death," 219)

- Castle smirks, "Four words – Eat, pray, love, kill. Little friendly advice- next time you kill someone, skip the part where you prove only you could've covered it up" in "Wrapped Up in Death" (219).
- Castle notes, "This guy is like Indiana Jones, but with space-age technology. Ooh! Which would've been such a better movie than that last one" ("Wrapped Up in Death," 219).
- Castle quips, "A little *Girls Gone Wild* jealousy turned deadly?" ("Wrapped Up in Death," 219)
- Castle insists: "This is the part where you say, 'and I would've gotten away with it, too, if it weren't for you meddling kids'" ("Wrapped Up in Death," 219). There are multiple *Scooby-Doo* references throughout the episode, including Castle's suggestion for the 'villain's' final words, and Beckett's reaction to Castle's assertion of the curse at the top of the stairs.
- While in the museum for the first time, Castle does a little homage to Indiana Jones. ("Wrapped Up in Death," 219)
- When the crew finds out that Bobby Mann visited Mickey Reed's apartment the night that he died Castle says "Oh Mickey, not so fine," referring to the song "Mickey" by Toni Basil from 1982, where she sings "Oh, Mickey you're so fine, you're so fine you blow my mind". ("The Late Shaft," 220)

BECKETT: "FTW"?

> CASTLE: "For the win." Means, "My tweet kicks your tweet's butt." Come on, Beckett. You got to keep up, hang with the cool kids. ("The Late Shaft," 220).

\ Castle notes, "Killing the king of late-night to take his throne – It's very *Richard III*" It appeals to the writer in me" ("The Late Shaft," 220).

\ When Castle and his friends like the special shaving cream, Lanie says, "It's like *Sex and the City*...only with boys" ("Overkill," 221).

> BECKETT: I cannot believe you asked for samples.
> CASTLE: What? They said anything we want. Plus these aren't for me: they are for Ryan and Esposito.
> BECKETT: Don't you mean Charlotte and Miranda.
> CASTLE: Wait, that would make me Carrie.
> BECKETT: You are so metrosexual for even knowing that.
> ("Overkill," 221)

\ In "A Deadly Affair" (301), Castle's meth-related line, "Just like that cable show," references *Breaking Bad*.

> CASTLE: Maybe you missed the part where I said she was shot dead. When I heard the noises coming from the next room, I thought whoever killed her was coming back. So I picked up the gun to defend myself. It seemed like a very good idea at the time. That's when you, Esposito and Annie Oakley *[gestures to the viewing room]* come bursting through the door.
> MONTGOMERY: Annie Oakley?
> RYAN: I kind of almost shot Castle. What? He had a gun.
> ("A Deadly Affair," 301)

\ Castle tells Beckett: "Oh, so you don't believe in fate, yet your "gut" has magical properties. That's cool ... Scully" ("He's Dead, She's Dead," 302).

\ "Driving in New York, it's like a *Mad Max* movie," Castle says ("Under the Gun," 303).

\ After Alexis rejects his smore-omlet, Castle says, "Ah ha, I knew you'd reconsider. It's like David Hasselhoff. At first you're repulsed but strangely you're drawn in" ("Punked," 304).

\ Castle is delighted that the victim has the new slot car app on her phone ("Anatomy of a Murder," 305).

\ Castle notes, "A known criminal living in a swanky hotel. Very Al Capone" ("Anatomy of a Murder," 305).

\ Castle explains: "Three reasons why Katonah is awesome. One, gorgeous countrysides. Two, it's where Doonsberry cartoonist Gary Trudeau went to school. And three, and perhaps most importantly, it's where Martha Stewart lives" ("Anatomy of a Murder," 305).

\ Castle calls an inmate's faked death "very *Pulp Fiction*" ("Anatomy of a Murder," 305).

> ALEXIS: Dad, those are for Theodore. He has a very specific diet I'm supposed to follow.
> CASTLE: Well, unless he's Ben I'm sure he won't hold it against me. (he pops a nut into his mouth as he turns away) If anyone needs me, I'll be in the park with a dead body.
> ALEXIS (to MARTHA): Who's Ben?
> MARTHA: Killer rat movie. Before your time. ("Murder Most Fowl," 308)

\ Castle says, "Surveillance equipment, clandestine meetings, a professional hit? Mix in the subway and we're looking at *The Taking of Pelham 123*, or better yet, *Money Train*. And one of these people could be a secret accomplice. That's what I love about the subway. Down here everyone's got a story" ("Murder Most Fowl," 308).

\ Castle cries of the government spooks: "They were Men in Black!" ("Close Encounters of the Murderous Kind," 309).

\ Listening to a SETI expert's speech, Castle notes, "He's like the Tony Robbins of alien abduction" ("Close Encounters of the Murderous Kind," 309).

> BECKETT: C'mon, Castle. You don't actually believe that Klingons are behind this, do you?

> CASTLE: Killer aliens is a reach, even for me. But government agents covering up the truth? Not so crazy.
> BECKETT: Yes it is. I mean, ("Close Encounters of the Murderous Kind," 309)

> LANIE: ...so I'd say no, this was no boating accident.
> CASTLE: *[Bending down]* Then we'd better close the beaches.
> [Lanie and Becket give him confused looks]'
> CASTLE: "No boating accident"? Chief Brody? Hooper? *[The women are still confused and Castle rises back up annoyed]* Seriously? ("Last Call," 310)

\ Rick's Café Américain is the name of the bar from *Casablanca*. It's Martha's suggestion, better than Castle's of "Castle-blanca." The quote "Here's looking at you, kid" is from the same movie ("Last Call," 310).

\ "Indy" is a nickname for Indiana Jones of course. *C.H.U.D.* (Cannibalistic Humanoid Underground Dwellers) is a 1984 horror/science fiction movie ("Last Call," 310).

\ "Alligators in the sewers" are a well-known urban legend dating back to the 1920's ("Last Call," 310).

\ The team all sing "Piano Man" together at the end ("Last Call," 310).

\ Castle tells Beckett, "Forget it. Fear does not exist in this dojo" ("Knockdown," 313)

> PAGE: What the hell, yo? That was slamming.
> CASTLE [Speaking into the intercom] "Three armed cops and a writer makes four.
> You're under arrest, so get on the floor" ("Lucky Stiff," 314)

\ Castle says, "Then it must have been Ernest Hemingway who said, "Man, I sure could use a drink right about now" ("The Final Nail," 315).

\ Castle says, "No, think of all the amazing things that are found in storage units at times like this. Ark of the Covenant, Dr. Jones?" ("Setup," 316).

- Castle watches *General Hospital* for research ("One Life to Lose," 318).
- When Beckett admits she watches soaps, Castle tells her, "My DVR would make yours look like *Masterpiece Theater*" ("One Life to Lose," 318).
- Castle explains of his newly written piece, "Th—this scene is going to expose the killer. The play is the thing wherein we'll catch the conscience of the king. *Hamlet*" ("One Life to Lose," 318). This is indeed the strategy he uses.
- Castle says, "That's just the tip of the iceberg. Are you ready for the Titanic?" ("Law & Murder," 319).
- Castle tells Beckett she can't play his *Angry Birds* if he can't try her police ap. ("Slice of Death," 320).
- Castle quips, "Now we know how Zack made his money. While he was out all night he was playing *Grand Theft Auto*" ("The Dead Pool," 321).
- Castle says, "Man born into hardship struggles to reach for something greater, only he can't escape the demons of his past. It's *Oedipus*. It's *The Godfather*. *The Beverly Hillbillies*" ("The Dead Pool," 321)

> JIMMY LENNON (eastern European accent): I know nothing.
> BECKETT: Not the best three words to have falling out of your mouth, Jimmy.
> CASTLE: I was half expecting Moose and Squirrel. ("The Dead Pool," 321)

- Castle comments, "This place looks like my first apartment. We used to have cockroach races. I wonder if that's how Kafka got the idea?" ("The Dead Pool," 321).

> CASTLE: Ah, Maurice is amazing, isn't he? I bet if I ordered the Ark of the Covenant he'd come through.
> BECKETT: Wouldn't you be afraid to open it?
> CASTLE: No. It only melts Nazis. ("To Love and Die in L.A.," 322)

CASTLE: Is that America's Dad, Bobby Stark? What's he doing here?
BECKETT: He's a pageant host. Oh please don't tell me you watch his sitcom.
CASTLE: *Family Foibles*? Half of what I know about being a father I learned from watching that show. ("Pretty Dead," 323)

BECKETT: I was my own private Vietnam. Our place smelled of hairspray, perfume and cigarettes. I'm surprised that we didn't spontaneously combust.
CASTLE I love the smell of hairspray in the morning. Smells like...victory. ("Pretty Dead," 323)

ALEXIS: What if I'm just cutting my losses on something that was never meant to be?
CASTLE Then we can be the father-daughter version of *Grey Gardens*. Life is a journey. And there is no predicting the outcome. The only thing you can control are your choices. And they'll... They'll define who you are. I would just hate to see you so focused on the problem right in front of you that you completely miss the entire picture. ("Pretty Dead," 323)

When Castle tells Beckett that he's 'always been the guy that says they can move the rubber tree plant' it's a reference to the Frank Sinatra song "High Hopes". The song talks about what makes an ant think he can move a rubber tree plant. ("Knockout," 324)

BECKETT: Our side doesn't execute criminals.
CHAD: See ... yeah, neither do I.
CASTLE: Except for last night's episode of two half men. ("Heroes and Villains," 402)

In "Heroes and Villains" (402), Castle mentioned that the victim being cut in half was "so *Game of Thrones*."

On discovering the cryogenics lab, Castle asks, "You got any celebrities in here? Ted Williams? Jack Frost?" ("Head Case," 403). When finding out the murdered scientist was conducting illegal patient trials, Castle quips,

"Maybe Frankenstein's monster came back and killed Frankenstein."

↘ "Head Case" (403) copies lines from *X-Files* almost verbatim, explaining why only the head is necessary for cryogenic preservation.

↘ On finding a body impaled on a Statue of Liberty statue in "Eye of the Beholder" (405), Castle quips, "Looks like somebody gave him liberty and gave him death."

> CASTLE: So you were kind of like the female Indiana Jones, only without the hat and whip.
> SERENA: Well, without the hat. ("Eye of the Beholder," 405)

↘ In "Eye of the Beholder" (405), a character jokingly calls Castle "Jason Bateman." Castle retorts that their similar looks got him out of a traffic ticket once. This actually happened to Nathan Fillion in real life. The joke is repeated in "An Embarrassment of Bitches" (413), where Castle is mistaken for Jason Bateman by some paparazzi. Castle complains that "this is getting old," to Beckett's amusement.

> CASTLE: Listen, if you're not scared, just say it.
> BECKETT: No!
> CASTLE: Come on, I know you want it.
> BECKETT: I don't wanna say it, Castle...
> CASTLE: For me, *please*...
> BECKETT: I ain't afraid of no ghosts... (*Ghostbusters theme playing*) ("Demons," 406)

↘ Castle tells Beckett real ghost hunters don't use proton packs ("Demons," 406)

↘ "Since the McClaren mansion was built in 1898, bodies have been piling up faster than a Tarantino movie," Castle says ("Demons," 406).

↘ Castle says, "They're here," the words from *Ghost Hunters* ("Demons," 406).

> BECKETT: And what could explain the picture suddenly going out like that?
> LULU: I don't know. It's never happened before.
> CASTLE: Well, there was that last episode of *The Sopranos*. ("Demons," 406)

❯ In "Cops and Robbers" (407), Castle uses his skills and love of *Die Hard* to get information about the bank hostage situation.

> CASTLE: Well, how about just a low-key evening with your girlfriends? You guys can have a John Hughes marathon and fill out a Cosmo quiz.
> ALEXIS: Dad, the '80s just called. It wants its plan back. ("Heartbreak Hotel," 408)

❯ In "An Embarrassment of Bitches" (413), Castle notes of the murder victim, "dog whisperer, check. People whisperer, not so much."

❯ Castle watches "Beverly Hills Chihuahua." With the dog he's caring for. ("An Embarrassment of Bitches," 413)

❯ In "Once Upon a Crime" (417), they discover that the victims were being blackmailed over a car accident they caused years ago. Castle immediately references *I Know What You Did Last Summer.*

❯ Castle advises Martha, "In the wise words of Don Vito Corleone, (he shoves part of a doughnut in his mouth and gravels his voice) you need to make her an offer she can't refuse" ("A Dance with Death," 418).

❯ Castle mentions cheering up pancakes are meant for *Dancing with the Stars* eliminations ("47 Seconds," 419).

❯ Castle says, "I bet Glitch thought he could make his bones by cutting the heads off of Westie enemies. Bet he planned on puttin' those heads in some high ranking Jamaican beds. Like a horse's head? *The Godfather?*" ("Headhunters" 421).

❯ Castle, under zombie attack, cries, "It's ground zero for *World War Z*" ("Undead Again," 422).

CASTLE: Being a fan of zombie lore, I get it. But what's the appeal of being a zombie? Like look at this guy. Who would want to be alive in a decayed, mindless state? Being a vampire, that I understand. That's the romantic route to immortality. The gentleman's monster, as it were.
BECKETT isn't really paying attention. She's holing up the photo from the security footage, trying to find a zombie that matches.
BECKETT: Speaking of monsters, none of these zombies match the photo of our killer.
CASTLE: Maybe he's trying out a new look. (he pauses, then turns to her) How about you? If you could be any supernatural creature, what would it be?
BECKETT: Van Helsing, no question.
CASTLE: (nods) Monster slayer. Befitting. ("Undead Again," 422)

Castle plans a John Woo marathon in "Always" (423). He is a Hong Kong film director, writer, and producer whose films (like *The Killer* and *Hard Boiled*) are often full of action, violence, and blood.

CASTLE: Look, I tried everything to get away. I-I hid under the counter. I was hiding in the bathroom. At one point I tried to pull a *Cape Fear* up under the piano.
BECKETT: Yet when I walked in, she was straddling you on the couch
CASTLE: Right? She's like the Terminator of sexpots.
BECKETT: What is that even supposed to mean? She just keeps on coming?
("Cloudy With a Chance of Murder," 502)

CASTLE: You know what I love about this case? Finding a pretty pink bracelet in my belongings.
RYAN: You know you're gonna have to return that —
CASTLE: [Exploding] I *know*, Ryan! I know that! I ju—Can you just let me have this moment?! This one, small, *Treasure Island Indiana Jones* moment?
RYAN: Right. Got it.
CASTLE: [Petulant] *Well*, it's too late now. It's ruined.
("Secret's Safe With Me," 503)

❧ "The 27 Club. Memberships include some of the greats. Jimi Hendrix, Jim Morrison, Janis Joplin. The list is extensive," Castle explains ("Swan Song," 504)

❧ Castle calls Ryan and Esposito "Tango and Cash" ("Swan Song," 504)

❧ In "After Hours" (508), Castle thinks the MacGyver trope is enough to help him fix an old radio:

> BECKETT: Did you find some tape?
> CASTLE: Yes, and I also found a box of tools and a broken CB radio, but I think I can get it to work.
> LEO: Great! You have an engineering degree or electronics experience?
> CASTLE: No, but I've seen every episode of *MacGyver*.

> CASTLE: I'm just saying, there have been worse dinners.
> BECKETT: Like what?
> CASTLE: Well, the dining scene from *Alien* comes to mind.
> BECKETT: Honestly, a creature bursting out of my dad's chest might have lightened the mood. ("After Hours," 508)

> GATES: Oh Lord, I hate the holidays.
> CASTLE: Yet another quality she has in common with the Grinch. ("Secret Santa," 509)

> BECKETT: Noah uses a fake identity, starts dating Michelle and then he disappears just after she's killed?
> CASTLE: It's *The Bachelor* meets *Homeland*. ("Significant Others," 510)

> CASTLE: Monster. Now that sounds like the kind of ganged up thug that would shoot you dead and leave you in a dumpster someplace. Probably half man, half mountain, full of prison tats. Or is he quietly dangerous? Like Javier Bardem in any movie where he's got weird hair.
> ESPOSITO: Just ... take a look for yourself.
> They walk into the observation room. In the interrogation room is a bored looking kid.
> ESPOSITO: Behold. Monster.
> BECKETT is confused.
> CASTLE: More like Cookie Monster. ("Under the Influence," 512)

RYAN: No, it makes sense. Some savvy criminals use minors to do their dirty work.
CASTLE: Of course. A Fagin to Joey's Oliver Twist.
RYAN: And if Holly's involved, that makes her the Artful Dodger. Or the Artful DJ.
CASTLE: Ooh, nicely played. ("Under the Influence," 512)

＼ Castle asks, "I mean, on a scale of one to Hannibal Lector, what are we dealing with here?" ("Scared to Death," 517).

＼ Castle describes a victim as looking "like an Edvard Munch painting. Really freaky" ("Scared to Death," 517).

＼ "So really Lady Maggie was Lady Macbeth. Only she was Irish, not Scottish," Castle says ("The Wild Rover," 518).

＼ You don't come to be a casino owner without making enemies. Look at Moe Greene in the *Godfather*," Castle quips ("Heartbreak Hotel," 408).

＼ Castle suggests, "Hey, what if I consult by phone? We could pretend I'm Charlie and you're my angels" ("The Lives of Others," 519).

＼ Castle says, "Uh oh. Someone's got some 'splaining to do," from *I Love Lucy* ("The Lives of Others," 519).

＼ Castle insists Alexis's art teacher "looked just like the guy from *America's Most Wanted*" ("The Lives of Others," 519).

CASTLE: Don't let Moonshine fool you. I'm betting he and his fellow (he uses air quotes) retirees are actually super intelligent apes plotting to take over New York City. They're going to round up all the people, put us in a sanctuary. (BECKETT gives him a skeptical look) Most likely Anne got on to them – (he gestures) – they took her out.
BECKETT: Now if this monkey cabal really wanted to get Anne out of the picture, why did they drop her off at the hospital?
CASTLE: Well obviously they were conflicted. It's a complicated relationship between man and primate. (he adds MOONSHINE'S photo to the murder board) Didn't you see *Rise of the Planet of the Apes*? Cautionary tale. ("The Fast and the Furriest," 520)

CASTLE: Yeah, she's still not taking my calls.
BECKETT: Well, can you blame her, Castle? You
practically turned her into a Smurf.
CASTLE: Na'vi would be a more contemporary reference.
("The Fast and the Furriest," 520)

RICHARD CASTLE: Now you're dead. You can suck it. Oh,
you want more? Come get it, buddy. 'cause I got something
special for you.
KATE (wearing just his shirt): "And I've got something
special for you, too."
Castle keeps playing his game and taunting his online
opponent.
BECKETT: Castle!
CASTLE: What?
BECKETT: Would you rather play with a kid in an imaginary
world, or with – (he tries to split his focus and she drops her
voice and strikes a sexy pose) – in the real world?
CASTLE: Uh ... (he keeps playing) ... I ... ooh. (he doesn't
put down the game) I – uh ... uh ...
BECKETT: Oh my God.
By the episode's end, he makes a gesture and cuts the
power cord to his Xbox. ("The Squab and the Quail," 521)

CASTLE: I'm sorry. You know how I get when I'm gaming. I
was – I was in the zone. I was like Gretzky.
BECKETT: Well at least Gretzky knew how to score. ("The
Squab and the Quail," 521)

"Last supper list. (off their look) You and a table of 12
with anyone from history. What is mine, you ask? I'm
glad you did. In order it is, Lincoln, Einstein, Ian
Fleming, John Lennon, Joan of Arc, Sinatra – (he notices
Beckett's face dropping) And you, of course." ("The
Squab and the Quail," 521)

CASTLE: Yeah, you're right. (sarcastically) Oh, except for
the fact when it was Bracken they weren't having a slumber
party at fancy hotel. And let's face it. Compared to Bracken
Eric Vaughn is like George Clooney.
MARTHA RODGERS (oblivious to Castle's jealousy): Oh,
no. Eric Vaughn is way sexier than Clooney. ("The Squab
and the Quail," 521)

> BECKETT: Castle, Vaughn is worth a billion dollars. He's not going to be running scams.
> CASTLE laughs.
> CASTLE: Oh Beckett. That's what they said about Bernie Madoff. Like Madoff, it's quite possible Vaughn's entire empire is a house of cards. ("The Squab and the Quail," 521)

➤ Castle quips of spies, "The secretary will disavow all knowledge of your actions. It's *Mission Impossible*" ("The Human Factor," 523).

➤ Castle says of a world of automated drones, "It really will be *Rise of the Machines*" ("The Human Factor," 523).

➤ "Maybe Erika was some kind of an online Erin Brockovich. You know, a crusader for good delving into the seedy underbelly of the legal system to uncover some seamy truth," Castle suggests ("Watershed," 524).

> BECKETT: New Zealand? Castle, are you using our honeymoon as an excuse to go and tour Middle Earth?
> He clasps his hands together joyfully.
> CASTLE: I'm game if you are.
> BECKETT: I was hoping for something more romantic and less … hobbity.
> CASTLE: Why does everyone always think those two are mutually exclusive? ("Disciple," 609).

➤ Castle, describing moving a body, says, "Sounds like a case of *Weekend At Bernie's* gone wrong. (they look at him) No. No, wait. That would mean there's such a thing as *Weekend At Bernie's* gone right" ("Deep Cover," 612).

➤ Castle confesses, "My only other experience with surgery involved a board game and a guy whose nose lit up when I made a mistake" ("Deep Cover," 612).

> LANIE: Based on lividity, between 12 and 2AM. I also recovered some blue hairs left on her neck by the attacker.
> LANIE hands BECKETT an evidence bag.
> CASTLE: Blue hairs. So she was killed by a little old lady. Or – Katy Perry.

> BECKETT hands the bag back to LANIE. LANIE gives
> CASTLE a look.
> LANIE: Animal hairs that were dyed blue, Castle.
> CASTLE: Or … a Dr. Seuss character.
> BECKETT: I don't recall any of them being homicidal.
> CASTLE: That's true. I need a new theory. ("Dressed to
> Kill," 614)

> BECKETT: A bug? Why would someone bug Ella's
> apartment?
> CASTLE: Because … she is La Femme Nikita and her job
> at Modern Fashion is just a cover.
> BECKETT: (shakes her head) She's not La Femme Nikita.
> ("Dressed to Kill," 614)

\ "So, where are we on Watergate?" Castle asks about some
electronic bugs ("Dressed to Kill," 614).

\ In the fashion episode, Castle comes up with the book
title "Murder is the New Black" ("Dressed to Kill," 614).

> CASTLE: She was thrown against the ceiling? That is a
> superhuman feat, bordering on physically impossible.
> BECKETT: (sighs) Okay, Castle. Let's hear it. What's your
> outlandish theory?
> He shrugs.
> CASTLE: Isn't it obvious? Madison made The Hulk angry.
> ("Smells Like Teen Spirit," 615)

\ Castle says, "Thank God for the Kindle or I'd be out of a
job in a couple of years. Kids just don't read actual books
anymore" ("Smells Like Teen Spirit," 615).

> BECKETT: No, Castle. I'm not choosing our song off of a
> list that includes – (she scans) Def Leopard's "Pour Some
> Sugar On Me".
> CASTLE: Uh … that song, I'm sure, ignited many a strip
> club romance in 1987. (he sighs) 1987. A year when The
> Bangles taught us how to walk like an Egyptian. Bon Jovi
> taught us to live on nothing but a prayer. And Rick Astley
> taught us how to laugh. ("Smells Like Teen Spirit," 615)

> BECKETT: Castle, I love you. But I will not marry you on a
> ride or up in space or on a slide.

> CASTLE: I bet Dr. Seuss got married somewhere fun.
> BECKETT: Yes. His wife's living room. ("The Greater
> Good," 619)

➘ Castle suggests, "The killer was looking for something. A pricey necklace. Ooh, a bunch of cash strapped to his chest like *Wolf of Wall Street*" ("The Greater Good," 619).

> BOYLE: Vince's advisor. His consigliere.
> CASTLE: You mean like Tom Hagen in *The Godfather*.
> (That '70s Show," 620)

➘ Castle is a Scrabble expert ("Law & Boarder," 621)

> CASTLE: What if that bad crowed refers to an evil cabal
> that pays extreme athletes to duel to the death, all for the
> benefit of depraved millionaires.
> BECKETT: You mean like the movie *Rollerball*?
> CASTLE: It would explain the motorcycle versus
> skateboard murder. ("Law & Boarder," 621)

➘ Castle says, "A shady law firm, a mysterious death, a young man righting wrongs. Maybe Logan Moore is like Erin Brockovich but with a skateboard instead of you know, other assets" ("Law & Boarder," 621).

➘ Castle says of his insomnia, "Maybe my subconscious has a pressing need to catch up on my Facebook likes" ("Time of our Lives," 705).

➘ In the alternate reality, Castle discovers he jumped on a Macy's parade float and sang "Let It Go" with Idina Menzel and then landed a hot air balloon naked in Central Park. He protests, "I didn't do these things, guys. Come on. I would never sing "Let It Go" as a duet" ("Time of our Lives," 705).

➘ Castle makes a gorgeous website for himself ("Private Eye Caramba!" 712)

➘ Castle tracks the star he's seeking through all the social media fansites ("Private Eye Caramba!" 712).

➘ Castle plays *Terra Quest* in several season seven episodes.

- Castle makes a trap of metal pots and pans and utensils that he's hung all around the room and tells Beckett, "And you thought zombie apocalypse survival camp was a waste of time" ("Clear & Present Danger," 703).
- Castle speculates that a stolen item was "Cold fusion technology. Genetically engineered super virus. Some secret unpublished *Harry Potter* manuscript" ("Hong Kong Hustle," 717).
- Castle asks Beckett, "You're not trying to break my high score on *Fruit Ninja*, are you?" when she uses his computer ("Hong Kong Hustle," 717).
- Castle bursts out, "There's a snake on the motherflying plane!" ("In Plane Sight," 721).

Pop Culture in the Novels
A man is killed falling from a great height. Rook quips, "It's raining men."
Nikki Heat didn't even turn. She just sighed his name.
"Rook." (*Heat Wave* 2).

- He then pesters Raley and Ochoa to guess who wrote the song.
- Rook says, "I always wondered where all those Martha Stewarts came from. They must breed them on a secret farm in Connecticut." (*Heat Wave* 8).
- When a stripper names herself Samantha, Rook comments that *Sex in the City* leads to poor role models (*Heat Wave* 20). He also describes the girl changing her name as getting a "Henry Higgins" from *My Fair Lady*.
- Jameson Rook protests Nikki Heat catching a suspect and saying "Go ahead," without adding "Make my day," comparing it to "Shave and a Haircut" without the ending (*Heat Wave* 59).
- Rook and Heat compare the victim and his wife to Donald Trump and Tara Reid (*Heat Wave* 51).
- Rook sends Nikki an art print of Carnation, Lily, Lily Rose, her favorite (*Heat Wave*, 79).

❮ Rook teases Nikki when instead of saying she has a friend to rely on, him, she says "I've got a ... flashlight" (*Heat Wave* 96). He suggests they offer James Taylor the new lyrics.

❮ Rook tells Nikki implausible stories about hanging out with Elton John, Tony Blair, and Prince Harry in London (*Heat Wave* 101).

❮ When paintings mysteriously vanish, Rook asks, "Do Penn and Teller have a burglary crew?" (*Heat Wave* 140).

❮ With their suspect vanished, Rook suggests he's out on a reality show titled "I'm a Mouth-Breathing Killer, Get Me Outta Here" (*Heat Wave* 143).

❮ Rook gives Casper the thief a custom ringtone from *Ghostbusters* (*Heat Wave* 163).

❮ Rook defines a man's accent as "Southern. Like Wilford Brimley...But not the look-at-that- Wilford Brimley's-doing-TV-commercials-now Wilford Brimley. Younger. Like from *Absence of Malice* or *The Natural*" (*Naked Heat* 113). The detective interviewing him writes "Southern" and Rook concedes that "the man's IMDB credits" aren't necessary.

❮ Rook gives Heat a John Singer Sargent poster and watches *Antiques Roadshow* (*Naked Heat* 116).

❮ In candlelight, he notes, "Sometimes I can come off kind of Mephistophelian when lit by flame" (*Naked Heat* 118).

❮ At Lauren's autopsy, Rook notes, "This is like late-show infomercials. 'But wait, there's more'" (*Naked Heat* 148).

❮ After identifying the Greek god of hindsight, Rook adds, "True fact. Alex, I'll take 'Moons of Saturn' for a thousand" (*Naked Heat* 213).

❮ Rook describes how he "dropped everything to rush to you in true ain't-no-river-wide-enough fashion" (*Heat Rises* 62)

❮ Rook interviews Heat using "Proust Interview" questions. As he adds, this was a popular parlor game "pre-Dance Dance Revolution" (*Heat Rises* 96). In the process, Heat reveals that her favorite authors are Jane Austen and

Harper Lee. Rook's are Charles Dickens and Dr.. Hunter
S. Thompson." They both love Odysseus. Heat's favorite
poet is "Keats...For 'Ode on a Grecian Urn.'" Rook's is
"Seuss. For 'One Fish, Two Fish.'" Her most impactful
musician is Chumbawamba. (97) His are Steely Dan,
James Taylor, and AC/DC (98).

\ After a suspicious break in, Rook says, "What do you
know. It's like Freud said. Sometimes a cable guy is just a
cable guy...Unless it's Jim Carey" (*Heat Rises* 205).

\ Snarking with Raley and Ochoa, Rook asks if they took
the time to stop at White Castle on their way to save
them (*Heat Rises* 220).

\ Rook has the line "When you say things like that to me, I
call it a Kardashian. Know why? Because I'm looking for
the but" (*Heat Rises* 225).

\ Rook mentions he loves the reality show *Payback Playback*
(*Heat Rises* 246).

\ Rook says, "To quote Charlie Sheen, Duh" (*Heat Rises*
262).

\ Rook tells her, "With apologies to Prince, we're going to
partner like it's 1999" about an old case (*Frozen Heat* 29).

\ Rook insists he was drawn into a fight by being
mesmerized and had to leave the car – "It's like *Close
Encounters* for me. Or the rose ceremony on *Bachelorette*"
(*Frozen Heat* 47)

\ Rook thinks Ravel's "Bolero" is the most erotic piece of
music, except for "Don't Mess with my Toot Toot"
(*Frozen Heat* 64).

\ Looking through Nikki's mother's photos, Rook says,
"It's like a mash-up Syfy Channel meets Lifetime movie
where a rip in the space-time continuum removes all
traces of the best friend (*Frozen Heat* 73)

\ On going to meet Heat's father, Rook quips about it
being *Father of the Bride* part four, "Diane Keaton puts
Steve Martin on a colon cleanse right before the
wedding." (*Frozen Heat* 87). He also quotes *King Lear*.

❧ Rook wonders why he and Nikki can't be happily in love like a Woody Allen movie but she always has to pummel him (*Frozen Heat* 123)

❧ Rook quips, "Take that, Chuck Norris" (*Frozen Heat* 250).

❧ Rook sarcastically compares them to Bogey and Bacall (*Frozen Heat* 256).

❧ Rook says, "I haven't seen this much blood in a hotel since *The Shining*" (*Frozen Heat* 258).

❧ Rook decides that typical dark cop humor is similar to "why the Three Stooges never hugged" (*Deadly Heat* 23).

❧ Rook gets some of his esoteric knowledge from Snapple cap (*Deadly Heat* 38).

❧ Rook's ringtone on Heat's phone is "Remind Me" (*Deadly Heat* 50).

❧ Rook says, "I went in the pet shop and got everyone out. Ever see *Pee-wee's Big Adventure*? I was this close to running out with two handfuls of snakes" (*Deadly Heat* 77).

❧ Rook often does the scene from *Forrest Gump* with all the shrimp (*Deadly Heat* 82).

❧ Rook calls the CIA van "like Air Force One's dinghy" and does a Harrison Ford "Get off my RV" (*Deadly Heat* 131).

❧ Rook quips of a prison escapee, "He didn't tear off somebody's face to use as a mask to get out, I hope." He adds, "Spoiler Alert: *Silence of the Lambs*" (*Deadly Heat* 250).

❧ Rook says, "There's an old Watergate catchphrase. 'Follow the money.' It was sort of the 'What's in your wallet' of its day" (*Deadly Heat* 260).

❧ Rook theorizes their victim jumped from a plane, *Point Break* style (*Raging Heat* 11). Rook also suggests a hang glider or wing suit (*Raging Heat* 13).

❧ Rook suggests many action figures he might resemble, adding that he ghostwrote a piece on Hasboro (*Raging Heat* 15).

❧ Rook decides Captain Irons is like Gregor Samsa, "a human cockroach, only freakishly mutated. Like that deviant species the discovered that survives chemical spills, nuclear meltdowns, and *Real Housewives* marathons" (*Raging Heat* 22-23).

❧ Rook imitates Groucho Marx, punning on "European model" (*Raging Heat* 37).

❧ Surrounded by dead chickens, Rook quotes Dickenson's "Hope is the Thing with Feathers" (*Raging Heat* 45).

❧ Rook calls a mansion "Downton Abbey's little brother, only of wood" (*Raging Heat* 53).

❧ After Heat takes down an assailant, Rook quips, "Apologies to Peter, Paul, and Mary, but now we know what you'd do if you had a hammer" (*Raging Heat* 122).

❧ Rook jokes when a production of *The Tempest* is canceled because of the storm. Heat tells him he's actually quoting *King Lear* (*Raging Heat* 215).

❧ Rook suggests their suspect was keeping a Kenyan birth certificate, an Obama joke (*Raging Heat* 199).

❧ When his friends call him the Bullet Whisperer, Rook jokes "I see lead people" (*Raging Heat* 193).

❧ Rook quips, "You can't have a situation in the situation room" from *Dr. Strangelove* (*Raging Heat* 269).

❧ Rook got the engagement ring made at a French shop that's been there so long it "probably designed those candlesticks Jean Valjean stole" from *Les Miserables* (*Raging Heat* 286).

❧ Rook loves his Hemmingway pen in *Driving Heat*.

❧ At Ron King's office, Castle asks if Hannibal Lector sent anyone seeking severed heads (*Driving Heat* 30).

❧ Rook learns takedowns from The Streets of San Francisco (*Driving Heat* 52).

❧ Rook adds, "Thank you nineteen-seventies" and feels he's in a Michael Douglas scene (*Driving Heat* 53).

❧ Describing a manacled criminal, Rook quotes *A Christmas Carol*'s "I wear the chain I forged in life" (*Driving Heat* 55).

❧ They squabble over whether invisibility cloaks exist and Rook calls Harry Potter his "sometime alter ego" (*Driving Heat* 61).

- Rook suspects investigating gaits will lead them to John Cleese (a quip on *Monty Python*'s Ministry of Silly Walks sketch) (*Driving Heat* 93).

- Rook hums the five notes from *Close Enounters of the Third Kind* during a drone attack (*Driving Heat* 102).

- Rook says the CEO Tangier Swift "has more stone walls around him than Fortunato" from "The Cask of Amontillado" (*Driving Heat* 113).

- Rook asks if the yacht has Dance Dance Revolution (*Driving Heat* 120).

- Rook quips that with the current case "Clooney's got his plot for *Ocean's 21* (*Driving Heat* 130).

- Rook quotes "We become what we hate" from Screeching Weasel, not Neizche (*Driving Heat* 144).

- Rook calls them an opera box away from being Muppets Statter and Waldorf (*Driving Heat* 156).

- On his rescue, Rook quips on PJ Clarke, orcs, and *50 Shades*, keeping his typical lightheartedness (*Driving Heat* 220).

- Rook jokes when a bullet hits a TARDIS bookshelf that it may get lost in time and space (*Driving Heat* 262).

- Rook plays six degrees of separation with the bad guys to determine how they met (*Driving Heat* 282).

- Rook suggests Zach Hammer wears an opera cape and sleeps in a coffin (*Driving Heat* 316).

- Rook jokes that his new bride's scars will make her look like Freddy Kruger. No one is amused (*Driving Heat* 317).

- Rook says being surrounded by snow made him say "Rosebud" and Beckett understood him (*Driving Heat* 324).

"Yes," Showers replied, impressed. "Unfortunately, there are about seventy-five million AK-47s being used right now in the world. The Soviet Union did a hell of a job exporting them to every terrorist and revolutionary group in the world, as well as every nut in the U.S. who found a way, legally or illegally, to get his hands on a firearm capable of firing six hundred rounds a minute."

"It sucks being Bambi nowadays." (*A Brewing Storm*, ch. 4)

➤ Castle describes growing up in the library reading "the classics: Edgar Allen Poe, Arthur Conan Doyle, and Carolyn Keene (What can I say? Nancy Drew was hot.)" (About the Author, *Deadly Storm*).

➤ Castle insists he attended Edgewyck Academy where he learned the Dark Arts in a *Harry Potter* reference (About the Author, *Deadly Storm*).

➤ "Who trained you, John Woo," Storm asks Strike (*Storm Season*).

➤ When asked if he's heard of Russian Ivan Azarov, Derrick Storm asks if he's the one who wrote science fiction books about robots, confusing him with Isaac Asimov (*A Calm Before Storm*).

➤ Trying to retire, Derrick Storm pictures a Michael Corleone joke about "Every time I think I'm out..." (*Unholy Storm*).

➤ Jones sends Derrick Storm James-Bond style spy gear but all in ACME boxes to reference the Roadrunner cartoons (*Storm Front* 84).

➤ Storm runs "past a quartet of TSA employees who were so concerned about ether or not people had their shoes on that they didn't immediately react to the most brazen security breech any of them had seen outside a training exercise" (*Storm Front* 291). He infiltrates a plane and defeats a hijacker, despite all the post-9/11 protocols.

➤ Storm appreciates the code name Mockingbird "because he so adored the Farrell Lee novel of a similar name" (*Wild Storm* 99).

➤ Storm calls his beloved .44 Magnum Dirty Harry, since it was popularized by Clint Eastwood.

➤ Storm begins an annoying movie quiz as a distraction (*Wild Storm* 209). He insists as a distraction a scientist fake epic "you've-just-watched-Kevin-Costner-in-*Waterworld*" seasickness" (*Wild Storm* 317).

❭ Storm calls a professor in their Egypt expedition "Professor Plum" (*Wild Storm* 195).

Other Pop Culture Homages

❭ Many entire episodes parody a show or genre, as described above. However, there are also smaller moments, described here.

❭ Hudson University is a fictional school that appears frequently in TV shows, originally invented as a fictional university for the DC Comics universe. In Castle, it appears in "The Mistress Always Spanks Twice," "A Deadly Game," "Close Encounters of the Murderous Kind," "Head Case," and "Dial M for Mayor."

❭ "Nanny McDead" (102) clearly references Nanny McPhee, in name if nothing else.

❭ "Hell Hath no Fury" (104) is from Shakespeare, suggesting a female criminal scorned.

❭ "A Death in the Family" (110) puns on the mob term but also discusses the death of Beckett's mother – the novel of this name describes a father's death.

❭ The plot of "The Double Down" (202) is based on Hitchcock's *Strangers on a Train,* with both the film and the novel by Patricia Highsmith getting a mention.

❭ "Vampire Weekend" (206) is named after a popular indie rock band.

❭ "Famous Last Words" (207) features the band The Blue Pill, a *Matrix* reference.

❭ In "A Rose For Everafter" (212) Castle's old flame's name Kyra Blaine is a nod to *Casablanca* as is the resolution of the love quadrangle and the quote: "Out of all the murders at all the weddings in all the cities in the world, you walk into mine."

❭ "The Mistress Always Spanks Twice" (216) is from *The Postman Always Rings Twice.* However, it has little in common with this noir film other than the murder.

❭ The pay phone at the beginning of "A Deadly Game," (224) is an homage to the spy movie *Three Days of the*

Condor. The clip that Castle is watching at the beginning is from *His Girl Friday.* The fake country Luvania was created for a survey in 2004 to see if people could identify which countries were joining the EU.

➤ Samuel Anders from *Battlestar Galactica* plays a romantic lead who doesn't work out, here and there.

➤ "He's Dead, She's Dead" (302) is from *He Said, She Said,* a 1991 American romantic comedy. As this is the psychic episode, it does explore different perspectives…

➤ "Punked" (304) references a practical joke reality show. Castle and his friends are certainly fooled several times over by the Victorian society and their ways.

➤ "Anatomy of a Murder" (305) is the title of a court drama movie starring Jimmy Stewart.

➤ 3XK (306) features a killer who's returned to his original hunting ground with a name echoing the Trinity Killer from *Dexter.*

➤ "Almost Famous" (307) is named for a film about a high-school boy profiling an up-and-coming rock band. Of course the hero here is an actor turned stripper and front man. It features a made-up businessman named Mandelay, a reference to *Seinfeld*'s fictional "Art Vandelay." "Almost Famous" also has a *Jersey Shore* reference where the names Sammy, Ronnie and Pauly are mentioned by a fake-tanned woman with a poof.

➤ "To Love and Die in LA" (322) has an obvious name homage. *To Live and Die in L.A.* is a 1985 American action thriller film with a sting by the Secret Service. The plot point of a voice lock opened by taping the CEO's voice during a date is from the movie *Sneakers.*

➤ In "Pretty Dead" (323), Baron's All American Beauty Pageant is put on by Victor Baron, a Donald Trump nod, complete with comb-over.

➤ In "Kick the Ballistics" (404) the scene where Esposito distracts the bodyguard in the library is based on a moment from *Beverly Hills Cop.*

❧ In "Cops and Robbers" (407) the robbers use the aliases Dr. Howser, Dr. Quinn, Dr. Huxtable (*The Cosby Show*), and Trapper John (*MASH*). There's also a mention of *Die Hard*, Dr. House, Dr. Shepherd (*Grey's Anatomy*), and Dr. Phil. Sal, the epileptic hostage, references *Dog Day Afternoon*.

❧ The episode "An Embarrassment of Bitches" (413) guest-stars Hilarie Burton, who played Peyton Sawyer in *One Tree Hill*. The episode title is probably a subtle reference to the aforementioned show and its initial title "An Unkindness of Ravens."

❧ "Dial M for Mayor" (412) is from *Dial M for Murder*, a Hitchcock film about an affair. This episode hints at one.

❧ "Once Upon a Crime" (417) references either the fairytale line or the fellow ABC show in an obvious nod. The story only uses fairytales to cover the crime, however.

❧ In "Once Upon a Crime," the victims were being blackmailed over a car accident they caused years ago, to the tune of *I Know What You Did Last Summer*.

❧ *Dead Again* (for "Undead Again" 422) is a 1991 British-American romantic mystery. The heroine has amnesia after trauma, a small parallel to the episode.

❧ "The Fast and the Furriest" (520) is the Bigfoot episode and thus has little in common with the action film *The Fast and the Furious*.

❧ In "The Squab and the Quail" (521), Ioan Gruffudd plays a genius-level inventor, billionaire and all-round innovator, much as he does when he plays Mr. Fantastic.

❧ In "The Human Factor" (523), Jared Stack mentions the local Counter-Terrorist Unit. His actor, Carlos Bernard, played CTU Agent Tony Almeida in 24.

❧ "The Good, The Bad & The Baby" (610) obviously riffs on "The Good The Bad and the Ugly," though there's little else in common with this Western.

❧ In "Limelight" (613), Alexandra Chando plays a child-star-gone-party-girl called Mandy Sutton. This nods to her last role before this, of Sutton Mercer.

\ "That '70s Show" (620) obviously references the popular retro show by that name. Castle and his friends also go retro in modern times. It also nods to its lead actress playing Nikki Heat.

\ "Law & Boarder" (621) riffs on *Law and Order*, punning on skateboards.

\ "Time of Our Lives" (706) is fittingly a love song. Castle and Beckett get married in this one.

\ "Bad Santa" (710) was a 2003 film about a naughty Santa, but the episode focuses on a murderer in a Santa suit, using little more connection than the pun.

\ "Private Eye Caramba!" (712) appears to be a pun on "Aye Carumba," Bart Simpson's classic expression. It's just a pun, one assumes.

\ "In Plane Sight" (721) takes place on a plane owned by Oceanic Air – the airline appearing on *Lost* and a few other shows that don't want to creep people out with an existing airline having troubles.

\ *In Plain Sight* is a drama following a U.S. Marshal as she ensures the safety of people in the Federal Witness Relocation Program "In Plane Sight" (721) simply appears a plane pun.

\ Robert Duncan (composer for season seven *Buffy*, *Tru Calling*, *Terriers*, and *Lie To Me*) composed the theme and incidental music on *Castle*.

\ Molly Quinn is a real-life cosplayer, famously playing a female Mal Reynolds during Comicon 2011.

\ The cast and crew nod to Ryan and Jenny being married in real life by creating a wedding website for them with the Devers' pictures.

\ Andrew Marlowe has suggested that the writer-muse balance of the show mirrors his relationship with fellow writer Terri Miller.

Castle on Superheroes

\ Fillion is one of four actors from *Firefly* who voiced superheroes on *Justice League* (2001), where he played the

Western-themed "Vigilante." The other Castle actors have had similar roles: Susan Sullivan played Queen Hippolyta on *Justice League*. Stana Katic voiced Lois Lane on *Superman Unbound* (2013) and Talia al Ghul in *Batman: Arkham City*. Molly Quinn voiced Supergirl on *Superman: Unbound*. Penny Johnson Jerald voiced Amanda Waller in *Justice League: Gods and Monsters Chronicles*. In addition, Susan Sullivan was in the pilot of *The Incredible Hulk*, and computer expert Tory was on *Agents of S.H.I.E.L.D.*

❋ When Beckett asked Castle how he knew Alexis missed him, Castle responds, "Spidey-sense" ("A Chill Goes through her Veins," 105).

> CASTLE: It reminds me of early Frank Miller.
> BECKETT: Which Frank – Epic Comic or Dark Horse years?
> CASTLE: Oh, my God. That is the sexiest thing I ever heard you say. I had no idea you were interested in comic books.
> BECKETT: Oh, Castle. The things you don't about me could fill a book ("Vampire Weekend," 206)

> BECKETT: I didn't think you were arrogant, Castle, I thought what you did was sweet and I will pay you back.
> CASTLE: Negative, Ghost Rider; small price to pay for a shot at your mother's killer. ("Sucker Punch," 213)

❋ Castle is called Captain America by a suspect ("Tick Tick Tick," 217)

> RYAN: Hey, we're thinking maybe you could talk to Montgomery about finding some room in the budget for those smart boards.
> BECKETT: Sure. While they're at it, maybe they could buy us batmobiles.
> ESPOSITO: That'd be cool.
> RYAN: Yeah. ("Boom," 218)

❋ Castle quips about the liquid nitrogen death, "The next time you decide to go all Mr. Freeze on someone, you should really clean up after yourself. We found your bowls in the sink" ("Food to Die For" 222).

❈ Castle observes, "We do have a box of bugs. It's the next best thing to a Bat Phone" ("Close Encounters of the Murderous Kind," 309)

❈ Castle references the magician's "fortress of solitude" and adds later, "Are you kidding me? He has an identical twin who wears glasses. That's the worst disguise since Clark Kent and you believe him?" ("Poof! You're Dead," 312)

❈ "You see, Wolverine, Batman, Betty and Veronica … sure, they were fine, in their day. But there is a new sheriff on the spinner rack. And his name is Derrick Storm," Castle brags ("Knockout," 324)

❈ Castle says his Spidey-sense is tingling and tells Alexis, "To quote Spider-Man, 'with great power comes great responsibility'. Not a lot of people get a chance to go to a school like this. You need to think about your dreams and what you want." ("Heroes and Villains," 402)

❈ On seeing a rapist bisected by a sword, Castle makes a Conan the Barbarian quip, then keeps going:

> CASTLE: Whoa. You smell that? Wafting scent of printed pages. Comicadia. Beckett, this place is the premier comic book shop. It's the Vatican to a Catholic. It's Mecca to a pilgrim. Upstream to a...
> BECKETT: I know, Castle! I bought my first comic here when I was 14. *Sin City. Dame to Kill For.*
> CASTLE: Hard core! Okay, whoa, okay. If you could be any comic book character in the world, who would you be?
> BECKETT: Elektra.
> CASTLE: Oh. A ruthless assassin who hides from her emotions.
> BECKETT: No, maybe it's because she's got badass ninja skills.
> Castle: Oh.
> BECKETT: What about you? Iron Man, Spider-Man? No wait, I know, Annoying Man.
> CASTLE: Try billionaire industrialist Bruce Wayne, aka, the Dark Knight. He's brooding, he'd handsome, and he has all the coolest toys.

BECKETT: Wow, digging deep on that one. ("Heroes and Villains," 402)

CASTLE: Conan probably saved her life. She doesn't want to throw him under the bus. Or under a Ben-Hur style chariot.
BECKETT: Yeah, but she saw the killer. Isn't she afraid for her life?
CASTLE: She probably knows he wasn't after her. Career felon smited in two? It's very Old Testament. This ... this plays like a vigilante killing. Think Dirty Harry with a sword. ("Heroes and Villains," 402)

BECKETT: You were eavesdropping?
CASTLE: Can I help it if I have superhuman Daredevil-like hearing? ("Heroes and Villains," 402)

BECKETT: NYPD! Do not move a muscle.
CASTLE: Unless you can move faster than a speeding bullet. ("Heroes and Villains," 402)

BECKETT: Sean Elt doesn't exist. His name is an alias.
CASTLE: Or a nom de plume, as we writers say. Though, why anyone would choose Sean Elt ... wait a minute. It's an anagram. Change the letters around and you get –
BECKETT: Stan Lee. Comic book genius.
CASTLE: (chuckles) Trust me. He is no Stan Lee. He's not even Sean Elt. ("Heroes and Villains," 402)

GATES: So he's a journalist like Peter Parker.
BECKETT: Actually, Peter Parker was a news photographer.
CASTLE: Yeah, our guy is more like Clark Kent. And he's mild mannered, just like... I... predicted. ("Heroes and Villains," 402)

"Heroes and Villains" involved a vigilante who dressed up as a superhero, so it was heavy on the Marvel Comics references, saying the killer drew his costume's inspiration from Spider-Man, Daredevil, Deadpool, and Black Panther. Disney owns ABC and Marvel, of course.

Remarks about Bruce Wayne and Clark Kent were much briefer.

- In the episode "Eye of the Beholder" (405) there's a thief named Serena Kaye, a reference to Catwoman, Selina Kyle. She even has a whip.
- Castle plays with the green screen, pretending to be a flying superhero ("Cloudy with a Chance of Murder," 502).
- When learning about a murder at the convention in "The Final Frontier" (506), Castle asks, "What happened, Doc Ock finally caught up with Spider-Man?" The episode actually aired just over a month before the start of *Superior Spider-Man.*
- Beckett quips that Castle should look like Dr. Manhattan on "The Final Frontier" (507).
- Castle says of a suspect, "Being a dancer could just … be his cover. And that way the lair could be like his Batcave" ("The Way of the Ninja," 618).

> BECKETT: Come on, Castle. You know that there are plenty of ways to access windows on high level floors without a fire escape.
> CASTLE: Yes. If you're Spiderman. ("Clear & Present Danger," 703)

- Rook proposes they "jump to Montrose's like Spider-Man. I mean the movie, not the musical" (*Heat Rises* 241).
- The first thing Rook says on coming out of his coma "was how pissed he was for not catching the bullet in his teeth, like the superhero he was, and spitting it back at the bad guy" (*Frozen Heat* 162)
- Rook quips about Beckett needing her Wonder Woman bracelets (*Deadly Heat* 208).
- When Rook boasts of saving the world unnoticed, Heat adds, "maybe you, Batman, and Lone Vengeance should form a support group" (*Deadly Heat* 278).
- Rook describes summoning Agent Bell with a Bat signal (*Driving Heat* 167).

- If a zip line wasn't used, Storm notes that the killer might have been Spider-Man (*Storm Front* 35)
- In the introduction to the comic *Deadly Storm*, Richard Castle explains, "Growing up without a father, my first real male role models were found in the pages of comic books. From a young age, I aspired to be one of those complicated, hard-charging heroes driven by circumstance and fate to do what was right, no matter the personal cost."
- Among various spy toys, Derrick Storm hopes for an invisible jet like Wonder Woman's (*Deadly Storm*).
- In his introduction to *Storm Season*, Castle describes Derrick Storm influences such as "Jim Steranko's bold and brassy take on Nick Fury."
- "Look out, Captain America. Stand aside, Hulk. There's a Storm coming," Storm quips (*Storm Season*).
- Being frisked, Derrick Storm makes a "Gigantor" quip (*A Calm Before Storm*).
- Confronting the villain, Fear, Storm thinks, "I feel ridiculous calling someone by a name like that. It's like wandering into the middle of a super hero movie" (*A Calm Before Storm*).
- Rook describes summoning Agent Bell with a Bat signal (*Driving Heat* 167).
- Rook quotes North by Northwest (*Driving Heat* 104).

Castle on *Star Wars*

> BECKETT: Yeah, I know. You were not-asking very loudly.
> CASTLE: I know. I'm like a Jedi like that.
> …
> BECKETT: Any more wisdom, Obi-Wan? ("Little Girl Lost," 109)

- Fillion models himself after Harrison Ford and adds, "I steal all the best stuff from him" (Nussbaum).
- Princess Leia escaping the Death Star is a reference to *Star Wars* ("Boom," 218).

- Castle complains to Beckett, "You pulled your Jedi mind trick on me" ("The Late Shaft," 220).
- "Now I finally know what Obi wan Kenobi felt like when Darth Vader turned on him," Castle says ("The Dead Pool," 321).
- Castle and his daughter have a beloved set of lightsabers.
- Castle says of Ryan's theory, "The student has become the master. Or at least, he tried. Actually, for a truly Castle-esque theory, it has to be fully thought through" ("Heroes and Villains," 402).
- Castle complains, "I didn't want to. Mother used her Jedi mind tricks on me" ("Secret's Safe with Me," 503).

> CASTLE: Ah, I used to come here a lot. Alexis and I would come here every year and dress up. You should have seen her looking like a little pint sized Princess Leia.
> BECKETT: And you were?
> CASTLE: Ah... Darth Vader, of course. ("The Final Frontier," 507)

- Castle wants a limited edition *Star Wars* lightsaber signed by George Lucas for Valentine's Day ("Reality Star Struck," 514).

> BECKETT: Castle! Castle, please. No more Wookie calls.
> CASTLE: It's not Wookie. I'm not doing Wookie. I can't do Wookie. Alexis does a really cute Wookie. ("The Fast and the Furriest," 520)

- When Nikki admits she's getting swept away in Rook's outlandish theories, he does a Darth Vader impression and calls her to "come to the Dark Side" (*Heat Rises* 265).
- Rook calls his physical therapist "the spawn of an unholy union between the Marquis de Sade and Darth Vader" (*Frozen Heat* 2).
- Rook says he slept with a reporter "once upon a time in a galaxy far far away" (*Frozen Heat* 81).
- Escorted by cops, Rook says, "I officially feel like I'm in *Star Wars*" (*Deadly Heat* 138).

↘ With a gas mask on, Rook breathes heavily and says, "Luke, I am your father" (*Deadly Heat* 272).

↘ When ordered to identify himself to US fighter jets, Storm explains that he's "just the orphaned nephew of a poor moisture farmer from the planet Tatooine" (*Wild Storm* 105).

Castle on *Star Trek*

↘ Many production staff members at *Castle* got their start with *Star Trek*. There are many visiting actors as well. Penny Johnson Jerald (Kasidy Yates) plays Chief Gates, Michael Dorn (Worf) is Beckett's psychiatrist, Tim Russ (Tuvok) plays Dr. Malcolm Wickfield, David Burke (Steven Price) appears as Chief John Brady, Robert Picardo (The Doctor) appeared as Doctor Death, and Ethan Phillips (Neelix) was in the episode "The Final Nail" (315). Penny Johnson Jerald also played Dobara on *TNG*'s "Homeward."

↘ Jonathan Frakes (William T Riker) directed the episodes "Kill the Messenger" (208) and "The Final Frontier" (506), and "The Fast and the Furriest" (520). He also directed Stana Katic in *The Librarian: The Curse of the Judas Chalice* (2008).

↘ Rene Echevarria of *TNG* & *DS9* wrote for the first two seasons.

↘ Castle says: "You have the bridge, Number One" (104).

↘ In "Ghosts" (108), the captain mentioned is Captain Pike.

↘ Nana Visitor (Major Kira on *Deep Space Nine*) guest stars in 413, "An Embarrassment of Bitches" as Dr. Patty Barker., who is in fact barkers.

↘ "The Final Frontier," (506) is clearly named for *Star Trek*. Its fictional show, Nebula 9, appears a mash-up between various versions of *Star Trek* and old-school *Battlestar Galactica*. Both get name-checks. The episode was directed by *ST: TNG* alum Jonathan Frakes (who cameoed) and featured Armin Shimerman (of *ST: DS9*). Castle imitates Kirk and Picard and chortles that the victim was killed by a phaser. Frakes plays Castle's Number One fan in a quick cameo.

> CASTLE: Oh! Um ... borg attack?
> BECKETT: Uh uh.
> CASTLE: Cylon skin job? Please say Number 6. ("The Final Frontier," 507)

✕ Castle announces he's checking his bucket list and asks, "Can either one of you introduce me to Bill Shatner?" ("Scared to Death," 517).

✕ "Wait a minute. Wait. We are demonstrating two dimensional thinking here, like Khan in *Star Trek 2: Wrath of Khan* ("Deep Cover," 612).

✕ Castle narrates: "Space - the final frontier. These are the voyages of Castle and Beckett. Their ongoing mission: to explore strange, new motives; to seek out new witnesses, new suspects for murder; to boldly go... Oh, right over here" ("The Wrong Stuff," 716).

✕ Rook met his top code breaker at a *Star Trek* convention (*Deadly Heat* 115).

Castle on *Sherlock Holmes*

✕ On their first meeting, Castle, an amateur, attaches himself to Beckett the brilliant detective, to partner with her and write about how she solves crimes, complete with the romance and sensational twist that Beckett and Holmes disapprove of.

✕ Castle also pulls a Sherlock-style scan of her background based on her appearance and watch in the pilot. He does something similar to 3XK.

> CASTLE: I could get a bloodhound. I could name him Sherlock, and then I could – I could bring him to crime scenes.
> BECKETT: No, you couldn't.
> CASTLE: Oh, what? It'd be adorable. I could get him to wear a little Sherlock hat, train him how to carry a little magnifying glass. Oh, see? Right there. Disapproving,

judgmental. You're totally my work wife. ("The Fifth Bullet," 211)

BECKETT: Okay Castle, I'm here; what's so important?
CASTLE: Your first clue is: "The Curious Incident of the Dog in the Nighttime".
BECKETT: Oh, Jeez, Castle, I haven't even had my coffee yet - (*he hands her a cup of coffee*) Thank you.
CASTLE: From the Sherlock Holmes stories, *Silver Blaze*. Holmes unmasks the murderer because of what didn't happen. The dog didn't bark. That's how he knew: the dog must have known the killer. ("Murder Most Fowl," 308)

- Slaughter calls Castle "Sherlock" for the entire episode ("Headhunters" 421).
- Castle says, "A game is afoot" (he means laser tag) ("Undead Again," 422)
- Castle is delighted when Beckett supports his private eye job with a gift of deerstalker hat and magnifying glass ("Castle, P.I.," 711).
- Castle plans to speak at the Sherlock Holmes Society in "In Plane Sight" (721).

Castle on *James Bond*

- The creator describes Castle's early novels as "noir James Bond" ("Murder They Wrote). His Storm novels definitely fit this.
- In "When the Bough Breaks" (205), Castle may be asked to write a "certain British agent," and he's desperately excited.
- "Secret underground headquarters? This is straight out of James Bond," Castle decides in the CIA storyline ("Pandora," 415).
- Castle's father basically is James Bond.

"Tada," said Rook. "From my new friends at the spy store, I got you this." He handed her a smart phone.
"That's it? Darling, I was hoping I could wear a wire."
"So *21 Jump Street*. This baby has state-of-the-art noise canceling and sound pickup. Just set it on the seat beside you and we'll hear everything. It also has a GPS. I had

better not need to track you, but if something happens, I want to be able to."
"I approve," Nikki said in a British accent. "Very thorough, Q." (*Heat Rises* 259)

❧ One of the suspects in *Heat Rises* insists he was at home because he had rented *Quantum of Solace* and mentions that Detective Heat would make a good Bond girl. Stana Katic played the intelligence agent at the end of *Quantum of Solace*.

❧ Rook mentions a Bond girl shaves Bond in *Skyfall*, and Nikki Heat gives Rook the same treatment (*Raging Heat* 64).

❧ Rook says the CEO Tangier Swift has a "James Bond villain boat" (*Driving Heat* 119).

❧ Rook loves Heat for her "excellent recall of Bond villainy" (*Driving Heat* 134).

❧ In James Bond style, Storm often partners with a good girl and bad girl. In *A Calm Before Storm* it's Clara Strike and Helen Pierce, both of the FBI. He waltzes with Clara in formal dress in *Unholy Storm*, to spy upon their adversary.

❧ Storm thinks of an adversary as "ugly James Bond" (*Deadly Storm*).

❧ In his introduction to *Storm Season*, Castle writes of seeing the James Bond film *Goldfinger* and getting "undeniably hooked." As he adds, "I knew what I was going to be when I grew up. I was going to be a spy."

❧ His handler Helen clobbers two guys and walks away, perfectly poised, high heels in hand (*Storm Season*).

Clara Strike had entered his life the next morning, appearing in his office with a sexy smile and a seductive invitation. Over breakfast, she'd explained that Grout was actually a CIA operative gone rogue. ... She'd asked for Storm's help and slipped him an unmarked envelope filled with hundreds. He'd been naïve that morning. He'd taken her money and jokingly asked her for a poison pill, a spy

camera, a pen that was a gun, and an invisible jet. She'd laughed. (*A Bloody Storm*, ch. 4)

Castle on Detective Stories

Andrew Marlowe explains:

> One of the reasons I wanted to do something like *Castle* is that I had grown up a fan of murder mysteries, not police procedurals. The ones on air – the *CSI*s and *Law & Order*s – approached subjects very darkly. I've always been a fan of shows like *Moonlighting* and thought taking that and putting it in a [romantic] sparks-fly arena could be a lot of fun. (Ng)

Castle plays poker with famous mystery writers, starting in episode one. Real-life writers Stephen J. Cannell, James Patterson, Dennis Lehane, and Michael Connelly appear as themselves. On September 30, 2010, Cannell died in real life, and the characters kept his chair empty for a year. The real *Heat Rises* afterward reads: "There is an empty chair at my weekly poker game. Connelly, Lehane, and I decided to keep dealing you in, Mr. Cannell, and somehow you keep winning. As it was in life, my friend and mentor. You had me at Rockford" (304).

The 12th Precinct of the NYPD is the same precinct that the 1970s police sitcom *Barney Miller* was set in. (and in a two-part episode they were made into a homicide-only unit.)

When Sorenson questions Castle as to why he doesn't "shadow a real detective", Castle responds by telling him that "the ones on TV seem awfully fixated on their sunglasses." This is most likely a reference to the *CSI: Miami* character Horatio Caine (played by David Caruso), which airs at the same time as "*Castle*" in the US ("Little Girl Lost," 109).

(Lanie is dusting for fingerprints)

CASTLE: You want me to put on some music? Whenever they do this sorta thing on CSI, they always do it to music in poorly lit rooms...kinda reminds me of porn.
BECKETT: Zip it, Castle. ("Deep in Death," 201)

CASTLE: We make a pretty good team, you know. Like Starsky and Hutch, Tango and Cash... Turner and Hooch.
BECKETT: You know, now that you mention it, you do remind me a little of Hooch. ("Deep in Death," 201)

↘ According to Andrew Marlowe's commentary, after Castle says that this is the coolest case ever, Montgomery was supposed to say "You think this is cool? Do you have any idea the amount of paperwork this just created? See, this is why I can't watch action movies. Shootouts, car chases, explosions. I sit in the theater and all I can think about is the damn paperwork someone's gonna have to fill out." But they had to cut it because the episode was running long. ("A Deadly Game," 224)

CASTLE: Sure. Wow, nice. You know I was thinking on the way over here. All the best cops, *Dirty Harry*, *Cobra*, guy from *Police Academy* who makes the helicopter noises. They all have one thing in common.
BECKETT: Plucky sidekick?
CASTLE: That and they do their very best work after they've been booted off a case. ("Knockout," 324)

↘ "The Blue Butterfly" (414) is a noir homage with many references. Castle and the other characters act noir-style, with Castle adding, "I mean, this guy sounds like a hard boiled PI right out of a Raymond Chandler novel."

CASTLE: Hey there.
BECKETT: I feel like I just walked into a bad episode of *Miami Vice*.
CASTLE: Okay, first, there are no bad episodes of *Miami Vice*. Second, who died? ("The Limey," 420)

↘ Castle's season seven vanishing with amnesia (blamed on a publicity stunt) echoes the real Agatha Christie.

➤ When Castle goes to second grade to investigate a murder, the teacher calls him Colombo ("Child's Play," 704).

> CASTLE: This feels different, doesn't it?
> BECKETT: What does?
> CASTLE: Rolling up to a crime scene as a married couple. Like Nick and Nora Charles.
> BECKETT: Ooh, like MacMillan and wife.
> CASTLE: Hart to Hart.
> BECKETT: Turner and Hooch.
> CASTLE: Turner and Hooch aren't even married.
> BECKETT: Yeah, but you still remind me a little of Hooch.
> ("Kill Switch," 708)

➤ Castle relaxes in his office, in detective noir style – feet propped up on his desk and a glass of scotch in his hand. Sitting, he listens to a voiceover of himself he's recorded: "We were all after the same thing: justice. Trouble is, when it came to me, Lady Justice had different plans. While Beckett and the boys closed in on the killer I'd been kicked to the gutter like yesterday's trash. It just didn't seem fair" ("Castle, P.I.," 711)

➤ The following episode also shows him doing this narration. He adds, "A purse? I'm sorry, this is not just an ordinary purse. This is a diamond encrusted clutch. It's on par with the priceless Maltese Falcon and I am on the trail" ("Private Eye Caramba!" 712).

➤ "You know, a little red hair and you could be that CSI guy," Rook tells Nikki Heat (*Naked Heat* 35).

> One of the messages was from the travel agent I referred Captain Montrose to. She said she can't believe the news, especially since she just talked to him yesterday. He booked an island cruise."
> "Yesterday?" When she affirmed, he clapped his hands once and said, "John le Carre!" He read her bewilderment and added, "You know John le Carre, right? *Spy Who Came in from the Cold, Constant Gardener...* Oh, and *A Perfect Spy* – transcendent, best ever! But...John le Carre's first novel was *Call for the Dead*. This secret agent is found.

Suicide, they say. But that theory unravels because he left a wake-up call the night before. See the logic? Who leaves a wake-up call if he plans to kill himself?"
"Right," she said. "And who books a cruise? Especially Montrose." (*Heat Rises* 147)

\ Describing internet research, Rook says he's "Not exactly Philip Marlowe gumshoeing bad guys in *The Big Sleep*, but it has its rewards. I can snack, for instance" (*Heat Rises* 201).

\ Rook suggest international jewel thieves are seeking two halves of a treasure map "Like *The Pink Panther*," Malcolm says (*Frozen Heat* 69)

\ Rook is excited that they've lost internet at the precinct. He compares them to *77 Sunset Strip*. Ochoa wants to be Starsky and Hutch (*Driving Heat* 130).

\ In his introduction to *Storm Season*, Castle describes Derrick Storm influences including Raymond Chandler and Mickey Spillane.

\ Storm and his handler debate who's Face and who's Murdock (*Storm Season*).

\ At book's end, Storm wants to call Strike "Deep Throat." She refuses (*Storm Season*).

\ Storm and Strike meet in the bar of the Winter Palace in Luxor, Egypt, where Agatha Christie was said to have written *Death on the Nile* (*Wild Storm* 171).

The *Castle* actors all made their rounds on police shows:
\ Stana Katic appeared on *CSI: Miami*, *ER*, *24*, *Alias*, *The Closer*, *Dragnet*, *JAG*, and *The Shield*.

\ Jon Huertas (Javier Esposito) is a real life Air Force veteran. Many of his onscreen credits are of Marines: Ramirez, a Marine Recon Sniper Spotter in *JAG*, Recon Marine Sergeant Espera in *Generation Kill*, retired Marine Sergeant Jack Kale in *NCIS*. He also appeared on *CSI* and *Terminator: The Sarah Connor Chronicles* alongside *Firefly* alum Summer Glau.

- Seamus Dever (Kevin Ryan) did *CSI*, *CSI; Miami*, *CSI: NY*, *NCIS*, and *JAG*.
- Ruben Santiago-Hudson (Montgomery) had multiple roles on *Law and Order*, and appeared on *Law & Order: Special Victims Unit* and *NYPD Blue*.
- Tamala Jones appeared on *CSI: Miami*.
- Penny Johnson Jerald appeared on *24*, *Bones*, *NCIS*, *Law and Order*, *24*, and *Colombo*.
- Scott Paulin (Beckett's father) was on *JAG*, *24*, and *NCIS: LA*.

Castle on Thrillers

- In a subtle nod to Hitchcock; the picture behind Castle's writing desk is a down-shot photo of a square spiral staircase, similar to the shots from *Vertigo*.

> CASTLE: Could it be that easy? "You take mine, I'll take yours."
> ESPOSITO: What are you getting at, Castle?
> CASTLE: Strangers on a Train.
> RYAN: The Hitchcock movie?
> CASTLE: I'm partial to the novel by Patricia Highsmith, but yes. 202

- Castle announces, "Wait, I know what this is. Lawyer puts criminal in jail, criminal feels wronged, criminal kills lawyer. It's *Cape Fear*" ("Love Me Dead," 209).
- In "Tick Tick Tick," taxidermy is referred to as Norman Bates' favorite pastime (A *Psycho* reference) (217).
- Castle says, "Stephen King wrote stories of bloodthirsty cars and sold millions of copies. I figure, why be limited by logic?" ("The Fifth Bullet," 211).
- "A Deadly Affair" (301) has a scene from *The Man with the Golden Gun*, with Castle in the hall of mirrors in a pistol fight.
- Two suspects in "Countdown" (317) are named Evan Bauer and Jack Cochran. In addition to the obvious

reference to *24*, Robert Cochran and Evan Katz helped write, create, and produce the series.

"Do you realize what this means? We're spies. This is like being in a Jason Bourne movie, only he's the bad guy and the CIA are the good guys," Castle decides in the CIA storyline ("Pandora," 415).

> CASTLE: Well, it was a nine man team. There's only eight here. He must be the missing lawyer.
> BECKETT: Or he's not a lawyer at all.
> CASTLE: Or he is a lawyer but ... he operates behind the scenes. He would be um ... of council. Like Michael Clayton. ("After the Storm," 501)

> CASTLE: Someone had a priest assassinated? It's like a Vatican conspiracy. Ah, it's like *The Da Vinci Code*.
> BECKETT: Or ... not. ("After Hours," 508)

> BECKETT: No. I mean, why would Walter help Billy kill his wife? Yeah, sure, they're friends, but what was in it for Walter?
> CASTLE: It's not like they agreed to kill each other's wives like *Strangers on a Train*. Though what we saw of Walter's relationship, I'm sure he thought about it. ("Significant Others," 510)

"Three deaths, all leading back to the law firm of Banks and Bauer. Is it just me, or is this starting to smell like a John Grisham novel? A single car accident with no witnesses? Guys, this is a classic conspiracy cover up," Castle says ("Watershed," 524).

> CASTLE: Which is why it was used to kill him. Lance was murdered because he's the Spanish Jason Bourne.
> BECKETT: Why, Castle? Because a B action movie star in a kimono said so?
> CASTLE: Because it makes sense. Lance was drawing on his experience as a ruthless CNI operative to play action heroes. But his shadowy past caught up with him. Maybe it was revenge for a hit he did back in the day. Kill him the way he killed. ("Last Action Hero," 709)

❖ "My guess is we're dealing with some kind of big-money fixer. A shadowy, gun for hire Michael Clayton type," Castle speculates ("Castle, P.I.," 711)

❖ Rook admits his latest theory is "a little *Mission: Impossible*" but he's right (*Heat Rises* 237).

❖ Rook compares Nikki's mom to Arnold in *True Lies* or Julia Child in World War II (*Deadly Heat* 24).

❖ Rook calls the Homeland Security head "Jack Bauer" and requests to meet Dr. Strangelove in their underground lair (*Deadly Heat* 24).

❖ Rook calls his spy trip to Paris "like a le Carré novel" (*Deadly Heat* 50).

❖ Rook quotes North by Northwest (*Driving Heat* 104).

Castle and *Firefly*

❖ Fillion is best known for his role in the sci-fi series *Firefly*, the Joss Whedon cult legend that was axed after a single season. (For a 10-year-anniversary panel at Comic-Con, 10,000 fans lined up around the block.) (Sheffield)

❖ Fillion adds, "The first time *Castle* put on gloves at a crime scene, they were blue: like "two two, hands of blue" I didn't ask, I just did it, and people live for that stuff. In the Halloween episode, I hid a prop from *Firefly* on the set [the catalyzer]. I put it on Twitter: can you spot it?" (Nussbaum).

❖ Jose Molina (from *Firefly*) is another recurring writer.

❖ Castle, discussing the prospect of his ex-wife Meredith moving back to New York, says that it would be a "very special brand of Hell" ("Always Buy Retail," 106). In *Firefly*, Malcolm Reynolds is threatened by the Preacher with the "very special level of Hell" if he takes sexual advantage of a young girl.

❖ Quoting *Firefly*, Castle says: "I really am ruggedly handsome, aren't I?" ("Always Buy Retail," 106). Ryan, looking at a cardboard cut-out of Castle, decides, "He really is ruggedly handsome. ("A Deadly Affair," 301)

CASTLE: Well I know who the killer is. Did you see how that gorilla looked at me?
BECKETT: Yeah, I think it was lust actually, Castle. You are ruggedly handsome. ("The Fast and the Furriest," 520)

Castle also calls himself this in "Scared to Death" (517). The seventh season finale uses this line repeatedly as Castle tires to pick an author photo.

❯ Rook calls himself "ruggedly handsome" in *Heat Rises* (164).

❯ Rook decides if his nose is broken "I'll be even more rugged in my rugged handsomeness" (*Frozen Heat* 123).

❯ A female fan wants Rook to tweet their picture and add the hashtag "ruggedly handsome" (*Deadly Heat* 7).

❯ Nikki Heat thinks of his "ruggedly handsome mouth" (*Raging Heat* 161).

❯ Nikki thinks of Castle this way (*Driving Heat* 53), Rook says it (*Driving Heat* 234), and finally she says it to him (*Driving Heat* 324).

❯ Everyone in *Storm Front* calls Derrick Storm "ruggedly handsome" including the narrator. It appears in the first scene and the last, among others. This is how he can be identified by readers while undercover. It's also dropped in *A Raging Storm* (ch. 4). Clara Strike calls Storm this (*Wild Storm* 194).

❯ When Castle and Beckett arrive at a party in "Home is Where the Heart Stops" (107), the Mayor greets Castle with, "Why didn't you tell me you were gonna be at this shindig?" This quietly salutes the *Firefly* episode "Shindig," in which Fillion's character went undercover to an elegant party, as he's doing now.

❯ Nathan Fillion wears his *Firefly* outfit as his "space cowboy" Halloween costume. His daughter points out he wore it five years ago (the movie timing) and adds, "Don't you think you should move on?" ("Vampire Weekend," 206). Castle's co-worker tells him he holds a fine shindig at his Halloween party

- In "Fool Me Once" (204), Castle fixates on the "Hands of Blue" blue gloves.

- Castle recycles the line "Yeah, you better run" in similar circumstances ("The Mistress Always Spanks Twice," 216).

- In "Boom" (218), after shooting Dunn, Castle says, "I was aiming for his head." This is a quote from *Firefly*'s "The Train Job."

- Castle knows Chinese from a "TV show I used to love" ("Close Encounters of the Murderous Kind," 309)

- Beckett wants something to make her feel "shiny," a *Firefly* line ("Lucky Stiff," 314).

- "You haven't heard of the Serenity?" Castle's mom asks innocently about a spa ("Setup," 316). He looks up, startled.

- Gina Torres guest-stars in "Reality Star Struck" (514).

- Andy Umberger played D'Hoffryn on *Buffy*, Dr. Ronald Meltzer in *Angel*'s "I Fall To Pieces" and the Dortmunder Captain in the *Firefly* pilot. He also appeared on "Head Case" (403).

> CASTLE: (as the dinosaur, with an accent) You are very beautiful, Nikki Heat. It is too bad I have to kill you now. (as the Barbie) Uglier men than you have tried, Draco. (the Barbie slaps the dinosaur, then switches to voice the dinosaur) You have slapped me. Now I will have to –
> MARTHA: Playing with dolls, are we?
> CASTLE: These are action figures. ("Headhunters" 421)

It's especially appropriate that he's doing this in the episode where Adam Baldwin guest-stars, as Wash played with dinosaurs as well.

- Baldwin appeared in the fourth season as Detective Ethan Slaughter, a rough cop with crude methods (much like Jayne) whom Castle does a ride along with in "Headhunters" (421). Significantly, he forces Castle to give him his brown coat.

The episode "The Final Frontier" (506) has Castle investigating a murder at SuperNova Con. When Castle hears there has been a murder there, he exclaims, "Shiny!" There, *Nebula 9* resembles many science fiction shows, but its "Captain Max Reynard," visits to the planet Ariel, Lieutenant Chloe (for first mate Zoe), and vicious cannibalistic "kreavers" are *Firefly*-specific. Finally, Nebula 9's astern closely resembles that of *Serenity*. Castle thinks *Nebula 9* is silly, as it only lasted twelve episodes, ten years previously, though there's talk of bringing it back as a film. He mentions he's a Joss Whedon fan. The "Silk trigger active return bolt laser pistol" from the *Firefly* episode "Heart of Gold" can be seen on Armin Shimerman's design table.

Rook visits a strip club and the owner eyes him:

> "Sure, guess I could give you a bullwhip and a fedora. We'd market you as Indiana Bones. Or maybe go sci-fi. You sorta look like that guy who roamed outer space everybody's so crazy about."
> "Malcolm Reynolds?" asked Rook.
> "Who? ... No, I'm thinking we give you a space helmet and some assless chaps and call you ... Butt Rogers. (*Heat Rises* 244)

In *Frozen Heat* and *Deadly Heat*, the extra detectives Nikki brings into the case are Malcolm and Reynolds. In the first, they call attention to their blue gloves by calling themselves the Blue Hands Group (257).

Rook says, "I can't put my finger on it, but there's something I like about Malcolm and Reynolds" (*Frozen Heat* 123).

Searching the world for the answer to a code "Rook even investigated a site devoted to the mutt languages of some TV series called *Firefly*" (*Deadly Heat* 88).

Rook suggests many action figures he might resemble, finishing with "I know. *Firefly*, I sort of feel a connection to him. Can't explain it" (*Raging Heat* 15).

Castle and Fillion's Other Shows

❧ Castle's book *Hell Hath No Fury* is about "angry wiccans out for blood," an accurate description of season six of *Buffy* ("Flowers for Your Grave," 101).

❧ In "Nanny McDead" (102), Castle reminisces about how he "got the plot of (his) first novel by watching *One Life to Live*." Nathan Fillion's first TV role was Joey Buchanan on *One Life To Live*. Fillion actually dropped out of college to do that show (Bierly et al.). Fillion adds, "There was a line in the show about him watching a soap opera, and I said, could we make it *OLTL*?" (Nussbaum).

> Though, at other times, just being Nathan Fillion has been enough to get the job. Recounts Lost exec producer Damon Lindelof, who cast the actor in an episode in 2006: "We were looking for someone charismatic and instantly likable to play the one guy who we would believe Kate would stop running from the law to marry, and I remember saying, 'We need to get a Nathan Fillion type!' to our casting director, who thought for a moment, then said, 'What about Nathan Fillion?'" The end result, in Lindelof's words: "It was rad." (Bierly et al.)

❧ Castle's first wife, Meredith, is played by Darby Stanchfield, who also played his wife in *Waitress*.

❧ In walking to drop off ransom money, Castle tells Beckett, "I'm five by five" ("Little Girl Lost," 109). This was Faith's favorite line in *Buffy the Vampire Slayer*. Nathan Fillion played a season seven villain on *Buffy*. Writer Jose Molina in season two was a *Buffy* alum.

❧ *Buffy* actors Marc Blucas, Ethan Erickson, Leonard Roberts, Bailey Chase and D.B. Woodside guest-star. Principal Snyder appears in the *Firefly* episode.

❧ *Dollhouse* actor Reed Diamond guest stars in "When the Bough Breaks," (205). A Whedon alum, he later appeared with Fillion in *Much Ado About Nothing*. *Dollhouse* is another Whedon product.

❧ Castle mentions TV series *Alias* and *Desperate Housewives* with regards to Helen Parker and Sarah Reid (210). Stana

Katic played a stewardess on *Alias* and Nathan had a recurring role on *Desperate Housewives* as Adam Mayfield.

\ Dina Meyer (Lady Irena of "The Mistress Always Spanks Twice," 216) and Nathan Fillion played husband and wife in the short-lived TV show *Miss Match* (2003).

\ Dana Delany in "Tick Tick Tick"/"Boom!" (217-218) played Fillion's wife on *Desperate Housewives*. This gives a new layer of meaning to Nathan's line "Except for my second wife, this is the most sexless relationship I've been in."

\ Gil Birmingham, Cacaw Te, played a bodyguard whose lifeforce was drained by the mummy in *Buffy* episode "Inca Mummy Girl" (204) and returned for "Wrapped Up in Death" (219).

\ Attempting molecular gastronomy in his home kitchen, Castle's costume, voice, demeanor and apparent ambitions, echo Nathan Fillion's nemesis (played by Neil Patrick Harris) in *Dr. Horrible's Sing-Along Blog*, ("Food to Die For," 222). He has an evil laugh, too.

\ The pastry chef – Spike Ridenhauer in "Food to Die For" (222) may be a Buffy reference.

\ Xander Doyle's name is a yet another reference to *Buffy the Vampire Slayer* (and its spin-off *Angel*), through the characters Xander and Doyle. Both were handsome "everyman" characters who the audience could identify with, and who kept the team together emotionally, like Castle ("A Deadly Affair" 301).

> CASTLE: Well, maybe he's old school? Didn't want to give up the badge he built his career on.
> LANIE: Castle, he's mid-20s.
> CASTLE: You ever heard of a brilliant doctor named Doogie Howser? ("Almost Famous," 306)

\ Doogie Howser's actor, Neil Patrick Harris, was Fillion's co-star in *Doctor Horrible*.

\ When they find the secret passage in the basement of The Old Haunt, Castle exclaims 'blam said the lady' ("Last

Call," 310). His catchphrase (that Nathan Fillion invented) is normally 'bam said the lady'. He also uses it in "The Double Down" (202).

> ESPOSITO: Perfect match.
> CASTLE: Bam said the costume lady.
> RYAN: Ooh ... she's not the only lady saying bam when it comes to Bobby Stark. ("Pretty Dead," 323)

Castle amends this to "Zap said the lady" on "The Final Frontier" (507).

➘ Apparently the scriptwriter for *Heat Wave* is Spike Rosenberg, named for Buffy characters Spike and Willow Rosenberg. Natalie Rhodes, the actress playing Nikki Heat, notes: "Spike Rosenberg is one of my favorite screenwriters. You know he did the un-credited final pass on *Hell's Crawlspace*" ("Nikki Heat," 311). This may also nod to Whedon's many uncredited script touch-ups.

➘ The episode "One Life to Lose" (318) is an homage to Fillion's first role in *One Life to Live*.

➘ "Talk about coming full circle – Peter and I shared a dressing room on *One Life to Live*," says Fillion when Peter Parros guest-starred in "The Dead Pool" (321).

➘ Kristen Lehman costarred with him in *Drive* before appearing in "Eye of the Beholder" (405)

➘ Beckett references "crazy wiccan powers," suggesting Willow from *Buffy* ("A Dance with Death," 418).

➘ *Dollhouse*'s Tahmoh Penikett plays the assassin who nearly kills Beckett at the end of season four. *Dollhouse* is even a show about government conspiracies.

➘ In "Time Will Tell" (605), when Simon disappears from lockup, Beckett asks where he is, Castle responds with "Not where, when," a modified version of Inspector Spacetime's catchphrase. Of course, Fillion guest-starred on *Community*.

➘ In "Room 147" (616), Castle mentions how he likes "the weird stuff." This works as a *Doctor Horrible* joke.

- Around the time of "That 70s Show" (620) Fillion plays a cop in old-fashioned dress in Joss Whedon's *Much Ado About Nothing*.
- Fillion appeared in *Blast from the Past* (1999). It's no wonder he keeps finding time travelers in his investigations.
- Fillion was Kevin Callis on *Lost*. In season seven, he flies on *Oceanic Airlines* from the show ("In Plane Sight," 721).
- Like Castle and Fillion, Rook is active on Twitter (*Deadly Heat* 216).

Other Actor and Creator Allusions

- Like his actor, Jon Huertas, Esposito is a military veteran.
- Susan Sullivan has a theater and Broadway background, like her character.
- Seamus Dever (Kevin Ryan) has been married to his wife on *Castle*, Juliana Dever, since May 27, 2006.
- The David Mamet reference ("A Death in the Family," 110) nods to Stana Katic's appearance on his TV series *The Unit*.
- In "Deep in Death" (201), Beckett discusses how she sometimes visits Little Odessa (Brighton Beach, Brooklyn). When she was Hana Gitelman on *Heroes*, she tended to be in Odessa, Texas.
- In "Deep in Death" (201), Castle grants Alexis permission to see *Fame* with her boyfriend "but I have dibs on *A Christmas Carol*." Alexis' actor, Molly Quinn, did voicework for the film.
- "Vampire Weekend" (206) has Esposito dress as a marine and Ryan as a doctor, nodding to their past television roles.
- In "The Third Man" (214), there is a close up shot of the "most eligible bachelors" on the cover of the *Ledger*. The names of some of the writing staff have been placed under several of the photos. Series creator Andrew Marlowe is number eight, beating Castle.

❯ While Agent Shaw claimed to Castle that the "Re-capitator case" in Phoenix, AZ had been hers, it in fact belonged to Moira Kirland the writer of both this episode of *Castle* & the Supervising Producer and writer of *Medium* ("Tick Tick Tick," 217).

❯ As Martha packs to move in with Chet, she nostalgically watches the pilot of *The Incredible Hulk*. The character onscreen, Dr. Elaina Marks, was played by Susan Sullivan (217).

❯ The scene at the carousel "with the smoke and the flashlights and the weirdly cheerful music" was a deliberate shout-out to *The X-Files,* made by Rob Bowman, producer on both shows ("Tick Tick Tick," 217)

❯ Susan Sullivan was reunited with her *Falcon Crest* co-star, William R. Moses, in "Overkill" (223).

❯ Seamus Dever (Kevin Ryan) played Dr. Ian Devlin on *General Hospital* (2008), involved with a drug-importing scheme. The *Grey's Anatomy* (305) episode certainly may be an homage.

❯ Beckett admires comic book writer/artist Frank Miller. In fact, Stana Katic appeared in Frank Miller's directorial debut *The Spirit* (2008).

❯ Scott Paulin (Beckett's father) amusingly was in *Turner & Hooch* (1989) and *The Right Stuff* (1983), both of which get memorable show references.

❯ Chris McKenna was replaced by Fillion on *One Life to Live*. He appeared on "The Final Frontier" (507).

> CASTLE: You know, the majority of this nation's comedy was born in the mind of these geniuses. (he spots a poster of the current writers) Except for this season. Those guys suck.
> BECKETT: Yeah, they were terrible. ("Dead from New York," 722)

➤ Katic's film, *Sister Cities* (made before season eight), deals with a mother's death, an event that consumes Beckett's life.

➤ One of the suspects in *Heat Rises*, the third book, mentions as his alibi that he was at home, because he had rented *Quantum of Solace*, and mentions that Detective Heat would make a good Bond girl. Stana Katic played the intelligence agent at the end of *Quantum of Solace*.

Episode List

Season 1

Episode #		Air Date	Title
1	101	09/Mar/2009	Flowers for Your Grave
2	102	16/Mar/2009	Nanny McDead
3	103	23/Mar/2009	Hedge Fund Homeboys
4	104	30/Mar/2009	Hell Hath No Fury
5	105	06/Apr/2009	A Chill Goes through her Veins
6	106	13/Apr/2009	Always Buy Retail
7	107	20/Apr/2009	Home is Where the Heart Stops
8	108	27/Apr/2009	Ghosts
9	109	04/May/2009	Little Girl Lost
10	110	11/May/2009	A Death in the Family

Season 2

Episode #		Air Date	Title
11	201	21/Sep/2009	Deep in Death
12	202	28/Sep/2009	The Double Down
13	203	05/Oct/2009	Inventing the Girl
14	204	12/Oct/2009	Fool Me Once...
15	205	19/Oct/2009	When the Bough Breaks
16	206	26/Oct/2009	Vampire Weekend
17	207	02/Nov/2009	Famous Last Words
18	208	09/Nov/2009	Kill the Messenger
19	209	16/Nov/2009	Love Me Dead
20	210	23/Nov/2009	One Man's Treasure
21	211	07/Dec/2009	The Fifth Bullet
22	212	11/Jan/2010	A Rose for Everafter
23	213	18/Jan/2010	Sucker Punch
24	214	25/Jan/2010	The Third Man
25	215	08/Feb/2010	Suicide Squeeze
26	216	08/Mar/2010	The Mistress Always Spanks Twice
27	217	22/Mar/2010	Tick, Tick, Tick... (1)
28	218	29/Mar/2010	Boom! (2)
29	219	05/Apr/2010	Wrapped Up in Death

30	220	12/Apr/2010	The Late Shaft
31	221	19/Apr/2010	Den of Thieves
32	222	03/May/2010	Food to Die For
33	223	10/May/2010	Overkill
34	224	17/May/2010	A Deadly Game

Season 3

Episode #		Air Date	Title
35	301	20/Sep/2010	A Deadly Affair
36	302	27/Sep/2010	He's Dead, She's Dead
37	303	04/Oct/2010	Under the Gun
38	304	11/Oct/2010	Punked
39	305	18/Oct/2010	Anatomy of a Murder
40	306	25/Oct/2010	3XK
41	307	01/Nov/2010	Almost Famous
42	308	08/Nov/2010	Murder Most Fowl
43	309	15/Nov/2010	Close Encounters of the Murderous Kind
44	310	06/Dec/2010	Last Call
45	311	03/Jan/2011	Nikki Heat
46	312	10/Jan/2011	Poof! You're Dead
47	313	24/Jan/2011	Knockdown
48	314	07/Feb/2011	Lucky Stiff
49	315	14/Feb/2011	The Final Nail
50	316	21/Feb/2011	Setup (1)
51	317	28/Feb/2011	Countdown (2)
52	318	21/Mar/2011	One Life to Lose
53	319	28/Mar/2011	Law & Murder
54	320	04/Apr/2011	Slice of Death
55	321	11/Apr/2011	The Dead Pool
56	322	02/May/2011	To Love and Die in L.A.
57	323	09/May/2011	Pretty Dead
58	324	16/May/2011	Knockout

Season 4

Episode #		Air Date	Title
59	401	19/Sep/2011	Rise
60	402	26/Sep/2011	Heroes & Villains
61	403	03/Oct/2011	Head Case
62	404	10/Oct/2011	Kick the Ballistics

63	405	17/Oct/2011	Eye of the Beholder
64	406	24/Oct/2011	Demons
65	407	31/Oct/2011	Cops & Robbers
66	408	07/Nov/2011	Heartbreak Hotel
67	409	21/Nov/2011	Kill Shot
68	410	05/Dec/2011	Cuffed
69	411	09/Jan/2012	Till Death Do Us Part
70	412	16/Jan/2012	Dial M for Mayor
71	413	23/Jan/2012	An Embarrassment of Bitches
72	414	06/Feb/2012	The Blue Butterfly
73	415	13/Feb/2012	Pandora (1)
74	416	20/Feb/2012	Linchpin (2)
75	417	27/Feb/2012	Once Upon a Crime
76	418	19/Mar/2012	A Dance With Death
77	419	26/Mar/2012	47 Seconds
78	420	02/Apr/2012	The Limey
79	421	16/Apr/2012	Headhunters
80	422	30/Apr/2012	Undead Again
81	423	07/May/2012	Always

Season 5

Episode #		Air Date	Title
82	501	24/Sep/2012	After the Storm
83	502	01/Oct/2012	Cloudy With a Chance of Murder
84	503	08/Oct/2012	Secret's Safe With Me
85	504	15/Oct/2012	Murder, He Wrote
86	505	29/Oct/2012	Probable Cause
87	506	05/Nov/2012	The Final Frontier
88	507	12/Nov/2012	Swan Song
89	508	19/Nov/2012	After Hours
90	509	03/Dec/2012	Secret Santa
91	510	07/Jan/2013	Significant Others
92	511	14/Jan/2013	Under the Influence
93	512	21/Jan/2013	Death Gone Crazy
94	513	04/Feb/2013	Recoil
95	514	11/Feb/2013	Reality Star Struck
96	515	18/Feb/2013	Target (1)
97	516	25/Feb/2013	Hunt (2)
98	517	18/Mar/2013	Scared to Death

99	518	25/Mar/2013	The Wild Rover
100	519	01/Apr/2013	The Lives of Others
101	520	15/Apr/2013	The Fast and the Furriest
102	521	22/Apr/2013	The Squab and the Quail
103	522	29/Apr/2013	Still
104	523	06/May/2013	The Human Factor
105	524	13/May/2013	Watershed

Season 6

Episode #		Air Date	Title
106	601	23/Sep/2013	Valkyrie (1)
107	602	30/Sep/2013	Dreamworld (2)
108	603	07/Oct/2013	Need to Know
109	604	14/Oct/2013	Number One Fan
110	605	21/Oct/2013	Time Will Tell
111	606	28/Oct/2013	Get a Clue
112	607	04/Nov/2013	Like Father, Like Daughter
113	608	11/Nov/2013	A Murder is Forever
114	609	18/Nov/2013	Disciple
115	610	25/Nov/2013	The Good, the Bad & the Baby
116	611	06/Jan/2014	Under Fire
117	612	13/Jan/2014	Deep Cover
118	613	20/Jan/2014	Limelight
119	614	03/Feb/2014	Dressed to Kill
120	615	17/Feb/2014	Smells Like Teen Spirit
121	616	24/Feb/2014	Room 147
122	617	03/Mar/2014	In the Belly of the Beast
123	618	17/Mar/2014	The Way of the Ninja
124	619	24/Mar/2014	The Greater Good
125	620	21/Apr/2014	That '70s Show
126	621	28/Apr/2014	Law & Boarder
127	622	05/May/2014	Veritas
128	623	12/May/2014	For Better or Worse

Season 7

Episode #		Air Date	Title
129	701	29/Sep/2014	Driven
130	702	06/Oct/2014	Montreal
131	703	13/Oct/2014	Clear and Present Danger
132	704	20/Oct/2014	Child's Play

133	705	27/Oct/2014	Meme is Murder
134	706	10/Nov/2014	The Time of Our Lives
135	707	17/Nov/2014	Once Upon a Time in the West
136	708	24/Nov/2014	Kill Switch
137	709	01/Dec/2014	Last Action Hero
138	710	08/Dec/2014	Bad Santa
139	711	12/Jan/2015	Castle, P.I.
140	712	19/Jan/2015	Private Eye Caramba!
141	713	02/Feb/2015	I, Witness
142	714	09/Feb/2015	Resurrection (1)
143	715	16/Feb/2015	Reckoning (2)
144	716	23/Feb/2015	The Wrong Stuff
145	717	16/Mar/2015	Hong Kong Hustle
146	718	23/Mar/2015	At Close Range
147	719	30/Mar/2015	Habeas Corpse
148	720	20/Apr/2015	Sleeper
149	721	27/Apr/2015	In Plane Sight
150	722	04/May/2015	Dead from New York
151	723	11/May/2015	Hollander's Woods

Works Cited

Primary Sources

Bendis, Brian Michael & Kelly Sue Deconnick. *Castle: Richard Castle's Deadly Storm*, New York: Marvel, 2013.
—. *Castle: Richard Castle's Storm Season*. New York: Marvel, 2012.
Bunn, Cullen, et. al. *Castle: Richard Castle's Unholy Storm*. New York: Marvel, 2014.
Castle: The Complete First Season. ABC Studios, 2009. DVD Boxset.
Castle: The Complete Second Season. ABC Studios, 2010. DVD Boxset.
Castle: The Complete Third Season. ABC Studios, 2011. DVD Boxset.
Castle: The Complete Fourth Season. ABC Studios, 2012. DVD Boxset.
Castle: The Complete Fifth Season. ABC Studios, 2013. DVD Boxset.
Castle: The Complete Sixth Season. ABC Studios, 2014. DVD Boxset.
Castle: Season Seven. ABC Studios, 2015. DVD Boxset.
Castle, Richard. *A Bloody Storm*. New York: Hyperion, 2012. Kindle.
—. *A Brewing Storm*. New York: Hyperion, 2012. Kindle.
—. *Deadly Heat*. New York: Hyperion, 2013.
—. *Driving Heat*. New York: Hyperion, 2015.
—. *Frozen Heat*. New York: Hyperion, 2012.
—. *Heat Rises*. New York: Hyperion, 2011.
—. *Heat Wave*. New York: Hyperion, 2009.
—. *Naked Heat*. New York: Hyperion, 2010.
—. *Raging Heat*. New York: Hyperion, 2014.
—. *A Raging Storm*. New York: Hyperion, 2012. Kindle.
—. *Storm Front*. New York: Hyperion, 2013.

—. *Wild Storm.* New York: Hyperion, 2014.
David, Peter and Robert Atkins. *Castle: Richard Castle's A Calm Before Storm.* New York: Marvel, 2014.

Secondary Sources

Andreeva, Nellie. "'Castle' Star Stana Katic On What Made Her Stay, Big Season 8 "Event" And Her Future On The Show & Beyond." *Deadline* 27 July 2015. http://deadline.com/2015/07/castle-stana-katic-season-8-abc-1201485528.
Bierly, Mandi. "Stupid Questions with... Nathan Fillion." *Entertainment Weekly* 1096 (2010): 66. Academic Search Complete.
Bierly, Mandi, James Hibberd, and Jeff Jensen. "Nathan Fillion Geek God." *Entertainment Weekly* 1147 (2011): 38-45. Academic Search Complete.
Falksen, GD. "Castle's 'Punked': A Love Letter to the Steampunk Community." *Tor.com.* Oct 12, 2010. http://www.tor.com/2010/10/12/castles-qpunkedq-a-love-letter-to-the-steampunk-community.
Fillion, Nathan, Michael Connelly, et. al. "Murder They Wrote." Featurette. *Castle: The Complete Third Season.* Disk Five. ABC Studios, 2011. DVD Boxset.
Highfill, Samantha. "Nathan Fillion Talks about 'Castle' Season 7 and his Dream Wedding" *Entertainment Weekly.* 26 Sept 2014 http://www.ew.com/article/2014/09/26/nathan-fillion-castle-season-7-preview.
Lee, Trymaine. "Dressed for Halloween? No, to Clean Up Times Sq." *The New York Times.* 29 Oct 2007. http://www.nytimes.com/2007/10/29/nyregion/29super.html?_r=0
Mitovich, Matt Webb. "*Castle* in Review: So Yeah, That Just Happened – and the Series Creator Explains Why." *TV Line.* 19 Sept 2011. http://tvline.com/2011/09/19/castle-season-4-premiere-review-preview.

—. *"Castle* Bosses Reveal Beckett's Big Move: 'We Wanted to Shake Things Up'." *TV Line.* 4 Aug 2015. http://tvline.com/2015/08/04/castle-season-8-beckett-captain/

—. "Castle Episode 100 Delivers Easter Eggs for Fans and a Lot of 'Caskett' Fun." *TV Line.* 1 Apr 2013.

Ng, Philiana. *"Castle* Creator: '100 Episodes Is a Miracle'." *The Hollywood Reporter* 31 March 2013. https://www.yahoo.com/tv/s/castle-creator-100-episodes-miracle-050000733.html?nf=1

Nussbaum, Emily. "The Vulture Transcript: Nathan Fillion on *Castle, Firefly,* and a *Dr. Horrible* Sequel" Vulture.com. 4 Oct 2010. http://www.vulture.com/2010/10/the_vulture_transcript_nathan.html

Robinson, Matthew. *How to Get on Reality TV.* New York: Random House, 2005.

Sheffield, Rob. *"Castle* Is The New 'Rockford Files'." *Rolling Stone* 1166 (2012): 54. Academic Search Complete.

Sullivan, Susan. "Martha's Master Class." Featurette. *Castle: The Complete Fifth Season.* Disc Five. ABC Studios, 2013. DVD Boxset.

Truitt, Brian. *"Castle* Enters the Realm of Graphic Novels." *USA Today:* Academic Search Complete.

Index

About the Author

Valerie Estelle Frankel is the author of many books on pop culture, including *Doctor Who – The What, Where, and How*, *Sherlock: Every Canon Reference You May Have Missed in BBC's Series 1-3*, *History, Homages and the Highlands: An Outlander Guide*, and *How Game of Thrones Will End*. Many of her books focus on women's roles in fiction, from her heroine's journey guides *From Girl to Goddess* and *Buffy and the Heroine's Journey* to books like *Women in Game of Thrones* and *The Many Faces of Katniss Everdeen*. Once a lecturer at San Jose State University, she's a frequent speaker at conferences. Come explore her research at www.vefrankel.com.

Made in the USA
San Bernardino, CA
14 August 2016